The Muvipix.com Guide to
Vegas Movie Studio
Platinum 14
Steve Grisetti

The tools, and how to use them, to make movies
on your personal computer using this amazing
video editing program from Magix.

About Muvipix.com

Muvipix.com was created to offer support and community to amateur and semi-professional videomakers. Registration is free, and that gets you access to the world's friendliest, most helpful forum and lots of ad-free space for displaying your work. On the products page, you'll find dozens of free tips, tutorials, motion backgrounds, DVD templates, sound effects, royalty-free music and stock video clips. For a small annual subscription fee that we use to keep the site running, you'll have unlimited downloads from the ever-growing library of support materials and media.

We invite you to drop by and visit our thriving community. It costs absolutely nothing to join – and we'd love to have you become a part of our neighborhood!

http://Muvipix.com

About the author

Steve Grisetti holds a master's degree in Telecommunications from Ohio University and spent several years working in the motion picture and television industry in Los Angeles. A veteran user of several video editing programs and systems, Steve is the co-founder of Muvipix.com, a help and support site for amateur and semi-professional videomakers. A professional graphic designer and video freelancer, he has taught classes in Photoshop, lectured on design and created courses for lynda.com. He lives in suburban Milwaukee.

Other books by Steve Grisetti

The Muvipix.com Guide to Sony Movie Studio Platinum 13
The Muvipix.com Guide to Vegas Movie Studio Platinum 12
The Muvipix.com Guide to Vegas Movie Studio HD Platinum 10 & 11
The Muvipix.com Guide to DVD Architect Studio 5.0
The Muvipix.com Guide to Adobe Premiere Elements 7, 8, 9, 10, 11, 12, 13, 14 & 15
The Muvipix.com Guide to Photoshop Elements & Premiere Elements 9, 10, 11, 12, 13, 14 & 15
Cool Tricks & Hot Tips for Adobe Premiere Elements

An Introduction

If you're a long-time fan of Movie Studio, you were likely as happy as we were to hear that Magix had picked up this excellent product, left orphaned by Sony nearly 3 years ago. And Magix has done a terrific job of reviving the program – infusing it with some very nice new features as well as a cool new look.

Movie Studio once again looks more like a professional desktop program. The interface has been given an elegant, dark look with a less-cluttered feel. Tools are small and unobtrusive, yet easily accessible.

Among the other new features in version 14 is a terrific Multicam Editor. Modeled after a similar feature in Vegas Pro, the Movie Studio Multicam Editor gives you the ability to gather and sync video from up to four video sources and then cut between them – making producing a professional-looking video of a wedding, sporting event or other live event easy, intuitive and fun.

You'll also find improvements in the Trimmer and in the Make Movie tools for uploading to social media sites, as well as an improved RAM render feature – and, depending on which version of the program you've purchased, some cool new effects from NewBlue and HitFilm.

As always, our goal with this book is to make all of the tools in this program as easy to understand as possible – and maybe even to introduce you to some potential functions you hadn't even considered along the way. We'll also throw in some tips for helping keep your whole moviemaking process running as smoothly as possible.

So, whether you're new to video editing and/or this program or you're looking to improve your experience by getting to know the program a little bit better, we're glad to have you along.

Here's to your having as much fun with Vegas Movie Studio as we're having!

Muvipix.com was created in 2006 as a community and a learning center for videomakers at a variety of levels. Our community includes everyone from amateurs and hobbyists to semi-pros, professionals and even people with broadcast experience. You won't find more knowledgeable, helpful people anywhere else on the Web. I very much encourage you to drop by our forums and say hello. At the very least, you'll make some new friends. And it's rare that there's a question posted that isn't quickly, and enthusiastically, answered.

And, of course, I'm there several times a day – willing to answer any questions you might have about this book or the program personally.

Our learning center consists of video tutorials, tips and, of course, books. But we also offer a wealth of support in the form of custom-created DVD and BluRay disc menus, motion background videos, licensed music and even stock footage. Much of it is absolutely free – and there's even more available for those who purchase one of our affordable site subscriptions.

Our goal has always been to help people get up to speed making great videos and, once they're there, provide them with the inspiration and means to get better and better at doing so.

Why? Because we know making movies is a heck of a lot of fun – and we want to share that fun with everyone!

Our books, then, are a manifestation of that goal. And my hope for you is that this book helps *you* get up to speed. I think you'll find, once you get over the surprisingly small learning curve, making movies on your home computer is a lot more fun than you ever imagined! And you may even amaze yourself with the results in the process.

Thanks for supporting the Muvipix.com mission, and happy moviemaking!

Steve
http://Muvipix.com

Table of Contents

Chapter 4

Order and Prep Your Clips in the Project Media Window 55

The catalog of your imported media

Chapter 5

Prepare Your Media in
the Trimmer Window 63

Previewing and pre-setting your clips

Chapter 6

Edit Video on the Timeline 75

Where your clips become a movie

Table of Contents

Chapter 7

The deeper toolkit

Chapter 8

Chapter 9

Table of Contents

Table of Contents

Chapter 16

Prep Your Movie for Output to DVD or BluRay Disc   239

Putting your movie on disc

Chapter 17

Make Your Movie 247

Sharing your project with the world

Chapter 18

An Appendix 259

Advanced Vegas Movie Studio 14 tricks

What have I gotten myself into?
Some basic questions and simple answers about Vegas Movie Studio 14 and how it works

What is non-linear editing (NLE)?

Non-linear editing is basically another term for editing video on a computer. "Non-linear" is in contrast to linear editing – the way video and film used to be edited in the days of tape and film reels. In those days, if you wanted to take a scene from the beginning of a reel of film or tape and you wanted to cut it with another at the end, you'd need to go through the entire reel to grab each scene. That's *linear* editing. In order to get from this piece to that piece, you have to go through everything in between.

In non-linear video, your scenes or clips appear in a catalog (the **Project Media** window) and you just grab and mix them in any order you want. A much easier way to work, don't you think?

What's the difference between Vegas Movie Studio, Vegas Movie Studio Platinum and Vegas Pro?

Well, in terms of the quality of the results, absolutely nothing. They all produce the same excellent quality of video outputs.

The Pro version, however, includes a number of higher-end features (such as support for RED ONE camcorders) and the ability to embed one project into another.

Vegas Movie Studio Platinum's bundle includes DVD Architect (a DVD/BluRay authoring program), a slideshow creator tool and advanced color correction tools that are not included with plain vanilla Vegas Movie Studio. The Vegas Movie Studio Suite includes DVD Architect, a cool 3D titler from NewBlue and some high-end effects from HitFilm.

Magix has a chart listing all of the major feature differences at: vegascreativesoftware.com/[us]/vegas-movie-studio/product-comparison/

Can I mix more than one type of video in my Vegas Movie Studio project?

You certainly can – and the results are usually very good (particularly if you tweak your **Project Properties**, as we recommend on page 261). However, you'll always get the best performance and the best results from the program when your project settings match your source video as closely as possible, as we discuss in **Chapter 2, Start a New Project**.

What is an Event?

Video and audio clips, while on your hard drive or in the **Project Media** window, are called **media** clips. Once they are added to your project's timeline, they become **events**. Timeline events can be split and trimmed, or they can be set up to interact with other events on the timeline.

Video editing in Vegas Movie Studio, by the way, is a *non-destructive* process. That means that nothing you do to the events on your timeline will have any effect on your original video and audio clips. They will not be changed or damaged in any way.

What is an Envelope?

When you create an **Envelope** on your Vegas Movie Studio timeline, you create a workspace in which certain audio and video levels can be set to vary over time. You can use envelopes, for instance, to vary the volume level at specific points on an audio track or to lower the opacity level of a video track.

We'll show you how to use an envelope to control audio levels on your timeline at specific points in **Chapter 9, Edit Audio on the Timeline**. And we'll show you how to use envelopes to control video properties in **Chapter 15, Vary Effects with Keyframes**.

What is keyframed animation?

Like an envelope, a **keyframed animation** can be used to vary the levels or other characteristics of an effect or transition over time. A keyframed animation, for instance, can be used to create a pan and zoom motion path in a slideshow or to create an effect or title that changes in intensity or shape over time. Using keyframes, you can create an animation in which a clip starts out normal, then morphs into a swirl – then goes back to normal again.

Keyframing is one of the most powerful tools for creating effects and mixing audio in this program. Fortunately, Movie Studio's tools for making, creating and editing keyframes and animations are very intuitive and easy to use.

We'll show you how to unleash the power of keyframing and animation in **Chapter 15, Vary Effects with Keyframes**.

What is an Instance?

An **Instance** is, basically, an open Vegas Movie Studio project. By opening several instances of Vegas Movie Studio at the same time, you can cut and paste events or even entire sequences from one project to another. We'll show you how to do this in **Chapter 7, More Timeline Tools**.

What's the difference between the Vegas Movie Studio Explorer window and the Project Media window?

The Vegas Movie Studio **Explorer** window shows you all of the media that is on your computer's hard drive. The **Project Media** window, on the other hand, lists only the video, audio clips or stills that you've *actually added to your Vegas Movie Studio project*.

We'll show you how to add media to your **Project Media** window in **Chapter 3, Get Media Into Your Project**.

What is a Media Bin?

Media Bins are folders and sub-folders that you create in order to organize the media clips in your **Project Media** window.

Media Bins can be very helpful if your project includes dozens of media clips. You can, for instance, create one **Media Bin** folder for your titles, another for your audio, another for video clips shot at the Grand Canyon, etc. Media Bins make it easy for you to manage and locate the media in your project.

We'll show you how to organize your clips with Media Bins in **Chapter 4, Order and Prep Clips in the Project Media Window**.

What is the Trimmer?

The **Trimmer** in Vegas Movie Studio 14 is hidden by default, but it launches automatically whenever it's needed. In the **Trimmer**, you can preview clips that are in the **Explorer** or **Project Media** window. You can also pre-trim your video or audio clips before adding them to your timeline (isolating a small segment of a longer clip, for instance) or save a pre-trimmed clip back to your **Project Media** window as a sub-clip.

We'll show you how to use the tools in this window in **Chapter 5, Prepare Your Media in the Trimmer**.

What is the Loop Region?

A **Loop Region** is a segment you define on your timeline. By isolating segments of your timeline as Loop Regions, you can define which portion of your movie will be rendered and/or output. For instance, when using this feature you can opt to output a video of only a portion of a longer movie.

We'll show you how to set up and use a **Loop Region** in **Chapter 6, Edit Video on the Timeline** and **Chapter 7, More Timeline Tools**.

What are the Snapping and Quantize to Frame features?

The **Snapping** feature controls how your media clips align when you place them on your timeline. When **Snapping** is enabled, any clips you add to or trim on your timeline will automatically "snap" to align themselves with the playhead, grid, other clips or the **Timeline**.

The **Quantize to Frames** feature ensures that any trims that you make to the video or audio on your timeline are no smaller than a video frame. As with **Snapping**, it's probably best to leave this feature toggled on except for special situations.

The **Snapping** and **Quantize to Frames** options are turned on or off by checking or unchecking them under the **Options** menu.

What is Pre-Rendering and why should I do it?

Pre-rendering means creating a fully-rendered preview of an event clip or timeline segment to which effects have been added. The program will then use the pre-rendered segment in place of the effects-laden segment to give you a smooth-playing look at your work-in-progress.

This is as opposed to "soft rendering," or letting your computer just play your timeline without rendering. If you've got a lot of clips on your timeline that have had effects added to them, playing them without pre-rendering them can really burden your computer. **Pre-rendering** your timeline as you work allows the program to work more efficiently.

Pre-rendering falls into the category of good housekeeping, and we highly recommend you do it whenever you've added visual effects, your system starts to lug or your timeline doesn't play back at full speed.

We discuss why and how to pre-render your timeline in much more detail in **Chapter 6, Edit Video on the Timeline**.

Where can I learn more about Vegas Movie Studio 14?

Our site, Muvipix.com offers both an extremely helpful forum and an ever-growing number of helpful tutorials for both basic and advanced functions of a number of popular video editing and DVD authoring programs (including DVD Architect). And be sure to check out our free Basic Training tutorials for both Movie Studio and DVD Architect. (Just go to our Muvipix.com home page and type the name of the program and "basic training" into the product search box.)

You'll also likely find me on our free Muvipix Community Forum, day or night, helping out where I can and answering questions.

Even if you're not finding the program challenging, I hope you'll drop by and say hello! We love to see our videomaker community grow!

Steve and the Muvipix team

Get to Know the Workspace

Customizing Your Workspace

Basic Editing Moves

What's New in Version 14?

Chapter 1

Get to know Vegas Movie Studio Platinum 14

What's what and what it does

Although the interface for Vegas Movie Studio may seem a bit intimidating at first, you'll likely feel very comfortable with it in a very short time.

Magix has done a wonderful job of both mimicking the look of a professional video editor and keeping the tools simple and easy to access.

The Trimmer
(a floating window)

The Preview Monitor

The Audio Meter/Mixer

The Menu Bar

The Toolbar

The Project
Media Window

The Explorer

Transitions

Video FX

Media Generators

The Timeline

Timeline Tools

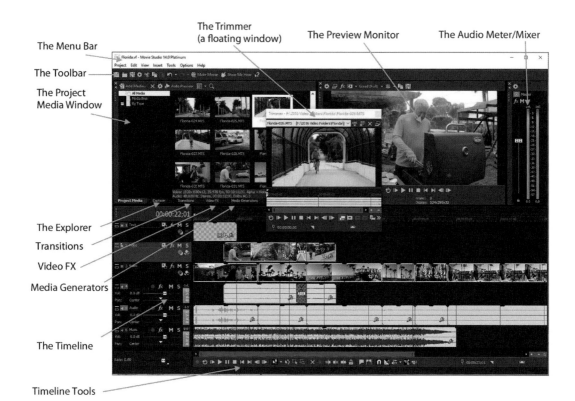

The Vegas Movie Studio 14 interface

Unlike many consumer-based video editing programs available today, Vegas Movie Studio looks and behaves like a full-blown professional editor. Its timeline looks and functions just like that of a professional editing system, its windows and toolbars offer access to a wealth of high-level features and its interface is crowded with easily-accessible tools.

In fact, once you've become familiar with what's here and how it all works, you'll likely find it relatively easy to transition to a professional editor like Adobe's Premiere Pro, Apple's Final Cut or, of course, Magix's Vegas Pro.

If you feel a need to, of course.

You may well find that this deep and affordable program is fully capable of doing everything you'll ever need!

Vegas Movie Studio's default workspace is designed to keep all of your tools within easy reach. Even its high-level tools are only a click or two away. Yet, as we'll soon demonstrate, it's also a very easily customizable workspace. And, once you have created a custom layout for your interface, you can even save that configuration and recall it whenever you'd like. In fact, you can save up to nine different interface configurations!

We'll look more deeply at the interface modes and how to use them to put together your movie in **Chapter 6, Edit Video on the Timeline**.

The Project Media panel displays the video, audio, music and stills that have been added to your project.

The Project Media window

The **Project Media** window, in the upper left of the interface, lists all of the media (video, audio, stills, etc.) that you've imported into your Vegas Movie Studio project.

Media can be added to your project in a number of ways, usually using the tools along the top of the window. You can:

- **Capture video from a tape-based camcorder.** When video is captured, it is streamed into the project in real time, and the video is recorded to your computer's hard drive as it is added to the project's media.

- **Download video or stills from a hard drive or memory storage camcorder.** When video is imported into your project using a tool like the **Device Explorer**, the video or other media files are simultaneously downloaded to your computer's hard drive and added to your Vegas Movie Studio project.

- **Rip video or audio from a disc.** This method saves the media from a DVD or CD to your hard drive while adding it to your project.

- **Import media from your hard drive.** In many cases, the video, still photos or audio files are already on your computer. Importing adds these files to your **Project Media** list.

We'll look into all of the methods of adding media to your project and when and how to use each in **Chapter 3, Get Media Into Your Project**.

The Explorer window

Sharing a tabbed space with the **Project Media** window, the **Explorer** is a browse screen for locating media files on your computer's hard drive.

The Explorer window gives you access to all of the media files on your computer. When files are dragged from the Explorer to the Timeline, they are automatically added to the Project Media window also.

As we'll show you in **Chapter 3**, video, stills, graphics and audio can be added directly from the **Explorer** to your timeline. Doing this automatically adds these media clips to your Vegas Movie Studio project and your **Project Media** list.

The Transitions window

The **Transitions** window (which also shares the tabbed space with the **Explorer** and **Project Media** windows) lists over 30 categories of Magix transitions (as well as third-party plug-ins), each of which includes a number of individual transitions, bringing the total number of transitions included with the program to close to 250!

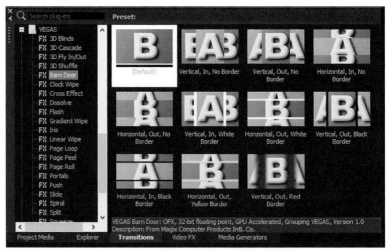

The Transitions window lists dozens of customizable transitional effects.

Each of these transitions can be customized in a number of ways, so there's really no limit to the number of possible transitions you can create for your movie!

We'll tell you all about transitions and how to use them in a Vegas Movie Studio project in **Chapter 13, Add and Customize Transitions**.

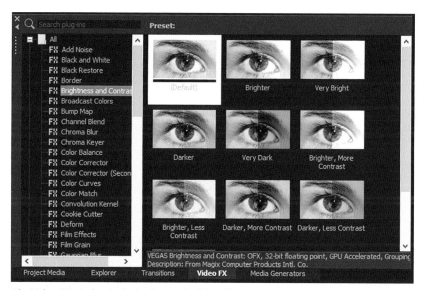

The Video FX window includes "presets" of the effects set loaded into Vegas Movie Studio. Like the effects themselves, these presets can be modified and customized as needed.

The Video FX window

Vegas Movie Studio Platinum comes loaded with over 300 preset video effects in over 50 categories. Like transitions, these effects can be customized in a number of ways and can even be combined in a chain to create any number of possible special effects.

The effects in the **Video FX** window are presets based on the Vegas Movie Studio plug-in effects set – a set you can easily add to, if you'd like. In fact, if you have the Platinum Suite version of the program, you'll find some additional effects from HitFilm among those listed.

We'll define each of these effects and show you how to use and customize them in **Chapter 12, Add and Adjust Video Effects**.

Media Generators

As illustrated at the top of page 10, **Media Generators** are pre-composed clips that you can add to your timeline as is or customize as needed. Among these are solid color clips, checkerboards and color test patterns as well as a number of title templates.

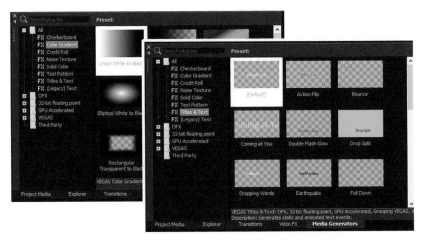

The Media Generator window includes customizable video clips as well as pre-created rolling and animated titles.

We'll show you how to use and modify clips from the **Media Generator** in **Chapter 3, Get Media Into Your Project**. And, in **Chapter 11, Add and Customize Your Titles**, we'll show you how to use **Media Generator** title templates to create basic, scrolling or even animated titles.

The Trimmer

Hidden by default but launched by selecting the **right-click** option on any clip in your project (and commonly positioned between the **Project Media** window and the **Preview** window), the **Trimmer** is a workspace in which you can prepare or pre-trim your media clips prior to adding them to your timeline. The **Trimmer** includes its own playback window as well as its own mini-timeline and tool set.

The Trimmer is a workspace for previewing and pre-trimming your media clips.

We'll show you all of the great things you can do in this workspace (and, if you'd like, how to position it permanently into the program's interface) in **Chapter 5, Prepare Your Media in the Trimmer Window**.

The Preview window

The **Preview** window, illustrated to the right, displays the playback of the video you've assembled on your timeline. This window also includes a number of important tools, and we'll show you how they all work in **Chapter 10, Preview Window Tools**.

The Timeline

The **Timeline**, illustrated below, is the main work area for assembling your movie. It's where your media clips are arranged, where most of the effects are added and where your clips interact with each other.

The Preview window displays the playback of the video you've assembled on your timeline.

In Vegas Movie Studio Platinum 14, you can have up to 200 video and a virtually unlimited number of audio tracks on your timeline, and you can arrange them in any order you'd like.

Since this workspace plays such a major role in the video editing process, no single chapter could say everything there is to say about it. So, in **Chapter 6**, we'll show you how to **Edit Video on the Timeline** and, in **Chapter 7**, we'll show you **More Timeline Tools**. Then, in **Chapter 9**, we'll show you how to **Edit Audio on the Timeline**.

Additional "Pop-up" windows

In addition to the windows that make up the basic interface, there are several windows that "pop up" as needed:

The Video FX dialog window

Whenever you add an effect to a video clip, the **Video FX** dialog window will pop open. On this window, you can add effects to or remove effects from your clip or event's "chain," customize the effect to your specific need or add keyframed animation.

You don't need to close this window, by the way, once you've made adjustments to an effect. Any adjustments you make are added to your clip in "real time," and the results immediately appear in the **Preview** window. In fact, if you've got room on your computer's desktop, you can leave this window open and it will automatically update when you add a new effect or edit an effect added to another clip.

We discuss this window in detail in **Chapter 12, Add and Adjust Video Effects**.

The Audio FX dialog window

The **Audio FX** dialog window functions similarly to the **Video FX** window. We'll show you how to add effects to your audio in **Chapter 12, Add and Adjust Audio Effects**.

The Video and Audio Plug-In Choosers give you access to all of the effects loaded into the program.

The Plug-in Chooser

The **Plug-in Chooser** lists all of the video effects, audio effects and transitions that have been loaded into your program. In fact, the effects listed on the **Video FX** panel (page 9) are actually just *presets* of the program's video effects plug-ins.

Whenever you select the option to add a video effect, audio effect or transition to a media clip, event, audio or video track or an entire project, the big **Plug-in Chooser** window will pop open. (There is one list of plug-ins for video effects, another for audio effects and another for transitions.)

Once you select the effect to apply, the **Plug-in Chooser** will close and you will have access to the **Video FX** or **Audio FX** dialog window (described on the facing page) in which you can customize the effect.

We'll tell you more about these effects and how to use them in **Chapter 12, Add and Adjust Video Effects** and in **Chapter 13, Add and Adjust Audio Effects**.

By the way, you can easily add more effects to your plug-in set. We show you how on page 186.

The Pan/Crop Motion dialog window

To add some interest and movement to your slidehows, you may want to pan and zoom around your still photos a la Ken Burns. The **Pan/Crop Motion** dialog window is Vegas Movie Studio's very intuitive workspace for creating animated motion paths around your video or stills.

We'll show you how to use this great tool for creating pans, zooms and crops around your clips in **Chapter 8, Work With Photos**.

Customize your workspace

Although the default set-up for the interface makes fairly efficient use of your computer desktop space, you can easily customize it (temporarily or permanently) so that you can focus on a particular window or two.

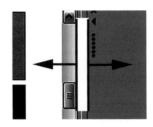

Resize the windows

To resize the program's windows, hover your mouse over the seams between them. When you see a double-headed arrow resize indicator (illustrated above), click and drag. As you drag one window larger, the other windows will resize to allow for it.

The Minimize/Maximize button instantly snaps the view of any window from its default size to the width of the entire interface – and instantly back again.

Maximize/Minimize the windows

The arrow buttons at the top left of each window are single-click ways to temporarily maximize or minimize a window's size.

For instance, click on the arrow at the upper left of the **Explorer** window, and it will snap to the full width of the program's interface. Click again on the arrow and the window snaps back to its original size.

Dock or undock the windows

If you click and drag on the ":...." at the top or left side of any window (officially called the "**gripper**"), you can pull that window completely free from the interface so that it becomes a "floating" window.

- Once you've dragged the window free from the interface, you can place it anywhere you'd like on your desktop. If you're using a two monitor system on your computer, you can undock any or all of the program's windows and arrange them any way you'd like across your desktop.

- If you hold down the **Ctrl** key and drag a window into any of the "drop zones" in the program (areas of the interface in which windows already reside), when you release your mouse button the window will drop right into this space – becoming a tabbed window set or a new window panel in the interface.

By dragging on the Gripper, you can undock a window and make it a floating panel.

Save and load a Window Layout

A very nice bonus feature in Vegas Movie Studio is its ability to save your various **Window Layouts**.

Occasionally, for instance, you may need to rearrange the windows in the program's interface in order to allow more space for the **Timeline**. Or you may want to sometimes make the **Preview** window larger so that you can see the detail in the playback.

To save or recall a custom layout, just go to the **View** menu at the top of the interface and select the option to save or recall a layout in the sub-menu **Window Layouts**.

Vegas Movie Studio 14 allows you to save up to ten different interface configurations in addition to the program's **Default Layout**.

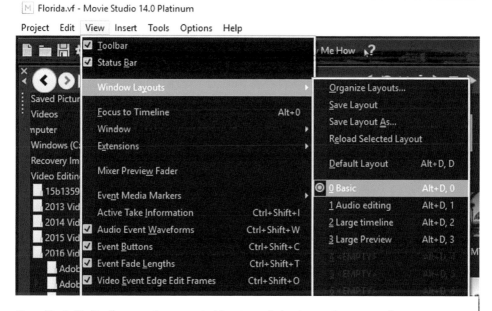

Vegas Movie Studio allows you to save up to 10 custom window layouts for easy recall.

Basic editing moves

No matter what you plan to do with your video and no matter how creatively you plan to do it, the video editing process itself will still follow the same basic structure.

Here's a brief walk-through of the basic steps you'll take for creating any video project in Vegas Movie Studio 14.

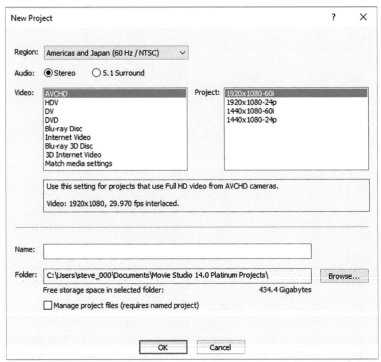

When you create a new project in Vegas Movie Studio, it's usually best to select the project properties that most closely match your source video.

1 **Start a project**

You can start a new project by selecting the option on the **Welcome Screen** or by selecting the option under the **Project** menu at the top of the program.

For best performance and results, your project should be set up to match, as closely as possible, the source footage you're using to build your movie. Vegas Movie Studio 14 even includes a "Match Media Settings" tool for automatically setting your project properties to match the specs of the video you'll be working with.

In **Chapter 2**, **Start a New Project**, we'll show you how to properly set up a new project and ensure that its settings provide you with the best performance and results possible.

2 Gather your media

The assets, or media, you gather to create your movie can come from a variety of sources. These assets can include video, audio, music, photos and graphics.

As you gather, or *import*, your assets into your project, they will appear in the **Project Media** window.

There are three basic ways to get your media into your project, and which method you'll use depends on where your media files are located.

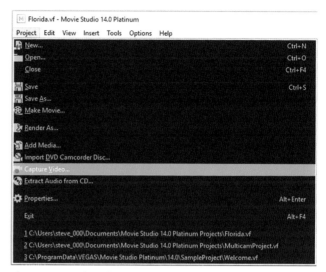

There are a number of ways to add media to your project.

- **Tape-based digital video is *captured* into your project.**

  MiniDV and HDV camcorders connect to your computer over a FireWire, or IEEE-1394 cable, connection. The camcorder's playback is controlled by Vegas Movie Studio's capture software, and the video segments you choose to capture are streamed onto your computer and into your project in real time.

- **Video, stills and other media are *downloaded* from hard drive camcorders, cameras and other devices.**

  Hard drive camcorders, including high-definition AVCHD units and those that record to flash memory cards, download their video to your computer as whole files rather than stream it in. Media files can also be downloaded from other sources, including DVDs, digital still cameras and phones. Vegas Movie Studio includes a **Device Explorer** tool (available under **View/ Window**) for locating and downloading media from hard drive camcorders and other media storage devices.

- **Media that is already on your computer is *imported* into your project.**

  Video, stills, music and other media files that are already on your computer are imported into your project by clicking the **Add Media** button on the upper left of the **Project Media** panel.

We'll show you how to use each of these methods to bring video, audio and stills photos into your project in **Chapter 3, Get Media Into Your Project**.

3 **Assemble your media clips on your timeline**

Once you've imported your media clips into a project, they will appear listed in the **Project Media** window and you can begin the process of assembling your movie. This process is as simple, and as intuitive, as dragging the clips from the **Project Media** window to your timeline and then arranging them in the order you'd like them to appear.

Once you add your files to your timeline, you'll have a number of options:

- **Trim your clips.** Trimming means removing footage from either the beginning or the end of a clip. To trim a clip, click to select the clip on your timeline and then drag inward either the beginning or end (as discussed on page 78).

- **Split your clips.** Splitting means slicing through your clips so that you can remove footage from the middle or delete one sliced-off segment completely. To split a clip, position the **Timeline Cursor** (playhead) over your clip(s) at the point at which you'd like the slice to occur and click the **Split** button below the timeline (as discussed on page 79).

- **Place your clip on an upper video or audio track**. On a multi-track timeline, your clips don't just follow one another – they also *interact* with each other. Your video tracks behave like layers of images. And how the clips are arranged on your upper tracks (or if they include transparent areas) determines how and how much of the clips on your lower tracks appear around or through them.

The use of multiple tracks of video is key, for instance, to the creation of many of the more advanced video effects, including the **Chroma Keyer** (see page 189).

We'll show you how to build a timeline and how to use multiple tracks of video in **Chapter 6, Edit Video on the Timeline**, and in **Chapter 7, More Timeline Tools**.

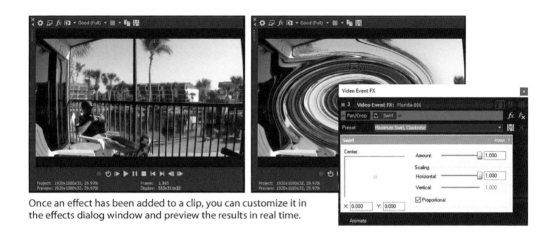

Once an effect has been added to a clip, you can customize it in the effects dialog window and preview the results in real time.

4 Add and adjust effects

Vegas Movie Studio comes loaded with dozens of video and audio effects. These effects can be added to a clip prior to adding it to the timeline, to an event or group of events on your timeline, to an entire video or audio track at once or to your project overall.

Once an effect has been added to your video or audio clip(s), a dialog window will open in which you can customize the effect or use keyframes to create an effect animation.

We'll show you how to work with effects in **Chapter 12, Add and Adjust Video Effects**, and **Chapter 13, Add and Adjust Audio Effects**.

In addition to video and audio effects, Vegas Movie Studio includes tools for creating motion paths – pans and zooms (or pans and crops) over your video or still photos. As with the other effects, you can use the **Pan/Crop Motion** tool to either create a pan and crop over an individual event on your timeline or use it to create this visual effect for an entire video track.

We'll show you how to work the **Pan/Crop Motion** tool in **Chapter 8, Work with Photos**.

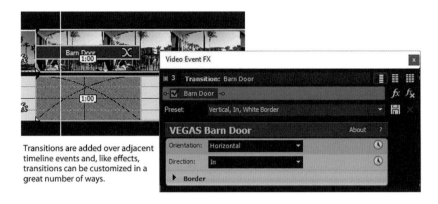

Transitions are added over adjacent timeline events and, like effects, transitions can be customized in a great number of ways.

5   Add and adjust transitions

Transitions are visual effects that take us from one timeline event to another. Some are subtle and nearly invisible – others are showy and draw attention to themselves.

As with effects, once you add a transition to your timeline, a dialog window will open, allowing you to customize your transition in a number of ways.

You might be surprised to learn how many different ways there are to add and customize transitions – and we'll show them to you in **Chapter 14, Add and Customize Transitions**.

6   Add titles

Titles are text placed over your clips to provide additional visual information for your video story.

There is more than one way to create a title. And, once you have created it, you can customize it in a number of ways.

Titles can be added to your project in a number of ways. And, like other media clips, your titles can be customized in many ways and can include animated effects and movement.

As with other video events on your timeline, you can add effects, like fade ins and fade outs, animation and even motion paths, to your titles.

We'll show you how to do lots of great tricks with your titles in **Chapter 11, Add and Customize Your Titles**.

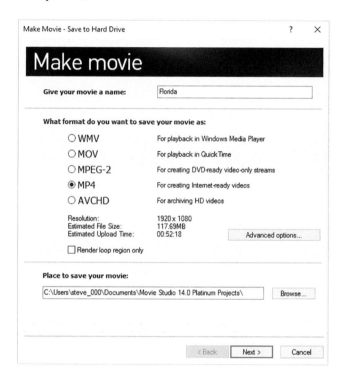

7 **Output your movie**

Once you've finished editing your Vegas Movie Studio project, you'll find lots of options for sharing it. From outputting your video for the web to exporting your movie to a portable device to sending your project to DVD Architect for production as a DVD or BluRay disc, Vegas Movie Studio 14 offers a wealth of options for making your movie.

We'll show you how to use these options and what the advantages of each output format are in **Chapter 17, Make Your Movie**.

And that's basically it!

You gather your assets, you assemble them on your timeline, you add effects, transitions and titles, you share it with the world. But between the lines of this simplicity are the countless variations that can elevate your movie project from the realm of a basic home movie to something truly amazing!

What's new in version 14?

Since inheriting Vegas Movie Studio from Sony, Magix has added a couple of very nice new features to version 14 of the program.

The first thing you'll likely notice is a return to the desktop-style interface. The version 14 interface is dark and elegant, and the tools are easily accessed and unobtrusive. Additionally, the new interface is designed to look great even on the newer, higher-definition monitors.

Beyond that, the program includes a number of cool, new features.

Improved RAM preview

Movie Studio now even more effectively uses your RAM to create clean preview renders of your work. RAM renders are a great way to preview how your advanced video composites and effects will look in your final output.

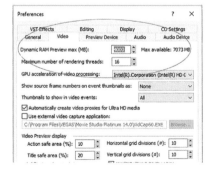

We show you how to create a **RAM preview** on page 91.

Extended upload to social media

In addition to tools for upload directly to YouTube and Facebook, version 14 of Movie Studio includes a tool for uploading directly to Vimeo. You supply the title and keywords and the program automatically produces an optimized video and sends it to the site.

We show you how to use all of the **Make Movie** options in **Chapter 17.**

Trimmer hover scrub

The **Trimmer** is a workspace for previewing and pre-trimming your video and audio before you add it to your timeline. A new feature in version 14 allows you to "hover scrub" – simply by dragging over the video preview itself – to quickly and intuitively locate a spot in your clip.

We show you how to use all of the tools in the **Trimmer,** including the new hover scrub feature, in **Chapter 5.**

Hover scrub playhead

Multicam Editing

Certainly the most noteworthy and exciting of the new features in version 14 is the **Multicam Editor.** Modeled after the **Multicam Editor** in Vegas Pro, this feature enables you to gather and sync footage from up to four video sources and then easily cut between each shot – tweaking your edit choices as needed – to produce a great-looking, professionally edited movie from a wedding,

sporting event or any other live event recorded from several video sources.

We show you how it works as well as how to sync up your audio and video on page 122.

DVD Architect

Included with the Platinum and the Suite versions of Vegas Movie Studio 14 is DVD Architect, a professional program for authoring and producing DVDs and BluRay discs based on your Movie Studio movie projects. Considering that the

cost of DVD Architect alone exceeds the price of the Vegas Movie Studio Platinum, that's a pretty good deal indeed!

We show you how to prep your movies and port them over to DVD Architect in **Chapter 16**.

If you'd like to learn all about this amazing program, we've got a whole book on the subject! *The Muvipix.com Guide to DVD Architect* is available at Amazon.com and at the Muvipix.com store.

The Welcome Screen
Selecting Project Properties
Match Media Settings
Project Properties

Chapter 2

Start a New Project

Smart beginnings

No matter how great the journey ahead, it all begins with a few key steps in the right direction.

And, no matter how simple or how complicated your movie project is, setting your project up correctly can go a long way toward ensuring a successful editing experience.

Your project settings determine how the program "digests" the media you load into your project.

In most cases, you'll want your project settings to match your source video as closely as possible. But, if you're mixing media in more than one format, your project settings can also determine how this other media is interpreted by the program.

Although Vegas Movie Studio allows you to change your project settings at any point in your work, it's always best to select the correct settings when you first create your project.

Start a new project

There are four ways to start a new project in Vegas Movie Studio:

- From the **Welcome Screen**, select the **New** option. (For more information on the **Welcome Screen**, see the sidebar below.)

- Select the **New** option under the **Project** menu or click the **New Project** button directly below the **Project** menu.

- Press **Ctrl+n** on your keyboard.

- Click on the 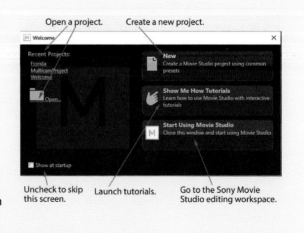 **New Project** icon on the **Toolbar** along the top of the interface.

The Welcome Screen

The **Welcome Screen** is the dialog screen that greets you when you first launch the program.

From this screen, you can start a new project, open an existing project or view basic tutorials for the program.

By unchecking the option in the lower left of this screen, you can skip the **Welcome Screen** and the program will, from then on, launch directly to the Vegas Movie Studio editing workspace.

Open a project.   Create a new project.

Uncheck to skip   Launch tutorials.   Go to the Sony Movie
this screen.   Studio editing workspace.

The **Welcome Screen** can also be re-launched at any time from within the program by selecting the **Welcome** option under the program's **Help** menu.

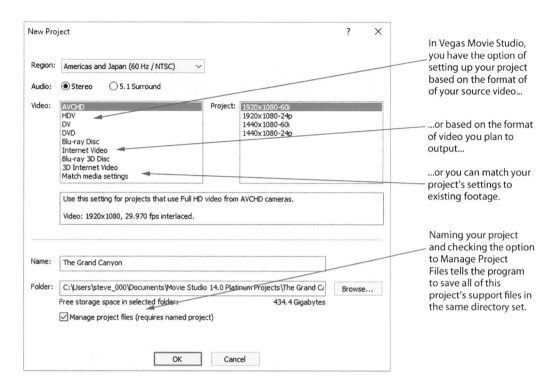

In Vegas Movie Studio, you have the option of setting up your project based on the format of of your source video...

...or based on the format of video you plan to output...

...or you can match your project's settings to existing footage.

Naming your project and checking the option to Manage Project Files tells the program to save all of this project's support files in the same directory set.

Select settings in the New Project dialog box

The **New Project** dialog box launches when you select the option to start a new Vegas Movie Studio project.

1 Select a Region

If you are in the United States, Canada or the rest of the Americas, or in Japan, you should select the NTSC option.

If you are in Europe or Asia, you should select the PAL option.

2 Select your Audio format

If your camcorder shoots in 5.1 audio or you plan to use 5.1 audio as an audio source, select 5.1 Surround. Otherwise, select Stereo.

3 Select your Video format

You can select your **Video** format either based on the type of camcorder your video came from or based on the format of video you plan to output.

For best results and the most efficient program performance, we recommend that you always set your project up based on the format of your *source footage* – the camcorder format that your video was recorded in – rather than the format you plan to output.

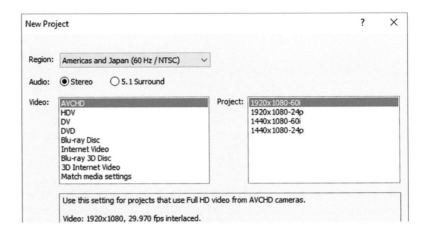

Set up your project based on your source footage

The first three presets are used when you set your project up based on the type of camcorder or other source your video came from.

> **AVCHD** is video from a high definition hard drive camcorder. AVCHD comes in two formats: 1920x1080 pixels and 1440x1080 pixels. Both of these formats are the same high-definition resolution. One format uses square pixels and the other uses pixels that are wider than they are tall. Check your camcorder specs to ensure you're selecting the correct settings.

> **HDV** is tape-based high-definition video. HDV can be full high-def 1440x1080 or "Lite" 1280x720. Again, check your camcorder's specs to ensure you select the setting that best matches your source video.

> **HDV project settings also include options for XAVC S video at 3840x2160 resolution, at 60p, 30p and 24p frame rates.**

> **DV** is video from a tape-based miniDV or Digital8 camcorder. DV video can be standard 4:3 or widescreen 16:9.

If you've no idea which **Video** setting to select, you can always choose to **Match Media Settings**, as discussed in the sidebar on the facing page.

If your video is shot in **24p**, be sure to select this also in your project settings. If your video is shot in **50p** or **60p**, it's best to do an additional tweak to the project's settings, as described in the sidebar on page 30.

Set up your project based on your planned output format

> **DVD** optimizes your project's video for output to either a standard 4:3 or widescreen 16:9 DVD, at standard or 24p frame rates.

What is 24p?

24p is video that plays at ~24 non-interlaced frames per second (as opposed to the standard, interlaced 25 or 29.97). 24p video tends to have a a more "filmic" look.

Match Media Settings

When you select the option to **Match Media Settings**, a **Browse** button will appear on the dialog screen. Use the **Browse** button to locate a sample clip of the video you will be using in your project. Vegas Movie Studio will automatically create a project setting that matches this video format as closely as possible.

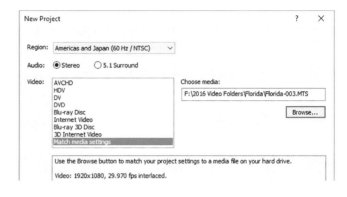

The program does a very good job of matching its project settings to your selected clip – but it's not perfect. Some video formats (such as video from Flip or other pocket camcorders, FRAPS programs or digital still cameras) often use codecs (compression methods) that aren't possible for the program to match exactly, while other video formats (DivX, for instance) are virtually uneditable and need to be converted to a more standard editing format before you'll be able to work with them in Vegas Movie Studio 14.

In these cases, when you bring the video into your project, the program may seem to perform sluggishly or require constant pre-rendering of your project. When this happens, it's often wiser to convert the video to a more traditional DV-AVI or MP4 before you begin editing.

Blu-Ray Disc optimizes your project's video for Blu-Ray output as either 1920x1080 or 1440x1080, at either standard interlaced or 24p frames rates.

Internet Video optimizes your video for display on a web site as either high-definition 1280x720 pixels, standard definition 640x480 pixels or widescreen 640x360 pixels as well as options for creating 24p video.

BluRay 3D Disc and **3D Internet Video** creates 1280x720 or 1920x1080 3D video optimized for output to BluRay disc or online display in either standard or 24p frame rates.

4 **Name your project**

It's not necessary to name and select a "save" location for your project at this point. (You can do so at any point in your work by going to the program's **File** menu and selecting **Save As**.)

But doing so allows you to manage your project files, as described in the next step.

At Muvipix we recommend that, whenever you start a new project, you create a new folder for it. This is just "good housekeeping," but it can make managing your project's media files much easier.

5   **Select the option to Manage Project Files**

When you select the option to **Manage Project Files**, a sub-folder will be created in your project folder into which the program will save your captured video and temporary render files.

This keeps all of your project's files in a single place – making it much easier to clear all of the files associated with a project when your project is done and you want to reclaim your hard drive space.

Set up your project for 50p and 60p video

Some newer camcorders have the ability to shoot in 50p or 60p. The "p" which follows these frame rates indicates that this video is shot in progressive scan rather than interlaced – meaning that 50 or 60 *complete* frames of video are displayed every second. (This is as opposed to more traditional 50i and 60i, in which each frame of video is created by interlacing information from two frames – displaying only 25 or ~30 actual frames of video every second.) Many people claim that these advanced frame rates (essentially doubling the number of frames that display every second) give your video a smoother and more life-like look.

60p is the progressive scan standard for NTSC video; 50p is the standard for PAL.

For best results when working with these progressive video frames, set up your project based on its resolution, as described on page 27. Then modify your **Project Properties** by clicking on the icon in the **Preview** window or by selecting **Properties** from the **File** menu, as described on the facing page.

On the **Project Properties** dialog window, go to the **Video** tab and select the appropriate resolution, format and frame rate for your video from the **Templates** drop-down.

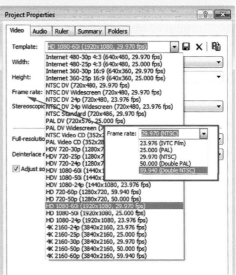

Change Project Properties

Even after you've started editing your project, you can change your current project's **Properties** by clicking on the cog at the top left of the **Preview** window. The **Project Properties** dialog window offers more detailed options than the **New Project** dialog.

In fact, there are a couple of properties here that you should set and lock in permanently:

Full Resolution Rendering Quality
We recommend you set this to **Best**.

Deinterlace Method
Make sure that this is set to either **Blend Field** or **Interpolate Fields**. (There is a lot of debate over which is better, although in truth the results are pretty similar – with **Interpolate Fields** usually recommended.)

Interlacing has to do with how your TV or computer draws a frame of video onscreen. An interlaced frame is drawn one horizontal line of pixels at a time, creating every other line in the first pass and then creating the lines in between them in the second pass. This happens 25-30 times a second, so it's too fast for your eyes to see.

Some video formats (AVIs, for instance) create their interlaced frames using the lower field (odd lines of pixels) first. Others (MPEGs, for instance) create theirs using the upper field (even lines of pixels) first. And some use progressive scan, which uses no interlacing whatsoever.

Selecting the option to use a **Blended** or **Interpolate Fields** deinterlacing method tells the program to minimize the differences between your source video and the project's settings.

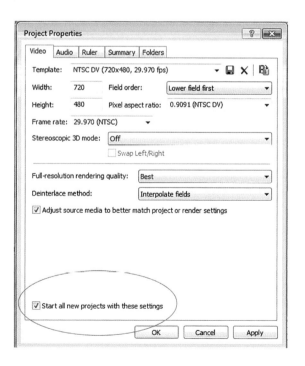

In addition, we recommend that you check the option to **Adjust Source Material to Better Match Project or Render Settings**.

Set Project Properties default
If you check the option to **Start All New Projects With These Settings**, your future projects will automatically be set up with the video and audio properties currently selected on this dialog window.

If you tend to work with similar video formats, this can simplify your projects' set-ups. You can then go right to the editing workspace for a new project by clicking the ■ button on the **Toolbar**.

Video, Audio and other Project Properties

On the **Project Properties** dialog, you can ensure that your video and audio are set properly for your project – and you can change them if you need to.

Under the **Video** tab, for instance, (as illustrated in the sidebar on the bottom of page 30), you can select one of any of 24 **Template**s from the drop-down menu, or you can manually set the individual properties.

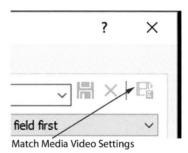

You can also select the **Match Media Video Settings** button on the upper right of this panel to set your project to automatically match the specs of your video, as described in the sidebar on page 29.

field first

Match Media Video Settings

Cut and paste between projects

If you need to, you can cut and paste clips, events or even entire sequences from the timeline of one Vegas Movie Studio project to another. This is done, essentially, by having both projects open at the same time.

1   **Select the clips you want to cut or copy**

    With one project open, select the events or clips you want to cut or copy.

    To select several events at once, hold down the **Ctrl** key as you select your clips on the timeline.

    You can also **Group** your clips so that they all stay together and you can grab them all at once (page 104) or use the **Selection Edit Tool** (page 96) to lasso your clips or events.

2   **Select the option to Copy or Cut**

    You can select the option to **Copy** or **Cut** from the **Edit** menu, select the option from the **right-click** menu or use the keyboard shortcut (**Ctrl+c** or **Ctrl+x**).

3   **Open a second instance of Vegas Movie Studio**

    Launch Vegas Movie Studio again from the Windows Start menu or by double-clicking on the desktop shortcut. The program will open as a second instance, independent of your original project.

    Open the project that you want to paste your clips into in the second program instance.

Vegas Movie Studio includes the option of having more than one instance of the program open at once, enabling you to cut and paste clips or even sequences between two projects' timelines!

4   Paste to the second project's timeline

To add the copied sequence to your other project, select the **Paste** option from that project's **Edit** menu, select the **Paste** option from the right-click menu or use the keyboard shortcut **Ctrl+v.**

Your video sequence will paste to the armed track at the position of the **Timeline Cursor** (playhead).

For information on arming a video or audio track, see page 77 of **Chapter 6, Edit Video On The Timeline.**

Capturing Tape-Based Video

Downloading Video from a Camcorder or Smartphone

Ripping Video from a DVD

Ripping Music from a CD

Importing Media into Your Project

Using Media Generators

Chapter 3
Get Media Into Your Project
Gathering your assets

Now that you've created your project, it's time to start putting media into it.

Your media can be video, audio, music, still photos or graphics. It can be streamed or downloaded from a device, ripped from a disc, downloaded from the internet or simply imported from your hard drive.

Your first step in building any video project is gathering your assets.

Gathering your assets – or getting your media – can involve capturing tape-based video, downloading stored video from your camcorder or smartphone or simply importing video, audio or still photos that are already on your computer into your Vegas Movie Studio project.

In any event, *all of the media you will use in your project must be on your computer's hard drive.* Using the tools included with Vegas Movie Studio, it's easy to simultaneously gather your media files onto your hard drive and add them to your project no matter where they are coming from.

Add media to your project

There are basically three ways media can be gathered into your project.

Video from tape-based camcorders is *captured*. Video from miniDV and HDV camcorders is captured, or streamed into your project over a FireWire (also called an IEEE-1394 or iLink) connection, and it is added to your hard drive in "real time." This means that you essentially play the videotape through your camcorder and it is recorded onto your hard drive using the capture software that is included with Vegas Movie Studio.

Video from non-tape camcorders is *downloaded* to your computer. Most modern camcorders store their video on a hard drive or flash memory card in the camcorder rather than on a tape. These video files are copied over to your hard drive and into your project over a USB connection using a Movie Studio tool called the **Device Explorer.** The program also includes tools for getting video and audio from DVDs and CDs.

Media already on your hard drive is *imported* into your project. If your video, still photos, music or other audio is already on your computer, it is merely added to your **Project Media** (see page 49).

So, although your video, still photos, graphics, music, audio and whatever else you plan to add to your project come in many different forms and from many different devices, the methods of getting the media into your project and/or onto your computer's hard drive are really just some variation of one of these three.

Titles and Media Generators

In addition to the media you will import into your project, there are a few types of media that are created right in the program.

Media Generators. Media Generators are specialized video clips that are created by the program, based on your settings. We'll show you how to use **Media Generators** on page 50.

Titles. Titles are the text overlays you will create for your movies. We'll show you more about creating, stylizing and even animating your titles in **Chapter 11, Add and Customize Your Titles.**

Capture video from a miniDV camcorder

Video from a tape-based miniDV camcorder is **captured** to your computer. Capturing is the process of recording your video to your computer in "real time" – which means that the video is recorded to your computer as your camcorder is playing it.

When video is captured from a miniDV camcorder, it is recorded to your computer as DV-AVI files. This is far and away the easiest and most efficient video format to edit on a personal computer.

To capture video from a miniDV camcorder:

1 **Connect your camcorder to your computer**

Your miniDV camcorder must be connected by a FireWire (also called an IEEE-1394 or iLink) connection. Vegas Movie Studio will not capture video over a USB connection. (Your camcorder may not have come with an IEEE-1394 cable. However, all miniDV camcorders have a FireWire jack. IEEE-1394 cables can be purchased online for $5-10 or at most "big box" stores for about $20.)

A FireWire connection is indicated with a Y-shaped logo.

Turn your camcorder on in **Play** or **VTR** mode.

Once your camcorder is connected, Windows should recognize the connection with a "bing bong" sound and your connection should be indicated by a camcorder icon on the right side of your Windows Task Bar.

Windows may also offer to auto-launch a capture program with a **Digital Video Device** option screen. Click **Cancel** to close this screen.

2 **Open the Vegas Movie Studio DV capture tool**

Open the Vegas Movie Studio **Capture** window by selecting **Capture Video** from the **Project** menu.

On the **Capture Video** option screen, select the **DV** option.

3 **Name your tape**

When you first open the **Capture** window, a pop-up dialog window will ask you to name the tape you're capturing from.

We recommend you don't just let the program name use the default "Tape 1." The name you give your "tape" here determines the name that Vegas Movie Studio gives your captured video file!

Use the transport controls to find the segment of your video tape you want to capture.

Click the Capture Video button to start capturing your tape.

Stop capture by either clicking the Pause or Stop button.

Optionally, you can set Vegas Movie Studio to capture your entire tape or only a still frame from it.

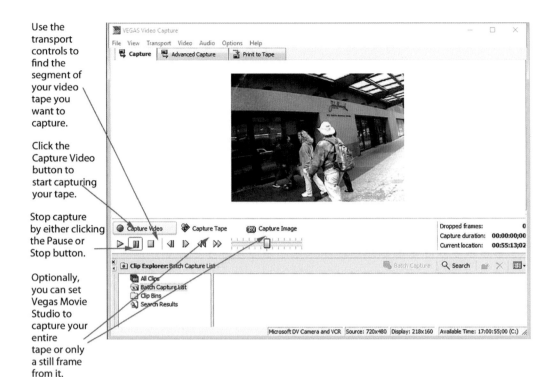

You can also elect to either have the program begin capturing your video immediately, or rewind to the beginning of the tape and automatically capture the entire tape, or you can elect to capture your video manually.

In most cases, you will select **Don't Capture Any Clips Right Now.**

When you click **OK**, you will be in the main **Capture** window.

If you do not see this pop-up menu, or if the transport buttons in the **Capture** window are grayed out, go to the **Capture** window's **Video** drop-down menu and ensure **Microsoft DV Camera and DV** is selected.

4   **Elect to use Advanced or simple Capture tools**

Under the **Capture** tab, you will find simple tools for capturing your video.

Under the **Advanced Capture** tab, you will find options for custom-naming your captured video clips and for setting up a **Batch Capture**. (More information on **Batch Capturing** can be found on page 40.)

5   **Locate a segment to capture**

Using the transport control buttons below the **Capture** window's **Preview** screen to control your camcorder, advance or rewind your tape to locate the segment you want to capture.

Pause the video at the point where you'd like to begin capturing.

6   **Begin your capture**

Click the red **Capture Video** button.

By default, your video will be captured into the **Documents** folder on your computer's hard drive. You can change where your video is captured to in the **Capture Preferences**, as discussed on page 262 of the **Appendix**.

Your captured video will automatically be broken into segments based on your recorded video's timecode.

In other words, at any point that the program recognizes that you paused or stopped your camcorder, it will create a new video segment.

If you'd like to turn this "scene detection" feature off, you can do so by going to the **Option** menu on the **Capture** window, selecting **Preferences** and, under the **Capture** tab, unchecking **Enable Scene Detection**.

7   **Stop capture**

To stop capturing your video, click the **Stop** or **Pause** button.

When you are finished capturing, you can then close this panel and return to the Vegas Movie Studio editing workspace.

Note that while it is not necessary to close the **Capture** window, leaving your camcorder connected to your computer can divert resources from your editing workspace. We recommend that, **once you've finished capturing, you disconnect your camcorder from your computer.**

MiniDV video is best edited in a Vegas Movie Studio project using the **DV** project settings (as discussed on page 27).

If you're having problems capturing your miniDV footage with Vegas Movie Studio, there are alternative tools (most of them free) that will capture your video in a format that's compatible with the program.

We list a number of them in our **Recommended Capture Utilities** on page 263 of the **Appendix**.

To Batch Capture, use the transport buttons to find the spot at which you want to begin capturing.

Mark it as your In Point.

Navigate to the spot on the video tape at which you'd like to stop capturing. Mark the Out Point.

Click Capture In/Out and the program will automatically rewind the tape and capture the segment you've indicated.

Batch Capture your video

Vegas Movie Studio includes a **Batch Capture** feature. This feature will automatically capture a section of your miniDV tape based on the start and end points you provide. **Batch Capturing** can save you the trouble of having to wait and watch as your tape is captured in "real time."

To set up a **Batch Capture**:

1 **Open Advanced Capture**

Open the **Capture** window by clicking on the camcorder icon along the top of the **Project Media** panel or by selecting **Capture Video** from the program's **Project** menu.

In the **Capture** window, go to the **Advanced Capture** tab.

2 **Set your Capture In Point**

Using the transport controls below the **Preview** window, cue your video tape to the spot you'd like your capture to begin.

Click the yellow flag **Mark In** button ⌐ as illustrated above.

3 **Set your Capture Out Point**

Using the transport controls, cue your video tape up to the spot you'd like your capture to end.

Click the yellow flag **Mark Out** button ⌐.

If you change your mind about the locations of these **In** and **Out** points, you can revise them at any time by re-cueing your video tape and re-clicking the **Mark In** or **Mark Out** button or by typing in the timecode manually.

4   **Click Capture In/Out**

The program will automatically rewind the tape and capture the segment you've designated, breaking the captured video into short clips based on when your camcorder was paused or shut off between shots.

As the video is being automatically captured, you can elect, at any point, to not capture a scene. To skip a scene, click the **Ignore This Section** button.

Capture video from an HDV camcorder

As with miniDV, video from a tape-based HDV camcorder is **captured** to your computer. Capturing is the process of recording your video to your computer in "real time" – which means that the video is recorded to your computer as your camcorder is playing it.

When video is captured from an HDV camcorder, it is recorded to your computer as M2T or M2TS files. (These M2T and M2TSs are high-definition MPEG2 video files.)

To capture video from an HDV camcorder:

1   **Connect your camcorder to your computer**

Connect your HDV camcorder to your computer with a FireWire (also known as an IEEE-1394 or iLink) cable.

Turn your camcorder on in **Play** or **VTR** mode.

Once your camcorder is connected, Windows should recognize the connection with a "bing bong" sound and your connection should be indicated by a camcorder icon on the right side of the Windows Task Bar.

Windows may also offer to auto-launch a capture program with a **Digital Video Device** option screen. Click **Cancel** to close this screen.

2   **Open the Vegas Movie Studio HDV capture tool**

Open the Vegas Movie Studio **Capture** tool by selecting **Capture Video** from the **Project** menu.

On the **Capture Video** option screen, select the **HDV** option.

Browse to save your captured video in a location other than the default.

As with miniDV capture, the HDV Capture window includes tools for setting up a Batch Capture.

To capture from an HDV camcorder, use the transport buttons to cue the tape to the spot you'd like to begin capture.

Click the red Capture button to begin capture.
Click the Stop or Pause buttons to stop capture.

The HDV capture screen is a bit more advanced than the miniDV capture screen, but they function essentially the same way.

The tools on the right hand side of the HDV **Capture** window can be used to **Batch Capture** your video, as discussed on page 40.

3   **Locate a segment to capture**

Using the transport controls below the **Capture** window's **Preview** screen, advance or rewind the tape to locate the segment you want to capture.

Pause the video at the point at which you'd like your capture to begin.

4   **Begin your capture**

Click the red **Capture** button.

By default, your video will be captured into the **Documents** folder on your computer's hard drive. However, this location can be changed by clicking the **Browse** button, as illustrated above.

However, by using the options at the top right of the HDV **Capture** window, you can designate a location to which your captured video will be saved.

If you're having problems capturing your HDV footage with Vegas Movie Studio, see our **Recommended Capture Utilities** on page 263 of the **Appendix**.

5   **Stop capture**

To stop capturing your video, click the **Stop** or **Pause** button on the Capture window's transport controls.

You can then close this panel and return to the Vegas Movie Studio editing workspace.

Note that while it is not necessary to close the **Capture** window, leaving your camcorder connected to your computer can divert resources from your editing workspace. We recommend that, once you've finished capturing, you disconnect your camcorder from your computer.

HDV video is best edited in a Vegas Movie Studio project using the **HDV** project settings (as discussed on page 27).

Capture video from an analog or non-DV source

The process used to capture video from an analog source (such as a VHS camcorder) is similar to the process used to capture video from a miniDV camcorder. The main difference is that, since there is no direct connection between the camcorder and your computer, you will need to manually control the camcorder's, VCR's or other video player's playback using the unit's transport controls. When your video is cued up and ready, click the **Capture** button in the Vegas Movie Studio Capture window.

At Muvipix, we recommend against using capture cards or USB-based devices like the Plextor or Dazzle digitizer to capture analog video. The best devices for capturing analog video for editing are called DV bridges. These devices connect to your computer with a FireWire (IEEE-1394) cable and save the captured video as DV-AVIs.

DV bridges range from relatively inexpensive to high-end professional devices with time base correction and other video optimizers. The best value on the market in DV bridges (and a Muvipix recommended "best buy") is the Grass Valley ADVC bridge, available for less than $200 – a great value if you expect to edit a lot of video from non-digital sources.

A discontinued device that's also a long-time favorite of Muvipixers (and still available online for as little as $100) is the ADS Pyro AV Link.

Both devices produce excellent results and are highly recommended.

An alternative to a DV bridge is a set-up called a pass-through, which essentially uses a miniDV camcorder as a DV bridge. (This feature is not available on all miniDV cams.)

To set up a pass-through capture, attach your analog camcorder or video player to your miniDV camcorder's AV inputs, and then link the miniDV camcorder to your computer via a FireWire cable. With the miniDV camcorder in play mode (but *without* a tape in the compartment), the analog video flows through the miniDV and into the computer, where it is captured as DV-AVIs.

Download your video from a non-tape based camcorder

Virtually all current camcorders save their video to a hard drive or other storage medium (such as a flash memory card) inside the camera rather than recording it to tape.

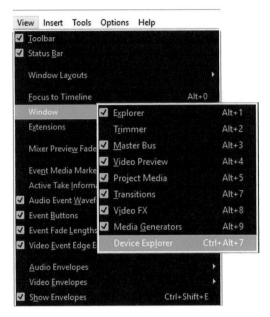

AVCHD video has become the standard for 1920x1080 high-definition consumer video. AVCHD camcorders range in price from inexpensive consumer cams to pricey semi-professional cameras, and the quality of it all is excellent.

Since the advent of smartphones and action cameras (like the GoPro), your video may also be coming from non-traditional camera sources, including drones and dashcams – and your video resolution can range from high-definition to 4K XAVC-S (3840x2160) and beyond.

Vegas Movie Studio can work with virtually all of these formats (plus professional formats like NXCAM and XDCAM EX).

Downloading this video from your camcorder onto your computer (and into your Vegas Movie Studio project) is fairly simple, thanks to Movie Studio's built-in **Device Explorer.**

To download your video from a non-tape based camcorder:

1   **Connect your camcorder to your computer**

   Connect your camcorder to your computer with a USB cable.

   Turn your camcorder on in **Play** or **VTR** mode. Once your camcorder is connected, Windows should recognize the connection with a "bing bong" sound. If it doesn't, check your camcorder's LCD display to see if you first need to activate your cam's USB connection. (Windows may also offer to auto-launch a capture program with a **Digital Video Device** option screen. Click **Cancel** to close this screen.)

2   **Open the Device Explorer**

   Go to the Vegas Movie Studio **View** menu. Select **Window**, then **Device Explorer**, as illustrated above.

3   **Select your camcorder**

   If there is more than one device listed in the **Device Explorer** (illustrated above), select your hard drive or video storage camcorder.

   The right-hand window will display thumbnails of all of the video clips in your camcorder's memory storage.

The Device Explorer interfaces with non-taped based camcorders like the AVCHD cam.

You can preview selected clips using the transport buttons.

The Device Explorer can be set to display all clips, only the clips you've imported or only new clips that have been added to the camcorder.

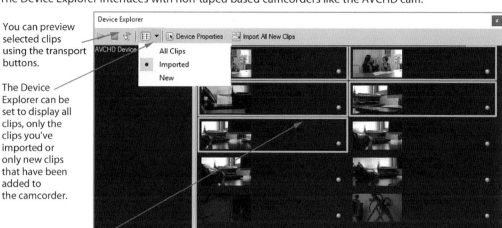

Select the clips you'd like to import into your project and click the Import button.

4   Indicate the clips you'd like to download

Using the transport tools in the top left of the **Device Explorer**, you can preview your camcorder's clips. When the 🎬 button is selected, your clips will play automatically when selected.

Click to select the clips you'd like to download into your project. To select more than one clip, hold down the **Ctrl** or **Shift** keys as you select.

5   Import your clips

Click the **Import** button (or select the option to **Import All New Clips**).

Your video will be downloaded to your computer and simultaneously added to the list in your open project's **Project Media** window.

As with any project, you'll get the very best performance from the program and the very best results if your project properties match your source video.

For AVCHD video, that means setting up a project using the **AVCHD** settings (as described on page 27 of **Chapter 2, Start a New Project**).

For other video formats, you should use the program's **Match Media Settings** tool, as described on page 29.

If the **Device Explorer** does not recognize your smartphone or action cam, it may be necessary for you to manually copy the video from your device to your computer using Windows Explorer and then import the video into your project using **Add Media**, as described on page 49.

Get video from a DVD or DVD camcorder

Whether you're getting your video from a DVD movie or from a disc produced by a miniDVD camcorder, the process is the same: You place the disc in your computer's drive and use Vegas Movie Studio's tools to "rip" the video files to your computer's hard drive.

As your video files are downloaded to your hard drive, they will be simultaneously added to your Vegas Movie Studio project.

To get video from a DVD:

1 Place the DVD in your computer's disc drive

If your disc was created by a DVD camcorder, be sure to **finalize** your disc in the camcorder before you place it into your drive.

If your disc drive is set to auto-launch, Windows will offer you a list of optional actions.

Click **Cancel** to close this window.

2 Select the Import DVD option

Go to Vegas Movie Studio's **Project** menu and select **Import DVD Camcorder**, as illustrated above left.

The **Import from DVD Camcorder** option window will appear.

3 Select your drive

If your disc doesn't appear on the **Import from DVD Camcorder** option window, select it from the drop-down menu at the top of the window, as illustrated below.

4 Import the DVD files

Click **Browse** to select a folder to download your files to, or use the default option.

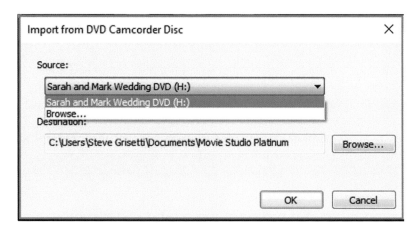

Click the **OK** button.

Vegas Movie Studio will import your video as MPG files.

VOB files (the format your video is stored as on a DVD) are actually MPEG2 files – so, aside from changing the suffix for the files, Vegas Movie Studio does not change these files in any way. It imports them essentially as is.

To set up a project to edit MPEG video, you should use the program's **Match Media Settings** tool, as described on page 29.

Extract audio from a CD

Although you can extract, or "rip," music from a CD with iTunes, Windows Media Player and a number of other music players, Vegas Movie Studio Platinum includes tools for ripping the music directly from the disc to your project.

Extract Audio from a CD with Power2Go

Power2Go is a free program that Magix bundles with Vegas Movie Studio 14 Platinum. If you'd prefer to use the built-in CD extractor in Vegas Movie Studio, see the following page.

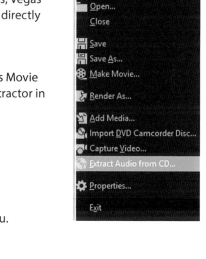

1   **Place your CD in your computer's disc drive**

Most DVD and BluRay disc drives can also read CDs.

2   **Select Extract Audio from CD tool**

Select **Extract Audio from CD** from the **Project** menu.

The **Magix Power2Go** program will launch.

3   **Indicate how you'd like your selection options displayed**

If your CD is not displayed on the **Extract Audio** screen, select the **Drive** in which your disc has been loaded from the drop-down menu.

4   **Select the tracks you want to extract**

Check the music tracks you'd like to rip to your project.

5   **Set the destination for your recording**

Under **Destination Folder**, click **...** to browse to the folder you'd like ripped music saved to.

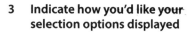
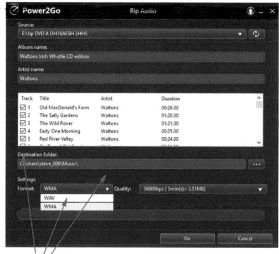

Select the songs you'd like to rip, the destination you'd like to save them to and the format you'd like to save them as.

6   **Select the Format and Quality for your recording**

Set the **Format** of your saved file to **WMA** (Windows Media) or the more universal **WAV** format.

If you'd like, change the **Quality** level – although the default 96000 kpbs is pretty standard for MP3s.

7   **Click Go to start the file rip**

Extract Audio from a CD with Vegas Movie Studio

1   **Open the Extract Audio from CD tool**

Select **Extract Audio from CD** from the **Project** menu. The **Extract Audio** dialog window will open.

If Power2Go opens, you can opt to close it and use the built-in Vegas CD Extractor.

2   **Indicate how you'd like your selection options to appear**

Select the view you would like to use to select which tracks you will rip.

Read by Track will display a list of the disc's individual tracks.

Read Entire Disc rips the entire disc to your project.

Read by Range gives you the option of selecting a segment of your disc for extraction by setting a start and end time.

4   **Select the tracks you want to extract**

Check the music tracks you would like to record. Click OK.

5   **Name and save your extracted file**

Your selected music will be added to your project and saved to your hard drive as WAV files.

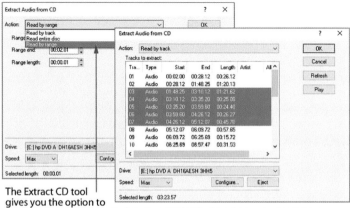

The Extract CD tool gives you the option to rip the entire disc, a selected range or individual tracks to your hard drive.

Import video and audio already on your computer

And of course a lot of the media you'll be adding to your project is already on your computer! To load these video, audio, music and still photo files into your project, you need only click the **Add Media** button in the upper left of the **Project Media** panel and browse to it!

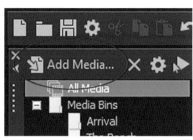

Add media from the Explorer window

By default, the **Explorer** window can be found sharing the tabbed window space with the **Project Media, Transitions, Video FX** and **Media Generators** windows in the upper right of the program's interface.

The **Explorer** window functions similarly to your operating system's Windows Explorer browse screen. In fact, it's essentially just another way to browse the media files on your computer.

Once you've located a media file or files you'd like to add to your project, you can right-click on the clip or clips and select the option to **Add to Project Media List**.

Alternatively, you can simply drag your media files directly from this window to your project's timeline. As you do, Vegas Movie Studio will automatically add the clips to your **Project Media** window's list.

Along the top of the panel are tools for changing or refreshing your view, previewing your media clips and removing files from your computer.

In the upper right of the panel you will find the **Get Media From Web** button and a toggle switch for changing how the media files are displayed in the panel.

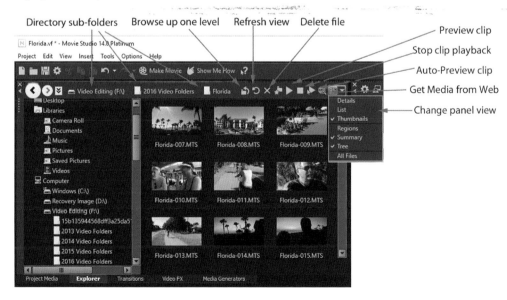

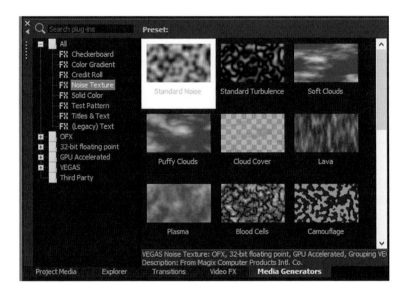

Create specialized media with Media Generators

The **Media Generators** window shares the tabbed window space with the **Project Media, Explorer, Transitions** and **Video FX** windows in the upper left of the program's interface.

Media Generators include pre-created media clips in the forms of patterns, colors, test patterns and even animated, rolling and still titles. Each of these media clips can be modified and, if you'd like, even animated with keyframes.

Preset media clips and textures

The major categories of non-text or non-title generated media textures are:

Checkerboard. A collection of patterns including checkerboards, diagonal diamond patterns and vertical and horizontal blinds.

Color Gradient. A collection of gradations of color, such as a linear gradient of black to white, a radial gradient of yellow to orange, a rainbow gradient and various patterns with feathered transparency at their centers.

Noise Texture. Abstract patterns like moss, wood and marble textures, camouflage, clouds, starfields and lightning strikes.

Solid Color. A collection of, as you'd expect, solid color clips.

Test Pattern. A collection of various color bars and other color test and calibration patterns.

Among their many uses, media clips and textures can be very useful as masks, as we discuss on page 118 of **Chapter 7, More Timeline Tools**.

Preset title templates

In addition, the **Media Generators** window includes a number of pre-created title templates:

Credit Roll. A collection of various animated rolling patterns.

Titles & Text. A collection of title templates, including a number that feature text animation.

(Legacy) Text. A basic set of title templates.

We'll discuss these title **Media Generators** in more detail in **Chapter 11, Add and Customize Your Titles**.

Customize generated media

Although **Generated Media** can be used "as is" in your video project, the clips are also easily customizable.

1   **Add a generated media clip to your timeline**

Drag a clip from the **Media Generators** window to your project's timeline.

A **Video Media Generator** dialog window will automatically open.

The options on this window will vary, depending on the effects that were used to create the media clip. Some **Video Media Generator** dialogs include several pages of options, accessible by clicking tabs along the top of the panel.

2   **Select a preset**

At the top of the **Video Media Generator** dialog window, there is usually a drop-down menu. This drop-down menu includes a list of presets for the panel's effects.

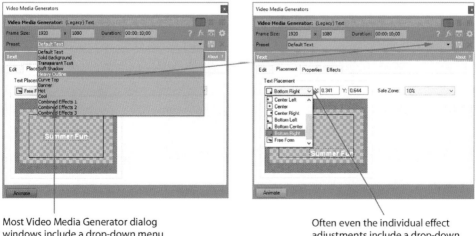

Most Video Media Generator dialog windows include a drop-down menu with several preset options for the effect.

Often even the individual effect adjustments include a drop-down list of presets.

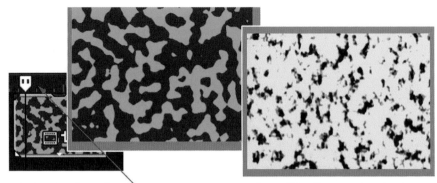

If the Timeline Cursor (playhed) is positioned over your clip, you'll be able to preview the changes you're making in the Media Geneator dialog in the program's Preview monitor.

Even if a preset doesn't get you exactly what you want, it can often get you close enough that it only takes a few tweaks to customize your precise effect.

If the timeline cursor is positioned over your **Media Generator** clip, you can preview any changes you make in the program's **Preview** window.

3 **Animate your clip's effects**

As with any effect in Vegas Movie Studio, the color, shape or any other property of your **Generated Media** clip doesn't have to be stationary. Clicking the clock-like animation buttons to the right of any property opens a **Keyframe Controller** along the bottom of the dialog window in which you can create movement in the clip and even have it shift from one set of colors to another.

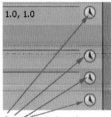

Property animation buttons

For more information on this process, see **Keyframe a Generated Media animation** on page 226 of **Chapter 15, Vary Effects with Keyframes**.

Set a Generated Media clip's length

By default, **Generated Media** clips appear on the timeline with a duration of 10 seconds.

You can trim a **Generated Media** event shorter on your timeline by dragging its end points in.

However, you can't make a **Generated Media** event play longer simply by stretching it longer on the timeline.

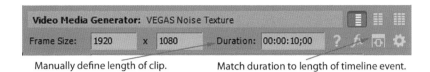

Manually define length of clip.   Match duration to length of timeline event.

There are two ways to set a **Generated Media** clip's length:

- Manually type in the **Length** in the box at the top of the **Video Media Generator** dialog window, as illustrated above; or

- Drag the ends of the clip on your timeline so that it is the length you desire, then click on the **Match Event Length** button at the top right of the **Media Generator** dialog window.

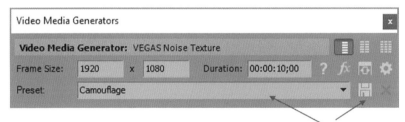

Your custom settings can be saved as a preset by typing a custom name onto the Preset menu and clicking on the Save Preset button.

Save Generated Media settings as a preset

Once you've created and customized your effect, you can save it as a **Video Media Generator preset** for later re-use.

To save your settings, type a name for your preset in the **Preset** box and then click the **Floppy Disc** icon in the upper right corner of the window.

Your new preset will then appear among the list of presets on the drop-down menu on the **Video Media Generators** dialog window.

Re-edit a Generated Media clip

To reopen a **Media Generator** clip and changes its settings, click on the filmstrip icon at the top of the clip's thumbnail on your timeline.

To re-open a Generated Media clip's Video Media Generator dialog window for re-editing, click the filmstrip icon on the event clip on your timeline.

Get to Know the Project Media Window

Organizing and Viewing Your Media

Pre-Applying Media FX

Managing Your Media Files

Chapter 4

Order and Prep Your Clips in the Project Media Window

The catalog of your imported media

The Project Media window displays a list of all of the media clips that have been added to your project.

The window also includes tools for managing and cataloging your clips as well as for importing more media into it.

The Project Media window can display thumbnails...

... lists, media clips or clip details.

Get to know the Project Media window

The **Project Media** window lists all of the media that has been added to your project by capturing or downloading them from your camcorder or by importing them from your hard drive.

The panel also includes a number of tools for gathering media into your project. (For more information on using Vegas Movie Studio's tools for adding media, see **Chapter 3, Get Media into Your Project**.)

Media clip views

As illustrated above, clips in the **Project Media** window can be set to display in a number of views, which can be selected by clicking the button in the upper right of the panel.

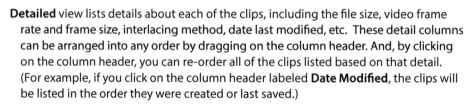

List view lists all of the media files in alpha-numeric order.

Detailed view lists details about each of the clips, including the file size, video frame rate and frame size, interlacing method, date last modified, etc. These detail columns can be arranged into any order by dragging on the column header. And, by clicking on the column header, you can re-order all of the clips listed based on that detail. (For example, if you click on the column header labeled **Date Modified**, the clips will be listed in the order they were created or last saved.)

Thumbnail view displays your clips as video thumbnails or, if audio, as icons indicating their audio file type. This is the default view for this window, and it is probably the easiest and most intuitive display view.

Preview your Project Media clips in the Trimmer

When you right-click a media file in your **Project Media** panel and select **Open in Trimmer**, your video will be displayed in the **Trimmer** window.

If you activate the **Auto-Play** button by clicking on it, your clips will automatically play in the **Trimmer** when selected. (For more information on the **Trimmer**, see **Chapter 5**.)

Organize your clips in Media Bins

Media Bins are folders and sub-folders that you can create and use to organize the media in your **Project Media** window.

This can come in very handy, especially if you have dozens of media clips in your video project!

To create and use a **Media Bin**:

1 **Select Create New Bin**

   Right-click on the **Media Bin** folder icon and select the **Create New Bin** option.

   You can also create a new **Media Bin** as a **sub-Bin** within an existing bin.

   You can even create a **sub-sub-Media Bin**!

2 **Drag clips into the Media Bins**

   Once you've created your **Media Bin**(s), click on **All Media** to display all of your clips.

   Adding media clips to your bins is as simple as dragging them from the **Project Media** browser window to one of your bin folders.

All of your clips will still be visible when you have **All Media** selected.

But, when you click on any **Media Bin**, the **Project Media** window will display only those clips that you've placed in that bin.

Media Bins are merely a cataloging system. The same clip can be added to more than one bin. And **Media Bins** do not affect the actual location of your clips on your hard drive.

Creating Media Bins (and sub-Bins) and storing your media clips in them can make managing a large number of clips much easier.

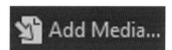

If media clips are imported while a Media Bin is selected, the clips will automatically be added to that particular bin.

Media Offline warning

Occasionally Vegas Movie Studio may warn you that a media file is no longer online. This is an indication that the link from your Vegas Movie Studio project to that media clip has been broken.

This can happen because the device on which the clip is stored has been removed. (If an external hard drive, for instance, has been disconnected.)

It can also happen if a clip has been renamed or moved to another location on your computer.

When this occurs, the Vegas Movie Studio warning window offers a number of options.

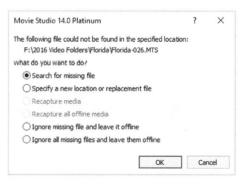

When a media file has been moved, removed or renamed, or the device the file is stored on is disconnected from your computer, Movie Studio will warn you that the link to your Project Media window listing has been broken and ask for your help resolving the issue.

If you would like to rebuild the link to that media file, select the option to **Search For Missing File**. This option will automatically search any location on your computer for your missing or unlinked file.

If the file has been renamed or moved, select the option to **Specify a New Location or Replacement File**. A browse screen will open, allowing you to browse to and locate the file.

You can also select the option to **Ignore the Missing File.** Then, if you no longer want the clip in your project, you can **right-click** on it in the **Project Media** panel and select the option to **Remove from Project**.

Locate a media clip on your hard drive

There are two ways to view a clip's location on your computer's hard drive, once it has been added to your **Project Media** panel:

Both options are available through a **right-click** menu:

- If you **right-click** on a clip and select **Explore Containing Folder**, a Windows Explorer browse screen will open, displaying the folder in which your original clip resides on your hard drive.

- If you **right-click** on a clip and select **Properties**, a **Properties** window will open, displaying various information about the clip. The location of your file will be displayed at the top of the **Media** panel.

You can easily locate on your hard drive a clip that has been added to your Project Media panel by right-clicking on it and selecting Explore Containing Folder or Properties.

Remove All Unused Media

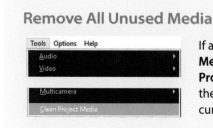

If at any point you want to clean out your **Project Media** window, go to the **Tools** menu and select **Clean Project Media**. This tool will automatically remove from the **Project Media** window all media clips that are not currently in use on your timeline.

The Stabilize tool can take some of the shake out of a handheld shot.

Pre-stabilize a media clip

If there's handheld camcorder shake in your video clip, Vegas Movie Studio can take some of the jiggle from the video before you even add it to your timeline. As we show you on page 60, once you've added **Media FX**, like **Stabilization**, to a clip in your **Project Media,** these effects will appear pre-applied to the clip whenever you use the clip on your project's timeline!

1   **Apply the Stabilize tool**

Right-click on a clip in your **Project Media** panel and select **Media FX** from the context menu. The **Plug-In Chooser** window will open.

Select **Magix Stabilize** from the list of available **Media FX Plug-Ins**.

2   **Select a Stabilize tool level**

On the **Media FX** option panel that opens, set the level of stabilization you'd like applied from the drop-down **Preset** menu.

Click **Apply.**

The **Stabilize** tool will analyze the clip and apply the necessary effect, and the **(Stabilized)** indicator will be appended to the clip's name in the **Project Media** panel.

In order to understand which stabilization level to select, it's important to understand how the **Stabilize** tool works.

To stabilize a clip, the program will zoom in on your video to some degree and, focusing on an object or color in the center of the screen, it will create motion paths over the clip to keep that element in the center of the screen.

This means that the tool must, by its nature:

• Remove some of the video around the edge of the clip, and

• Compromise some of your video's resolution.

In other words, the more stabilization you apply, the more you will compromise the quality of your video. Selecting the ideal stabilization level, then, means balancing how much stability you want applied to your clip with how much of the clip's quality you are willing to sacrifice.

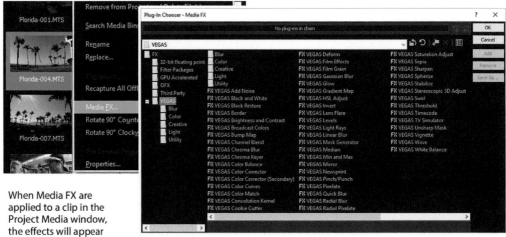

When Media FX are applied to a clip in the Project Media window, the effects will appear pre-applied to your clip whenever the media file is used in your Movie Studio project.

Pre-apply an effect to a "media" clip

There are four ways to apply an effect to your movie project:

- Apply an effect to an individual "**event**" on your timeline, in which case the effect will be applied *only* to that individual use of the clip.
- Apply an effect to an entire video or audio **track** on your timeline, in which case the effect will be applied to *every clip* on that video or audio track.
- Apply an effect to your entire video project.
- Apply an effect to a "**media**" clip in the **Project Media** panel.

When an effect is applied to an audio or video clip in the **Project Media** panel (at which point it is called a "media" clip), the clip is "pre-effected," meaning that this clip will appear with the effect already applied whenever you use it in your project.

To apply an effect to a **Project Media** clip:

1   **Select the option to add Media FX**

    Right-click on the clip in the **Project Media** panel and select the **Media FX** option.

    The **Plug-In Chooser** dialog window will open, as illustrated above.

2   **Select an effect**

    Click to select an effect in the **Plug-In Chooser** and then click **OK**.

    The **Plug-In Chooser** will close, revealing the **Media FX** dialog window.

3   **Customize the effect**

    Adjust the individual properties of the effect, as described in **Chapter 12, Add and Adjust a Video Effect** or **Chapter 13, Add and Adjust an Audio Effect**.

You can also pre-apply keyframed animation effects to your media, as described in **Chapter 15, Vary Effects with Keyframes**.

You will not be able to see the results of any effects you've added to your clip until the clip is added to your timeline and the timeline cursor (playhead) is positioned over the clip. In fact, as you create the effect, you may want to temporarily place your clip on the timeline as you add and adjust its effects.

Because the effect is being added to the "media" clip (while still in the **Project Media** window) rather than an event, the effect will remain pre-applied to the clip, even after you remove it from the timeline.

Once an effect is added to a media clip, the effect can be customized or keyframed to create an animated effect.

Tools for working with still photos

The **Project Media** window includes a couple of tools that are particularly useful for preparing still photos for use on your timeline.

Red-Eye Reduction
The **Red-Eye Reduction** tool darkens and desaturates those flaming red eyes that sometimes show up in photos of people or pets when they're taken with a flash in dim light.

To use the tool, **right-click** on the photo in your **Project Media** window and select **Red-Eye Reduction**. In the dialog window that opens, drag to lasso the red-eye areas on your subject. Using the **+** and **-** buttons in the lower left of the panel, you can zoom in or out.

Your results won't show in the **Trimmer** or in the **Project Media** window, so you'll likely need to temporarily put the image on your timeline and position the **Timeline Cursor** (playhead) over it so that you can see what you're doing in the **Preview** window. You can then delete the clip from the timeline and the effect will still remain applied.

Rotate Clips
To rotate a video clip or still image, **right-click** on it in the **Project Media** window and select either **Rotate 90 Degrees Clockwise** or **Rotate 90 Degrees Counter-Clockwise**.

Remove a clip from your Project Media

To remove a clip from your **Project Media** panel, **right-click** on it and select **Remove from Project**. The clip will be removed from your project – but will remain on your computer's hard drive. (You can also simply click on a media clip and press **Delete** on your keyboard. The clip will be removed from **Project Media** but will *not* be deleted from your computer.)

If you **right-click** on a clip (or clips) in your **Project Media** panel and select **Remove from Project and Delete File(s)**, the clip will be completely removed from your computer.

If your clip is currently on your timeline when you select one of the **Remove** options, a dialog window will appear reminding you that the clip is currently in use and asking you to confirm your decision to delete the file.

Replace a clip in your Project Media

Replacing a clip swaps the current clip in use in your project for another on your hard drive. **Replacing** a clip replaces every use of the clip in your timeline.

Replacing a clip is a key step in **proxy editing**, as we discuss on page 264 of the **Appendix**.

A number of options are available when you right-click on a media clip in the Project Media panel.

Recapture All Off-Line Media

In the event that a video clip in your project was captured from a miniDV or HDV camcorder and is accidentally deleted from your computer, you can opt to have the program automatically re-capture the video from your camcorder.

To recapture your video

1 **Connect your camcorder**

    Place the tape containing the clip in your camcorder and connect it to your computer via a FireWire/IEEE-1394 connection.

2 **Select the re-capture option**

    Right-click on the thumbnail representing the off-line clip in the **Project Media** window and select **Recapture All Off-line Media**.

The program will automatically locate the missing clip on the tape, based on its timecode, and **Batch Capture** it back into your project, replacing the clip currently selected in **Project Media**.

For more information on **Batch Capturing**, see page 40 in **Chapter 3, Get Media Into Your Project**.

Opening Media in the Trimmer

Pre-Trimming a Media Clip

Creating a Sub-Clip

Adding Audio-Only or Video-Only

Options for Adding Media from the Trimmer

Chapter 5

Prepare Your Media in the Trimmer Window

Previewing and pre-setting your clips

Available only in Advanced mode, the Trimmer is primarily a monitor for previewing your video and audio clips in your Project Media panel.

But it's also a dynamic workspace for pre-trimming and preparing your clips before – and after – you add them to your project's timeline.

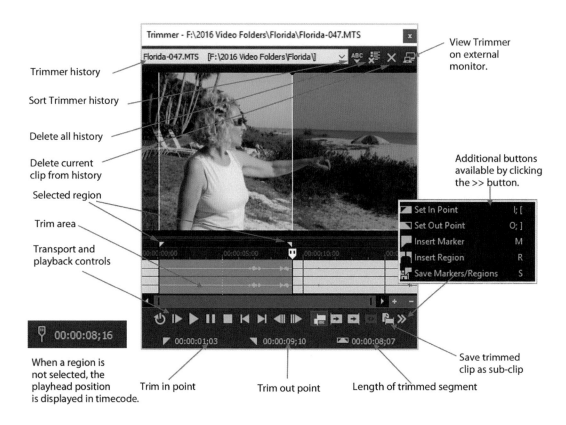

Trimmer - F:\2016 Video Folders\Florida\Florida-047.MTS

Florida-047.MTS   [F:\2016 Video Folders\Florida\]

View Trimmer on external monitor.

Trimmer history

Sort Trimmer history

Delete all history

Delete current clip from history

Selected region

Trim area

Transport and playback controls

Additional buttons available by clicking the >> button.

Set In Point   I; [
Set Out Point   O;]
Insert Marker   M
Insert Region   R
Save Markers/Regions S

00:00:08;16

00:00:01;03   00:00:09;10   00:00:08;07

When a region is not selected, the playhead position is displayed in timecode.

Trim in point

Trim out point

Length of trimmed segment

Save trimmed clip as sub-clip

The **Trimmer** is launched by **right-clicking** on a clip in either **Project Media** or on the **Timeline** and selecting **Open in Trimmer**.

The **Trimmer's** main purpose is to preview your individual media clips before they are added to your timeline. However, it is also a dynamic workspace, and it includes tools for preparing and pre-trimming your clips prior to adding them to the timeline as well as for saving these pre-trimmed clips as new **sub-clips** in your **Project Media** panel.

Open a clip in the Trimmer

The **Trimmer** can open both media clips in the **Project Media** window and event clips on the **Timeline**:

Open in Trimmer
Open Parent Media in Trimmer
Add as CD Track
Add at Project Frame Rate
Select Timeline Events
Match Project Video Settings

To open a media clip in the **Project Media** window, **right-click** on the clip and select the option to **Open in Trimmer**.

To open an event clip on the **Timeline**, **right-click** on the clip and select the option to **Open in Trimmer**.

If a clip you've selected is a sub-clip of a longer clip (as discussed on page 68), you will also have the option to **Open Parent Media in Trimmer**. This will open the *original* media clip from which the sub-clip was created.

Launch the Trimmer with a double-click

By default, when you **double-click** on a clip in your **Project Media** window in Vegas Movie Studio, the clip will be added to the "armed" track on your timeline as an event. (For more information on arming tracks, see **Arm a video or audio track** on page 77.)

However, in many other video editing programs, **double-clicking** on a clip in the media panel opens it in the **Trimmer** instead.

If you would like to set up the program so that **double-clicking** on a media clip opens it in the **Trimmer**, you can set this preference by going to **Options** on the Menu Bar and selecting **Preferences**. Under the **General** tab on the **Preferences** dialog window, check the option **Double-Click on Media Files Loads Into Trimmer Instead of Tracks.**

Trimmer history

Clips previously opened in the **Trimmer** can be re-opened by selecting them from the history drop-down menu at the top left of the **Trimmer** window.

The **Trimmer** history can be sorted by clicking the ▦ button at the top of the window. Clicking on this button will list all previously-opened clips in alpha-numeric order. **Ctrl-clicking** on this button will list these clips in *reverse* alpha-numeric order.

Trimmer history can be cleared completely by clicking on the ▦ button.

Individual clips can be removed from the **Trimmer** history by selecting them and then clicking the ✕ delete button.

Hover scrub a clip in the Trimmer

New to version 14, your clips can now be "hover scrubbed" through.

In other words, in addition to simply playing your clip in the **Trimmer** or even dragging the playhead along the clip's timeline (traditional "scrubbing"), you can also scrub through a clip simply by dragging your mouse over the video preview.

This makes it easier than ever to move to a specific spot in your clip.

When you hover scrub your clips, your playhead position is represented by a vertical line which drags through the video preview.

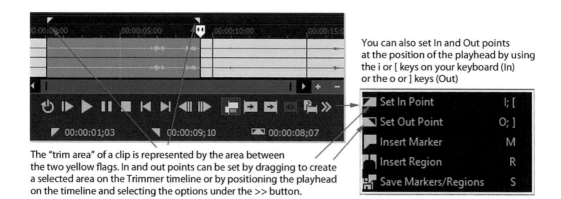

You can also set In and Out points at the position of the playhead by using the i or [keys on your keyboard (In) or the o or] keys (Out)

The "trim area" of a clip is represented by the area between the two yellow flags. In and out points can be set by dragging to create a selected area on the Trimmer timeline or by positioning the playhead on the timeline and selecting the options under the >> button.

Set In Point	I; [
Set Out Point	O;]
Insert Marker	M
Insert Region	R
Save Markers/Regions	S

Pre-trim a clip in the Trimmer

One of the primary functions of the **Trimmer** is – as its name would imply – to trim or pre-trim your media clips before you add them to your timeline.

Trimming means removing footage from either end of a clip so that only a select segment of the clip actually appears when it is added to the timeline. A pre-trimmed clip can also be saved as a **Sub-clip** in your **Project Media** window.

To pre-trim a clip:

1 **Open the clip in the Trimmer**

Right-click on a clip in the **Project Media** panel (media) or on the timeline (event) and select the option to **Open in Trimmer**.

The clip will open in the **Trimmer** window.

The trimmed area of a clip can be defined either by dragging across the **Trimmer's** timeline or by manually setting the in and out points, indicated with yellow flags on the upper left and upper right of the trimmed area.

To manually set the in and out points for your trimmed clip:

2 **Set an "in" point**

Position the **Trimmer's** playhead to the point at which you'd like your clip to begin.

Press the **i** or open bracket **[** key on your keyboard or select the **Set In Point** option from the **More Buttons**. A yellow flag will appear above the **Trimmer** window's timeline indicating the beginning of the trim area.

3   Set an "out" point

Position the **Trimmer's** playhead to the point at which you'd like your trimmed segment to end.

Press the **o** or closed bracket **]** key on your keyboard or select the **Set Out Point** option from the **More Buttons**. A yellow flag will appear above the **Trimmer's** timeline indicating the end of the trimmed area.

The "trim area" of your clip is indicated by the heavier gray area between these two yellow flags above the **Trimmer's** timeline, as illustrated on the facing page.

The trimmed area can be revised or redefined at any time by either repeating the steps above – or by simply dragging on the yellow flags.

The trimmed clip can then either be added to the timeline or saved as a new **Sub-Clip** in your **Project Media** panel (see page 68).

To add a trimmed clip to your movie, click on the trimmed area on the **Trimmer** timeline and drag it to your project's timeline. (Also see **Add Audio Only or Video Only from the Trimmer** on page 68.)

If you opened this clip in the **Trimmer** by **right-clicking** on an event clip on your timeline, the event clip already on your timeline will not be affected by your trims.

Event clips on the timeline are trimmed using the method described on page 78 of **Chapter 6, Edit Video on the Timeline**.

The trimmed area will remain defined on a clip in your **Project Media** window.

Zoom into and out from the Trimmer timeline

As when you're working on your project's timeline, there are times when you'll want to zoom in very close to the individual frames in your video clip and there are times when you'll want to step back and see it all at once.

As with the main Vegas Movie Studio timeline, you can zoom in and out of the **Trimmer's** timeline with a couple of keyboard shortcuts.

The **Up Arrow** zooms into the timeline.
The **Down Arrow** zooms out from the timeline.

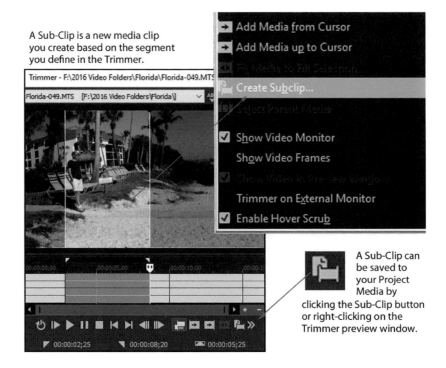

A Sub-Clip is a new media clip you create based on the segment you define in the Trimmer.

A Sub-Clip can be saved to your Project Media by clicking the Sub-Clip button or right-clicking on the Trimmer preview window.

Create a sub-clip

Once you've trimmed a clip and defined a segment of a clip in the **Trimmer,** you can save it as a **Sub-Clip** in your **Project Media** window. Several **Sub-Clips** can be created from a single longer clip.

To save a trimmed segment of a media clip as a **Sub-Clip**:

1 Trim a clip

Define a segment of a clip, as described in **Pre-trim a clip in the Trimmer** on page 67.

2 Select Create Sub-Clip

Click on the ▣ button at the top of the **Trimmer** window, or **right-click** on the preview displayed in the **Trimmer** window and select **Create Sub-Clip** from the context menu.

If you have a **Media Bin** selected in the **Project Media** panel (see page 59) when you create a **Sub-Clip**, the **Sub-Clip** will be added to this bin.

To open the original clip that the **Sub-Clip** was created from, **right-click** on the clip on the timeline or in your **Project Media** window and select **Open Parent Media in Trimmer.**

When you right-click on the Trimmer timeline, you can set the toggle so that you drag the Video Only, the Audio Only or both the clip's Video and Audio to your project's timeline.

Add Audio Only or Video Only from the Trimmer

It is possible to add only the audio portion or only the video portion of a media clip in your **Trimmer** to the timeline. **To use this feature, you must drag over the Trimmer timeline to indicate the portion of the clip you want to drag to your timeline.**

To add only the audio or only the video from a clip:

1   **Select the Audio Only or Video Only option**

    With your media clip open in the **Trimmer, right-click** on the selected region of the **Trimmer** timeline and check the option **Select Video Only** or **Select Audio Only**.

2   **Add your clip to your timeline**

    Click on the **Trimmer** timeline and drag the clip to a video track or audio track on your project's timeline.

It's important to note that toggling one of these options changes the default setting for this method of adding a clip to the timeline. In other words, *whichever option you select from this right-click menu will remain selected until you select another option*.

If you set the toggle to **Select Video Only,** for instance, you will add to your project's timeline only the video portion of any clip dragged from the **Trimmer** timeline until you set the toggle back to **Select Video and Audio.**

Add Audio Only or Video Only from Project Media

To add the audio portion or the video portion only of a media clip from the **Project Media** panel, drag the clip to a track on your timeline with a **right-click** rather than a left-click.

When you release the right mouse button, a pop-up menu will offer you the option of adding the **Video Only** or **Audio Only** portion of the media clip to your movie.

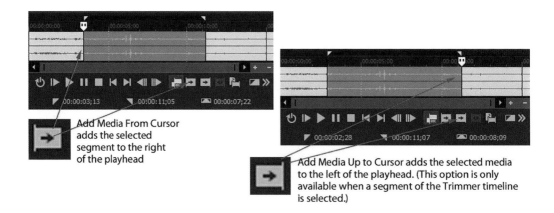

Add Media From Cursor adds the selected segment to the right of the playhead

Add Media Up to Cursor adds the selected media to the left of the playhead. (This option is only available when a segment of the Trimmer timeline is selected.)

Add Media From Cursor or Add Media Up To Cursor

There are a number of ways to add the video directly from the **Trimmer** to your timeline. If you have a segment of the **Trimmer's** timeline selected, you can simply click on the selected region and drag it directly to your timeline, placing it on whichever video or audio track you'd prefer. (You may also elect to add only the audio or only the video segment of a media clip, as discussed on the facing page.)

The following tools automatically add media from your **Trimmer** to your timeline's armed tracks at the position of the **Timeline Cursor** (playhead). For more information on arming a track, see **Arm a Video or Audio Track** on page 77.)

Add Media From Cursor
Add Media From Cursor adds to your timeline the segment of the clip displayed in your **Trimmer** to the *right* of the playhead.

1 **Position the playhead at the beginning of your selection**

   Position the playhead at the point on the **Trimmer's** timeline at which you'd like your added media to begin, or drag from right to left over a segment of the **Trimmer** timeline so that the playhead is to the *left* of your selection.

2 **Select the Add Media From Cursor option**

   Click the **Add Media From Cursor** button on the **Trimmer,** or **right-click** on the selected region of the **Trimmer** timeline and select the option to **Add Media From Cursor.**

Add Media Up To Cursor
Add Media Up To Cursor adds to your timeline the segment of the clip displayed in your **Trimmer** to the *left* of the playhead.

1 **Position the playhead at the end of your selection**

   Drag from left to right over a segment of the **Trimmer** timeline so that the playhead is to the *right* of your selection.

Add the Trimmer to the program's interface

Although by default the **Trimmer** in Vegas Movie Studio 14 is hidden until launched (by selecting **Open in Trimmer** from a **right-click** menu) or selected from the **View/Window** menu, many editors prefer it docked to the interface, between **Project Media** and the **Preview** windows.

To add the **Trimmer** as a separate window in the program's interface:

1   Open the **Trimmer** by selecting it from the **View** menu's **Window** sub-menu.

2   Hold down the **Ctrl** key and drag the **Trimmer** to the area between the **Project Media** and the **Preview** windows.

A new window/panel space will appear and your **Trimmer** will drop into it.

Resize the panels (as described on page 14) as necessary to allow you to view all of your panels.

Launch the Trimmer and drag it into position.

When the Trimmer is placed over the center top of the interface as you hold down the Ctrl key, a new panel will open and the Trimmer will drop into it.

2   Select the Add Media Up To Cursor option

Click the **Add Media Up To Cursor** button on the **Trimmer,** or **right-click** on the selected region of the **Trimmer** timeline and select the option to **Add Media Up To Cursor.**

Timeline Overwrite options

The **Timeline Overwrite** button affects how the existing clips on your timeline behave when video is added from the **Trimmer** by selecting the options to **Add Media From Cursor** or **Add Media Up to Cursor** (as discussed on the previous page).

- When **Timeline Overwrite** is enabled, the segment of the video you add to an existing series of clips will **insert** into the existing clips – splitting the clips at the position of the **Timeline Cursor** (playhead) and inserting the **Trimmer** media within the split.

- When **Timeline Overwrite** is not enabled, adding your video clip to an existing timeline will **overlay** the video onto the existing video clips.

An overlay clip works like a clip on an upper video track. Although it appears to replace the event it overlays, it can be dragged to a new position without affecting the event or events it overlays.

Armed video track   Timeline Cursor (playhead)

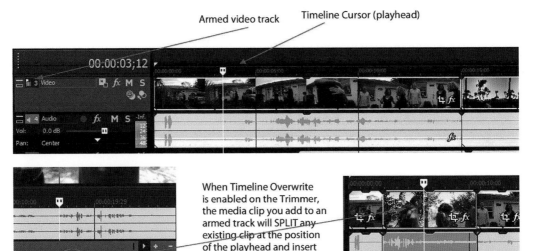

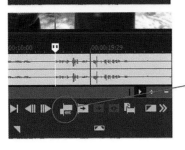

When Timeline Overwrite is enabled on the Trimmer, the media clip you add to an armed track will SPLIT any existing clip at the position of the playhead and insert the Trimmer clip.

When Timeline Overwrite is disabled on the Trimmer, the media clip you add to an armed track will OVERLAY onto any existing clips at the position of the playhead.

How the timeline behaves when new clips are added to it (i.e., whether the other clips remain in place or slide aside when a new clip is added) depends on how the **Auto Ripple** feature is set. For more information on **Auto Ripple** settings and how they affect the movement of clips on your timeline, see page 100.

Show Trimmer in external or second monitor toggle.

View the Trimmer on an External Monitor

When toggled, the **Trimmer on External Monitor** switch displays your **Trimmer** monitor on a second or external video monitor.

You can set which device this video displays on by going to the **Options** menu and selecting **Preferences**. On the **Preferences** option screen, select the **Device** you'd like the **Trimmer** displayed on from the drop-down menu under the **Preview Device** tab.

For information on setting up and configuring an external monitor, see page 158.

Adding Video to Your Timeline

Trimming and Splitting Event Clips

Separating Audio and Video on a Clip

Speeding Up, Slowing Down and Reversing a Clip

Adding Fade Ins and Fade Outs

Working with 3D Video

Pre-Rendering Your Timeline

Chapter 6

Edit Video on the Timeline

Where your clips become a movie

Of all the workspaces in Vegas Movie Studio, the Timeline takes up the most real estate.

And with good reason too.

The Timeline is where your clips are assembled, and where they interact with each other. It's where your media clips become a movie!

The **Timeline** is where the individual media clips you've gathered in your **Project Media** window and prepped in your **Trimmer** are finally gathered into a movie.

The **Timeline** is where all of the pieces come together. It's where you'll add transitions and most of your special effects. It's where your clips interact with each other.

In fact, because the **Timeline** window is such a powerful and important workspace, we've divided our discussion of its tools into three chapters.

In this chapter, we'll look at the basic tools for building the timeline for your movie. Then, in **Chapter 7**, we'll look at some of the more advanced **Timeline** tools. In **Chapter 8**, we'll look at some of the **Timeline's** tools for working with audio.

The Vegas Movie Studio **Timeline** is a slightly scaled down version of the interface in Vegas Pro. In fact, should you ever decide to move up to Movie Studio's big brother, you should find the transition fairly easy.

Add media clips to your timeline

There are a number of ways to add media to your timeline:

Drag a clip from the Project Media window. Far and away the most common way to add a media clip to a timeline is to simply drag it into position from the **Project Media** panel.

Double-click a clip in Project Media. By default, **double-clicking** a clip in the **Project Media** panel adds it to the armed track (see the sidebar on the facing page) on your timeline, at the position of the **Timeline Cursor** (playhead).

Drag a clip from Windows Explorer. A clip can be added to your timeline directly from a Windows Explorer browse screen. When a clip is added using this method, it is also added automatically to your **Project Media** panel.

Drag a clip from the Trimmer timeline. If you've trimmed a clip in the **Trimmer**, you can drag this pre-trimmed segment to your timeline from the **Trimmer** timeline. For more information on adding media clips directly from the **Trimmer**, see **Chapter 5, Prepare Your Media in the Trimmer**.

For information on adding only the audio or only the video portion of a media clip to your timeline, see page 69.

The clips you add may be inserted between clips on your timeline or overlayed onto them. Clips can also be overlapped so that they create a **Cross-Dissolve**.

How the clips on your timeline behave when other clips are added near, over and atop them are defined by the **Timeline** preferences:

- For information on inserting a clip between clips that are already on your timeline, see **Automatic Ripple Modes** on page 100.

- For information on enabling the **Cross-Dissolve** feature when clips are overlapped, see the sidebar **Create an Automatic Cross-Dissolve between events** on page 81.

- For information on creating more video and audio tracks, see **Add a Video and Audio Track** on page 107.

Arm a video or audio track

When you **arm** a track, you set it as the default track to which your video or audio clips will be added. In other words, when you add a clip to your timeline by **double-clicking** it, the clip will automatically be loaded to the armed track, at the position of the **Timeline Cursor** (playhead).

The flashing white light indicates that Track 2 is armed.

To arm a track, click on the colored square indicating the track's number on the upper left corner of the track header.

An armed track is indicated by a flashing white square on this colored square.

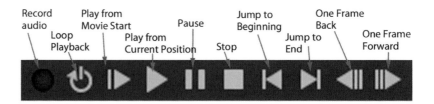

Record audio   Loop Playback   Play from Movie Start   Play from Current Position   Pause   Stop   Jump to Beginning   Jump to End   One Frame Back   One Frame Forward

Preview your timeline

The transport controls for playing your timeline are located along the bottom of the **Preview** window. (You may see a partial display of these controls if your **Preview** window is too narrow to display the entire set.)

The timeline's playback will be displayed in the **Preview** window.

A common keyboard shortcut for playing the timeline is the **Spacebar**. Pressing the **Spacebar** on your keyboard will start playback of your timeline. Pressing the **Spacebar** again will stop it and return the playhead to where it was when your playback began. Alternatively, pressing **Enter** while playing your video will pause the playhead where it is.

Included among the transport controls is a **Record** button. We discuss its function in **Record narration into your project** in **Chapter 9, Edit Audio on the Timeline**.

Trim an event clip on your timeline

Once a clip has been added to your timeline, you can easily trim it – removing footage from the beginning and/or end of the clip so that only a segment of the clip is actually included in your movie.

To trim an event clip on your timeline, hover your mouse over the beginning or the end of the clip until you see the **Trim** indicator.

When the **Trim** indicator appears, click and drag on the end of the clip to shorten or extend it.

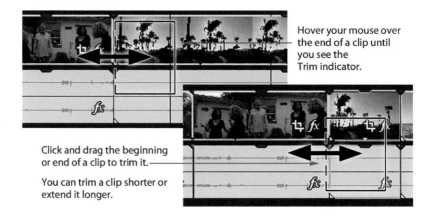

Hover your mouse over the end of a clip until you see the Trim indicator.

Click and drag the beginning or end of a clip to trim it.

You can trim a clip shorter or extend it longer.

Trim from beginning of an event to the position of the timeline cursor (playhead).

Trim all but selected region from the timeline.

Trim from position of the timeline cursor to the end of the event.

Split event at position of the timeline cursor.

Movie Studio also includes shortcut buttons, along the bottom of the **Timeline**, for trimming your event clips with a single click.

The button labeled **Trim** removes all except for the selected region of your movie's timeline, and is only activated when a selection on your timeline is created by dragging across it.

How trimming a clip affects its position on the timeline depends on whether or not the timeline is set to ripple, as discussed in **Automatic Rippling modes** on page 100.

Clips can also be pre-trimmed, prior to adding them to your timeline. For information on pre-trimming a media clip, see page 66 of **Chapter 5, Prepare Your Media in the Trimmer**.

Splitting an event clip (by pressing the S key) slices the clip at the position of the Timeline cursor.

Split an event clip on your timeline

Splitting an event clip means slicing it into two or more segments.

To split a clip, position the **Timeline Cursor** (playhead) over the clip and click the ▥ button along the bottom of the **Timeline**.

Alternatively, you can select **Split** from the **Edit** menu – or press the **S** key on your keyboard.

- **If you have a clip selected on your timeline**, only that clip at the position of the **Timeline Cursor** will be split.

- **If you have no clips selected on your timeline**, every clip on every track at the position of the **Timeline Cursor** will be split.

If you split an event clip in two spots, you can cut or delete the segment between the splits by clicking to select it and then pressing the **Delete** key on your keyboard.

If you want to remove or undo a split, you can use **Undo** (**Ctrl+z**) immediately after you split your clip(s). You can also restore a segment you've sliced off by **un-trimming** the clip, as described on the facing page.

Adjustments to your split's location can also be made using **Slipping** and **Sliding**, as described on page 103.

When you right-click on a clip and select the option to remove it from a Group, you will be able to manipulate its audio and video elements separately.

Separate a clip's audio and video

There may be times when you want to unlink a clip's audio track and video track so that they can be separately manipulated on your timeline or so that one can be removed, creating an audio only or a video only event.

By default, the audio and video for a media clip are **grouped**. This means that, when you add, position or move the clip on your timeline, both the audio and video move as one.

To break apart the audio and video for a clip, **right-click** on the clip and select **Group**, then **Remove From** (or press the **U** key on your keyboard).

The danger of over-extending an event clip

It's important, if you are un-trimming (extending) an event clip, that you are careful not to over-extend it beyond its actual duration.

The ends of a clip are indicated on a timeline by angled, blue corners on the upper left and upper right of the clip. If you over-extend a clip, this angle will appear as a V-shaped cut in the top of the clip.

If you accidentally over-extend a clip, the clip will play through and then repeat.

An angled dip along the top of a clip indicates that it is extended beyond its true duration.

The audio and video segment will then be treated as two separate clips. By clicking to select one or the other, you can move or remove it (by pressing the **Delete** key) without affecting the other part.

Alternatively, you can opt to add only the audio or only the video of a clip from the **Project Media** window. For information on this process, see the sidebar **Add Audio Only or Video Only from Project Media** on page 69.

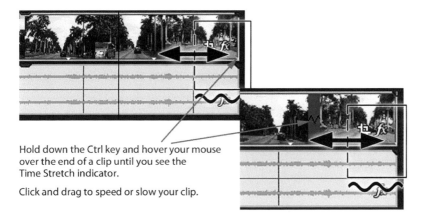

Hold down the Ctrl key and hover your mouse over the end of a clip until you see the Time Stretch indicator.

Click and drag to speed or slow your clip.

Speed up or slow down an event clip

It's very easy to change the speed at which a clip plays on your timeline. By using the **Time Stretch** tool, you can make your event clip play very fast or set it to play in slow motion.

To **Time Stretch** an event clip, hold down the **Ctrl** key and hover your mouse over the end of a clip, as if to **Trim** it (page 78).

Create an Automatic Cross-Dissolve between events

A **Cross-Dissolve** is a basic transition between audio and video clips on your timeline in which one event slowly dissolves into the next.

To enable **Cross-Dissolves** on your timeline, ensure that the **Automatic Cross-Dissolves** feature is toggled on along the bottom of the **Timeline**.

Once this feature is enabled, creating a **Cross-Dissolve** is as simple as dragging one event clip in so that it overlaps another.

The length of the overlap indicates the duration of the transition.

The length of the cross-dissolve is indicated on the overlap.

When the **Time Stretch** indicator appears (as illustrated above), click and drag on the end of the clip to "trim" it longer or shorter.

The shorter the clip, the faster it will play.

To see the speed at which your event is playing, **right-click** on the clip and select **Properties**.

The clip's **Playback Rate** will appear under the **Video Event** tab.

In fact, this indicator on the **Properties** window is dynamic. In other words, if you manually type in a **Playback Rate**, you can set your event clip's playback speed precisely.

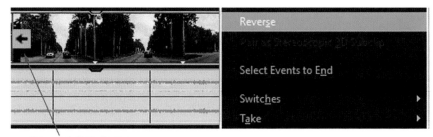

Reversed clip indicator

Play an event clip in reverse

To set an event clip to play in reverse, **right-click** on it and select the **Reverse** option.

Once you've reversed a clip's playback, you can also **Time Stretch** it, as described above.

Basic Timeline controls and views

Zoom in or out on your timeline

Sometimes you'll want to zoom out of your timeline so that you can see your entire project at once. Other times you'll want to get in close enough to edit the individual frames of an event clip.

To zoom out from your view of the timeline, click on the — button in the lower right of the **Timeline** window, press your keyboard's **Down arrow** or roll your mouse roller backward.

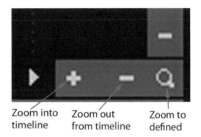

To zoom into timeline   Zoom out from timeline   Zoom to defined

To zoom into your timeline, click on the **+** button in the lower right of the **Timeline** window, press your keyboard's **Up** arrow or roll your mouse roller forward. (You will zoom into the location where the **Timeline Cursor** [playhead] is positioned.)

To zoom into a precise area of your timeline, click on the **Magnifying Glass** button in the lower right of the **Timeline** panel (or on the **Toolbar** at the top of the interface) and click and drag it to define the area on your timeline you want to zoom into.

One word of warning though: Zooming in with the **Magnifying Glass** tool can make the **Tracker Headers** (left of the tracks) disappear! (Actually, they've just been temporarily hidden.) To get them back, hover your mouse over the left side of the **Timeline** window until a double-arrow appears and then drag to resize them smaller (as described on page 108).

Scrub the timeline

Scrubbing means, essentially, dragging the **Timeline Cursor** (playhead) over your timeline in order to test an effect or transition or to re-position the cursor. There are a number of ways to scrub your timeline:

Manually drag the Timeline cursor's playhead. To scrub, click on the playhead itself rather than on the vertical line that stretches down across the timeline. To scrub more quickly, hold down the **Ctrl** key as you drag the playhead. To scrub without sound, hold down **Ctrl+Alt**.

Drag on the Scrub Control in the lower left of the **Timeline** window. The further to the left or right you drag the **Scrub Control**, the faster you will scrub the timeline. The position of the orange triangle sets the speed increments of your scrub.

The Scrub Control

Use the J, K, and L keys on your keyboard. The **J** key will scrub your timeline in reverse, the **L** key will scrub it forward and the **K** key stops the scrub. Tap the **J** or **L** key more than once and the playback speed will increase. The longer you hold down the **J** or **L** keys, the faster the timeline will be scrubbed.

Position the Timeline Cursor on your timeline

Beyond scrubbing, the **Timeline Cursor** (the official name for the playhead and vertical line that indicates your playback position on your timeline), can be positioned in a number of ways:

Drag on the vertical line below the playhead to set the cursor to any position on your timeline.

Likewise, if you **click on any spot** on the timeline, the cursor will jump to that position.

To create a Fade In, hover your mouse over the upper left corner of a clip until the Fade In indicator appears and drag down.

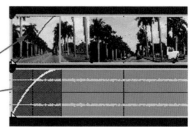

The changing level of a clip's opacity or volume is indicated by a sloping line.

Add a Fade In or Fade Out to a video event clip

A **Fade In** or **Fade Out** at the beginning or end of an event is added to both video and audio clips essentially the same way.

To add a **Fade In** to a clip.

1   Hover over the beginning of a clip

Hover your mouse over the upper left corner of a clip until the **Fade Offset** indicator appears, as illustrated above.

2   Create your Fade In

Click and drag down from the corner to create the **Fade in**.

Your **Fade In** will be indicated by a curved slope line, representing the fading up of the video level from the beginning of your clip. The longer this curved slope is, the longer your **Fade In** will last.

A **Fade Out** is created exactly the same way, except over the end of a clip.

This video level line, by the way, is actually an indicator of the video clip's **opacity** (the opposite of transparency). At the beginning of a **Fade In**, the clip will have 0% opacity, which means that it will be invisible. The curved slope represents the opacity rising to 100% over the course of the fade.

It's important to understand this if you are using a **Fade In** or **Fade Out** on an upper video track. Since changing opacity over the course of a fade is actually a change in *transparency*, you may find that **Fading In** or **Fading Out** a video clip will appear as a *dissolve* over any video that may be on the track below your fading clip.

In other words, a **Fade In** or **Fade Out** will fade in or out to black *only if there is nothing on the video track below* your clip. Make sense?

Adding a **Fade In** or **Fade Out** to an *audio* clip involves the very same moves, as discussed on page 139. The curved slope line on an audio track fade indicates a rising or lowering volume level.

Edit 3D video

Vegas Movie Studio 14 includes tools for editing, fine-tuning and outputting 3D stereoscopic video.

Stereoscopic video works by providing two video sources – usually shot by a special camcorder that simultaneously shoots both video images through lenses that are the same distance apart as your eyes. (It can also be shot with two separate camcorders, mounted side-by-side, as discussed in the sidebar below.) The result is essentially two video channels rendered as a single "multi-stream" video, each channel providing a slightly different point of view of the scene.

Anaglyphic 3D displays your stereoscopic video channels as bluish and reddish tints.

When viewed with special glasses, these images are seen as two slightly different views of the same scene, providing a 3D view of that scene. (The boxed version of Vegas Movie Studio Platinum comes with a free pair of 3D glasses that can be used for previewing your work.)

Because 3D vision is the result of two separate views of the same subject, the effect is most pronounced on subjects between three and ten feet from your camcorder. Distant objects do not make for good 3D subjects.

3D formats and Anaglyphic video

There are a number of ways to combine and then separate your two channels of video, some of it requiring special equipment for playback and viewing. Working with many of these formats is a bit beyond the scope of this book (and some of it beyond the off-the-shelf capabilities of Vegas Movie Studio Platinum).

The simplest and most common 3D system – and the one you'll more likely be working with most – is **Anaglyphic 3D**. This system displays your two stereoscopic video channels as tints of red and cyan (or blue). When viewed through special glasses (one lens tinted red and the other blue), the two video channels create a very effective stereoscopic viewing experience.

The beauty of the **Anaglyphic 3D** is that no special equipment is required, other than the glasses themselves. **Anaglyphic 3D** can be displayed on any TV or computer and can even be posted online to sites like YouTube.

Set up your video project for 3D

To set your Vegas Movie Studio Platinum project for 3D:

1   **Open Project Preferences**

The **Project Preferences** dialog window can be opened by clicking on the ⚙ (cog) button on the **Preview** window, or by selecting **Properties** from the **Project** menu.

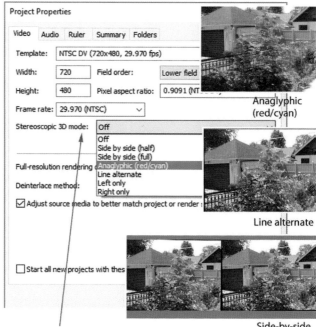

Anaglyphic (red/cyan)

Line alternate

Side-by-side

Activate 3D mode and set 3D view in the Project Preferences.

2   **Set the Stereoscopic 3D Mode**

Under the **Video** tab, select a view option from the **Stereoscopic 3D** drop-down menu.

These views will be used to align your 3D stereoscopic video channels (as discussed on the following page).

When working with **Anaglyphic 3D**, select the option for **Anaglyphic (Red/Cyan)**.

When you click **OK** or **Apply**, your 3D video should appear in the **Preview** window with the two channels slightly offset, one channel tinted red and the other tinted cyan/blue.

Align your 3D video channels

Aligning the two video images is a little like focusing a camera. It's very important that the two video channels overlay correctly and align or the 3D effect will be compromised (and will look very fuzzy).

The best way to align your video channels is to view the **Preview** video while wearing a pair of **red/blue** Anaglyphic glasses. You may even want to view your **Preview** full-screen on a separate monitor or viewing device (see page 158).

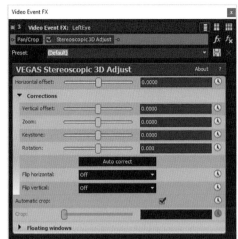

With your 3D glasses on, add the Stereoscopic 3D Adjust effect and tweak the Horizontal Offset as necessary. (Usually it's the only setting for this effect that needs tweaking.)

To align your two stereoscopic video channels:

1   Apply the Stereoscopic 3D Adjust effect

Click on the 𝑓𝑥 icon on the event clip you're going to adjust. The **Video FX Plug-In Chooser** will open.

Click to select the **Magix Stereoscopic 3D Adjust** effect, then click **OK**.

The **Video Event FX** dialog window will open, as illustrated above.

2   Adjust the offset

With wearing your 3D glasses, use the **Horizontal Offset** slider to fine-tune the position of the red channel until the 3D effect looks perfect in the **Preview** window.

If necessary, click on **Corrections** and further adjust the position of the red channel.

Output your 3D video

The program includes options for outputting **MVC** 3D video at 1280x720 and 1920x1080. MVC is the format used to create 3D BluRay discs. Special 3D equipment is required in order to display and view this 3D.

To output video for use in a 3D BluRay project in DVD Architect, go to **Project/Render As** and select the **Sony MVC/AVC** template for either 1280x720-60p, 1280x720-50p or 1920x1080-24p at 25 Mbps.

If you select the option to **Make Movie/Upload to YouTube**, the program will automatically detect your 3D project settings and will upload your video as **Anaglyphic 3D. Anaglyphic 3D** does not require special equipment (other than an inexpensive pair of red/blue glasses) and can be viewed on any computer or TV.

Add a 3D effect to a title

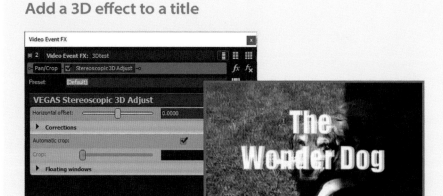

The wider the Horizontal Offset applied to your title, the closer it will appear to your viewer (to a point, of course).

Vegas Movie Studio Platinum creates stereoscopic 3D.

This is not to be confused with graphic 3D (the process used in programs like After Effects), in which a 3D illustration of text or an object is manipulated, along with layers of graphics and video, in three-dimensional space – rotating it, for instance, or creating camera moves around it.

However, even within those limitations you can create flat titles that appear to float in space or appear to move nearer to or farther from your viewer.

The trick is to manipulate the left and right channels of the title.

1   **Create a title**

    Create any text title, as described in **Chapter 11, Add and Customize Your Titles**.

2   **Adjust the 3D video channels**

    As discussed on the facing page, apply the **Stereoscopic 3D** effect to this title event on your timeline and adjust the **Horizontal Offset**.

The basic principle of stereoscopic 3D is that the difference between the left eye and right eye views is greater the closer the object is to the viewer.

So, by widening the **Horizontal Offset**, you can make the text appear to be closer to the viewer than the video background. (Naturally, you'll want to make these adjustments while wearing your red/blue 3D glasses to ensure your effect is successful.) You can even use keyframed animation with this effect to make it appear that your title is moving toward or away from your viewer!

Render and pre-render your video project

As you add transitions, effects and layers of video and audio, you may find your project's playback lugging a bit. It may seem to skip frames or play only a few frames per second.

In fact, whenever the **Display** rate (in the lower right of the **Preview** window) shows your video playing at less than a full 29.97 frames per second (or 25 fps, for PAL video), it's likely an indicator that you need to pre-render your video.

The problem is that all of those transitions, effects and video tracks are currently being rendered "on the fly" by the software. This means that, as you play your timeline, the program is using all of your computer's resources to apply and render all of the effects you've added to it.

Rendering all or portions of your timeline creates temporary video files of your project that the program can use in place of the work-in-progress for your playback. Pre-rendering your project can greatly improve your playback and allow the program and your computer to work much more efficiently.

There are three ways to render all or portions of your timeline's video.

Selectively pre-render your video

Selectively Pre-rendering your video is the most common way to render your timeline. To **Selectively Pre-render** your timeline:

1 **Create a Loop Region**

This is optional. You can, of course opt not to select any of the timeline, in which case *every* segment of your movie project that needs to be rendered will be pre-rendered.

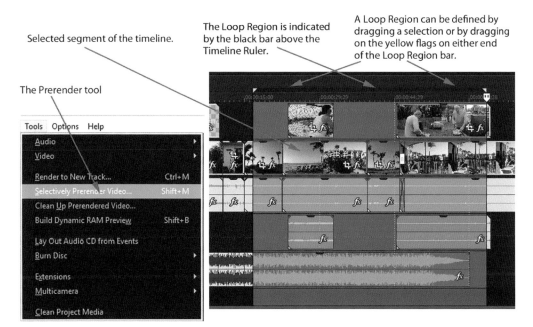

Selected segment of the timeline.

The Loop Region is indicated by the black bar above the Timeline Ruler.

A Loop Region can be defined by dragging a selection or by dragging on the yellow flags on either end of the Loop Region bar.

The Prerender tool

To define a segment – or **Loop Region** – of your timeline, click and drag over a section of your timeline.

Alternatively, you can define a **Loop Region** simply by dragging on the yellow flags on either end of an existing **Loop Region**, as illustrated.

The selected area of your timeline will be indicated in light blue, and the **Loop Region** will be indicated by a heavy gray line above the **Timeline Ruler**, as illustrated at the bottom of the facing page.

2 **Click on Selectively Pre-Render**

Go to the **Tools** menu at the top of the interface and choose **Selectively Pre-Render Video** (or press **Shift+m** on your keyboard).

A **Pre-render Video** dialog window will open.

3 **Select a render template**

Often you'll choose a format that matches your current project properties. However, you may also select a lower quality or lower resolution video template for your preview. Lower quality and lower resolution previews are generated much more quickly.

To render only the **Loop Region** of your timeline, ensure that **Render Loop Region Only** is checked.

Also, so that your rendered video is not letterboxed in your **Preview** window, ensure that **Stretch Video to Fill Output Frame Size** is checked.

Click **OK**.

The program will analyze the **Loop Region** you've selected and pre-render all segments that need rendering.

If your video format is perfectly matched to your project settings and you have few or no video effects applied, this process can go very quickly.

However, an effects-heavy video or one that is not well matched to your project's settings can take a long time to render – particularly if it is a high-definition video project.

Pre-rendering is done in 300 frame segments – approximately 10 seconds long each. As the program completes the rendering of each segment, you'll see indicators of the render along the top of your timeline.

Because a pre-render is done in segments, if you make changes to one area of your timeline you may not need to re-render your entire timeline. Only the changed segment will need to be re-rendered.

Prerendered segment indicator

Dynamic RAM Rendering

Short of creating a hard pre-render of your video, you can create a quick **Dynamic RAM Render** in order to preview a brief effects sequence. A **RAM Render** uses a portion of your computer's RAM to store a temporary render of your timeline so that you can watch your effects-heavy movie at as close to full preview as your computer can handle.

To create a **Dynamic RAM Render** of your video:

1 **Define a Loop Region**

To define a segment – or **Loop Region** – of your timeline, click and drag over a section of your timeline.

Alternatively, you can define the **Loop Region** simply by dragging on the yellow flags on either end of the existing **Loop Region**.

The selected area of your timeline will be indicated in light blue, and the **Loop Region** will be indicated by a heavy gray line above the **Timeline Ruler**, as illustrated above.

2 **Click on Build Dynamic RAM Preview**

Go to the **Tools** menu at the top of the interface and choose **Build Dynamic RAM Preview** (or press **Shift+b** on your keyboard).

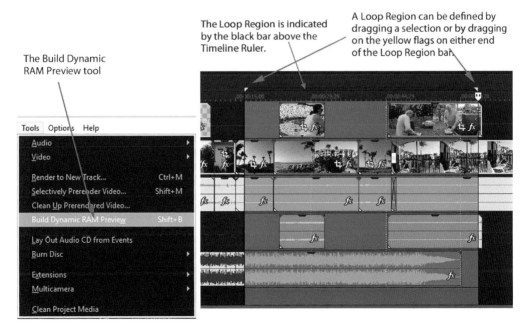

The Loop Region is indicated by the black bar above the Timeline Ruler.

A Loop Region can be defined by dragging a selection or by dragging on the yellow flags on either end of the Loop Region bar.

The Build Dynamic RAM Preview tool

The **Timeline Cursor** will move quickly down your timeline, analyzing your movie and creating and storing a temporary preview of as much of the **Loop Region** as your computer's memory allows.

When your **Dynamic RAM** allocation is full, the program will stop rendering and indicate the rendered portion of your timeline with a light blue highlight. This segment of your video should now play at full preview speed.

How much of your timeline the program is able to render into RAM (and how fast it does it) is determined by a combination of how much RAM you have allocated for your **RAM Preview** and what resolution your video project is. (You can store a lot less high-definition video in memory than you can standard definition video.)

The amount of RAM allocated as **Dynamic RAM Render** space is set in the program's preferences. To manually increase the amount of **Dynamic RAM Render** space the program uses, go to the **Options** menu and select **Preferences**. Under the **Video** tab on the **Preferences** dialog window, designate the **Dynamic RAM Preview Max** in the space provided. (To allow enough leftover RAM to keep your computer stable, we recommend you allocate about 3000-4000 MB less than the **Max Available**, as listed to the right of this preference listing.)

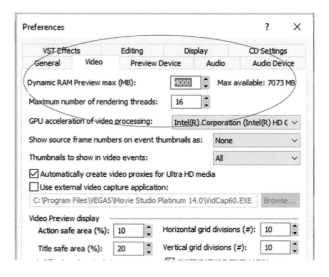

Render to a New Track

Finally, if the number of effects you've added to a clip is really slowing your timeline playback to a crawl, you can select the option to render your video to a new track.

This process creates a hard render of a segment of your video and then permanently adds it to your project on an upper video track.

The program then uses this rendered segment instead of your effects-heavy timeline segment for your preview playback.

To **Render to a New Track**:

1 **Define a Loop Region**

   This is optional. You can, of course, opt not to select any of the timeline, in which case your entire timeline will be rendered as a new track.

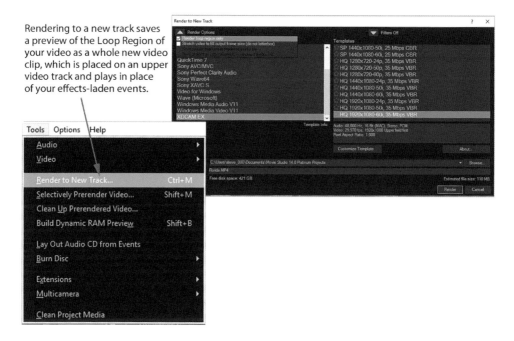

Rendering to a new track saves a preview of the Loop Region of your video as a whole new video clip, which is placed on an upper video track and plays in place of your effects-laden events.

Alternatively, you can define the **Loop Region** simply by dragging on the yellow flags on either end of the existing **Loop Region**.

The selected area of your timeline will be indicated in light blue, and the **Loop Region** will be indicated by a heavy gray line above the **Timeline Ruler**, as illustrated at the bottom of page 91.

2   **Click on Render to New Track**

Go to the **Tools** menu at the top of the interface and choose **Render to New Track** (or press **Ctrl+m** on your keyboard).

A **Render to New Track** option panel will open.

Render only one track of video to a new track

Usually, when creating a **Render to New Track**, you'll want to create a preview render of all of the tracks in a segment of your timeline. However, it is possible to create a render of only one track of video.

To render only one track of video to a new track, follow the steps above in **Render to a New Track**. However, before selecting the tool from the **Option** menu, click on the **Solo** button on the header of the track you want to render.

The **Solo** toggle hides all of the other video or audio tracks on your timeline.

3   **Select an Output Format**

On the **Render To New Track** option panel, choose a **Render Format** for your preview video.

Often, you'll choose a format that matches your current project properties. However, you may also select a lower quality or lower resolution video template for your preview. Lower quality and lower resolution previews are generated much more quickly.

4   **Select a Render Option**

If you have set a **Loop Region** on your timeline, check the option to **Render Loop Region Only.**

Click **Render.**

The program will render your **Loop Region** and, when it is done, it will create a new video track at the top of your timeline and place the rendered video there.

This process can take a while – especially if you are working on a high-definition video project! But, particularly if you've added lots of effects to this segment of your video, it's ultimately a very good investment of your time.

When you play your timeline, you will view this new video track rather than your effects-heavy timeline segment.

Chapter 7

More Timeline Tools

The deeper toolkit

The Timeline includes way too many tools to cover in a single chapter.

Here are some of the more advanced video editing tools you'll find in this feature-packed workspace.

The **Timeline** window is more than just a workspace for mixing, trimming and splitting your media clips.

It also contains a host of tools for doing advanced video editing work, as well as a number of tools for controlling how the **Timeline** workspace looks and behaves.

Select segments of events on your timeline

There are a number of reasons you may want or need to select a portion of your movie – either a segment of the timeline or one or more individual event clips – including:

- To apply an effect to several clips at once.
- To create a **Loop Region** in order to pre-render a portion of your timeline or output a segment of your video.
- To group several events or cut them and paste them to a new location, as discussed on page 104.

There are two tools for selecting and manipulating the events on the toolbar running along the bottom of the **Timeline**. A third is available under the **Edit** menu.

The Normal Edit Tool   The Envelope Edit Tool

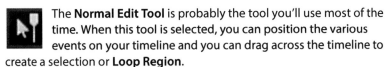

The **Normal Edit Tool** is probably the tool you'll use most of the time. When this tool is selected, you can position the various events on your timeline and you can drag across the timeline to create a selection or **Loop Region**.

The **Envelope Edit Tool** is used for creating envelopes on your timeline. **Envelopes** are level indicators that can be keyframed to, say, raise or lower the volume at specific points on an audio track. We discuss envelopes in **Use Audio Envelopes to adjust audio levels at specific points** on page 142 and in **Use Video Envelopes to set levels at specific points** on page 235.

The **Selection Edit Tool** (available under the **Edit** menu, inside the **Editing Tool** sub-menu) is a more specific version of the **Normal Edit Tool**. The primary purpose of the **Selection Edit Tool** is to allow you to select individual event clips (or several events at once) on your timeline. When you drag across your timeline with the **Selection Edit Tool**, for instance, rather than creating a **Loop Region**, you will "lasso" any clips you drag over.

A Loop Region can be defined by either dragging the Normal Edit Tool across the timeline to highlight a region or by manually positioning the two end flags on the Loop Region bar above the Timeline Ruler.

Create a Loop Region

A **Loop Region** is a segment of your timeline, indicated by a heavy gray bar above the **Timeline Ruler**. Once you've defined a **Loop Region**, you can elect to pre-render only that segment of your timeline (as discussed on page 89) or you can use one of the output options to export only the **Loop Region** you've defined for your timeline (as discussed in **Chapter 17**).

There are two ways to create or edit a **Loop Region**:

 With the **Normal Edit Tool** selected, drag over the timeline. Your selected region of the timeline will be highlighted in bright blue and this area will automatically be defined as your **Loop Region**.

With any of the three timeline **Tools** selected, drag on the yellow flags (illustrated above) on either end of the **Loop Region** bar to define your **Loop Region**.

Select individual event clips on your timeline

Selected event clips on your timeline display with dark colored frames. Unselected event clips display with light gray frames.

There are two ways to select individual event clips on your timeline.

 With either the **Normal Edit Tool** or the **Selection Edit Tool** selected, click to select the individual event clips on your timeline. To select a number of clips in a sequence, hold down the **Shift** key and select the first and last clip in the sequence. To select several individual clips, hold down the **Ctrl** key as you click on each.

 With the **Selection Edit Tool**, drag over the event clips on your timeline to select one or more. Hold down the **Shift** key as you drag to add more clips to your selection

Selected event.　　Unselected event.

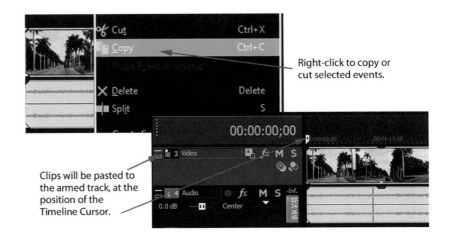

Right-click to copy or cut selected events.

Clips will be pasted to the armed track, at the position of the Timeline Cursor.

Cut, Copy and Paste clips on the timeline

To cut, copy and/or paste a clip on your timeline:

1 **Select a clip or clips**

   Click on an event clip on your timeline to select it. Hold down the **Shift** key and select the first and last clips in a sequence to select the entire sequence. Hold down the **Ctrl** key to select several non-sequential clips.

   You can also click to select the **Selection Edit Tool** on the **Toolbar** at the top of this interface and drag across the timeline to select a set of clips.

2 **Cut or Copy**

   To cut a clip, **right-click** on it and select **Cut** or press **Ctrl+x** on your keyboard.

   To copy a clip, **right-click** on it and select **Copy** or press **Ctrl+c** on your keyboard.

3 **Paste**

   To paste your video or audio clip(s) to your timeline, **right-click** on the timeline and select **Paste** or press **Ctrl+v** on your keyboard. (Note that the **Paste** option will only be available on the right-click menu if you are *not* clicking on an existing event clip.)

Your video will be pasted to your timeline at the position of the **Timeline Cursor** (playhead) onto the **armed** track. (For information on arming a track, see page 77.)

If you have several tracks of clips copied to your clipboard, they will be pasted in the same track order, beginning on the armed track.

Paste Event Attributes

Copying attributes is an easy way to take effects, motion paths and even keyframed animations that have been created for one event clip and paste them onto another (or to several others).

To use this feature:

1   Copy an element's Attributes

   Right-click on an event clip on your timeline and select **Copy**.

2   Paste the Attributes to another event

   Select one or several similar event clips on your timeline (by **Ctrl+clicking** or **Shift+clicking**) that you'd like to apply that same look to.

   Right-click on these elements and select **Paste Event Attributes**.

All effects and keyframed animations that have been applied to the original event clip will be applied to the selected event clips.

Cut, Copy and Paste between projects

Because Vegas Movie Studio allows you to have several instances of the program open at once, cutting and pasting clips or even entire sequences from one project to another is as easy as cutting and pasting to the same timeline!

To open more than one instance of Vegas Movie Studio, launch the program and open a project.

Then launch the program again.

Both instances of the program – in fact, several instances of the program – can be open at the same time, and each can have a different project open.

You can cut, copy and/or paste between projects as easily as you can cut, copy and paste within the same project, as described on the facing page.

Delete events from your timeline

Removing clips from your timeline is as easy as selecting them and deleting them. But how the timeline behaves when you remove a clip depends on which **Auto Ripple** mode you have selected, as discussed below.

To delete one or more clips on your timeline, select an event clip by clicking on it or select a sequence of clips as described on page 97, then **right-click** on the clip(s) and select **Delete** – or simply press **Delete** on your keyboard.

Auto Ripple modes

Rippling refers to the movement of the clips on your timeline when an event is added or deleted. When your timeline is set to ripple, the removal of an event from the timeline causes the other event clips to move left to fill in the gap. When a clip is added, the other clips slide aside so that the clip can be inserted between events.

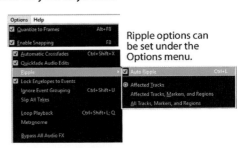

Ripple options can be set under the Options menu.

Ripple options can also be selected from the pop-up menu along the bottom of the Timeline.

Vegas Movie Studio includes a number of **Auto Ripple** modes, as illustrated above. These modes are set under the **Ripple** button on the **Options** menu. The **Timeline's Auto Ripple** function can be toggled on or off – or, when toggled on, it can be set to any of three different modes.

With some settings, regions and marker positions are affected as well as other video and audio events. **Regions** are segments of your movie that you designate and mark for easy reference (see page 240). They are created by selecting a portion of your timeline and choosing **Region** from the **Insert** menu.

For more information on **Timeline Markers**, see **Chapter 16, Prep Your Movie for Output as a DVD or BluRay Disc**.

Auto Ripple disabled

When the **Auto Ripple** function is turned off under the **Options** menu or by deselecting the option under the **Config** button, the clips will always remain in position on your timeline.

> **When a new clip is added into an existing event sequence** on the timeline, this new clip will **overlay** onto the existing sequence. The new clip will cover up or appear to replace the video of the event clip when the timeline is played. This overlayed clip can be dragged to any other position on the timeline or deleted and, when it is, the clip that it had previously overlayed will be restored.

> **If your new clip is longer** than the clip you are overlaying it upon, or you place it between clips and you have **Automatic Cross-Fades** enabled (page 206), the new clip will combine with the existing event to become a **Cross-Fade**.

> **If you delete an event clip** from your timeline, the remaining events will remain in position.

 When Auto Ripple is disabled, removing an event leaves a gap in the timeline.

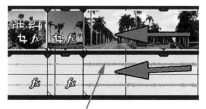

 When Auto Ripple is enabled, the other clips fill the gap when a clip is deleted.

 When Auto Ripple is disabled, a clip added to a sequence will overlay the sequence.

 When Auto Ripple is enabled, the new clip is inserted between existing events.

Auto Ripple/Affected Tracks

When **Auto Ripple** is enabled for only the affected track(s), adding and removing clips will affect only the audio or video tracks to which or from which the clip is added or removed.

> **When a new clip is added to an existing sequence**, all video and audio events *on that track only* will slide to the right in order to allow the clip to be inserted within the sequence.

> **When an event clip is removed** from an existing sequence, all video and audio events *on that track only* will slide left to fill in the gap.

Auto Ripple/Affected Tracks, Markers and Regions

When **Auto Ripple** is enabled for only the **Affected Tracks**, adding and removing clips will affect only the audio or video track(s) to which or from which the clip is added or removed.

> **When a new clip is added to an existing sequence**, all video and audio events *on that track only*, as well as all regions and markers, will slide to the right to allow the clip to be inserted within the sequence.

> **When an event clip is removed from an existing sequence**, all video and audio events *on that track only*, as well as all regions and markers, will slide left to fill in the gap.

Auto Ripple/All Tracks, Markers and Regions

When **Auto Ripple** is enabled for **All Tracks**, adding and removing clips will affect all video and audio tracks as well as any regions and timeline markers.

> **When a new clip is added to an existing sequence**, all video and audio events on *all tracks*, as well as all regions and markers, will slide to the right to allow the clip to be inserted within the sequence.

> **When an event clip is removed from an existing sequence**, all video and audio events on *all tracks*, as well as all regions and markers, will slide left to fill in the gap.

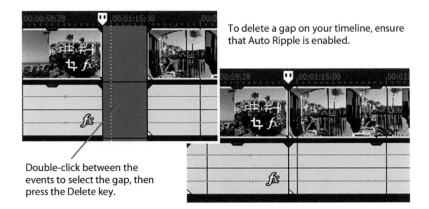

To delete a gap on your timeline, ensure that Auto Ripple is enabled.

Double-click between the events to select the gap, then press the Delete key.

Delete and Close Gap

If you've removed an event from a timeline sequence, leaving a gap in your timeline, you can have your clips move left to fill in the gap:

1 **Toggle on Auto-Ripple**

    Ensure that the **Normal Edit Tool** is selected (see page 96) and that your preferred **Auto Ripple** mode is enabled (page 100).

2 **Select the gap**

    Double-click on your timeline, in the gap between your event clips.

    This selected segment will be indicated by a light blue highlight

3 **Delete the gap**

    Press the **Delete** key on your keyboard.

    Your clips will slide left to fill in the gap.

Post-Edit Ripple

If you had **Auto Ripple** disabled when you moved or removed an event clip from your timeline, you can still elect to apply a **Post-Edit Ripple**.

Immediately after making your edit, go to the **Edit** menu and select **Post-Edit Ripple.** Then, from the sub-menu, select an **Auto-Ripple** mode, as discussed on page 101 (or use a keyboard shortcut like **Ctrl+Shift+f.**).

Slip or Slide an event clip or cut/transition

There are two advanced editing moves that change the in or out trim points on a clip or clips without changing the relative position or length of these clips on your timeline.

Slip a clip

Slipping changes the point at which a clip begins and ends without changing the overall length of the clip. In other words, if you've trimmed a clip down to a five second event (say, starting at one second into the original clip and ending at 6 seconds) you can **Slip** the content within that five-second event so that the clip begins at 3 seconds in and ends at 8 seconds in.

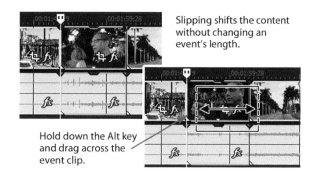

Slipping shifts the content without changing an event's length.

Hold down the Alt key and drag across the event clip.

An example may help you better understand. In the illustration above, a 5-second event clip begins with the girl's finger on the camera and ends with the girl and her father seated back in the car.

By holding down the **Alt** key and dragging to the left across the clip on the timeline, I am able to **Slip** the contents of the clip so that it now begins a few seconds later (with the girl already sitting back in her seat) and ends a few seconds later – yet, within the sequence, the clip still takes up the same 5-second space!

Slide a cut or transition

Sliding a cut means moving a cut or a transition between two clips so that it simultaneously comes earlier on one clip and later on the other or vice versa. In this way, for two clips that, together, take up, say, 10 seconds on a timeline, you can shift the cut's location between them and yet still maintain a combined length of 10 seconds.

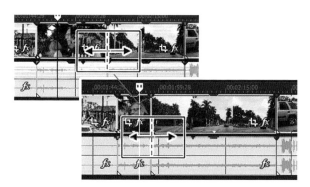

Sliding (by holding down Ctrl+Alt and dragging over a cut) changes the position of a cut or transition between events by simultaneously shortening one clip and lengthening the other.

As an example, I've got two clips – each 5 seconds long – on my timeline.

Holding down the **Ctrl+Alt** keys and hovering my mouse over the cut (or transition) between these clips until I see the **Slide** indicator, I can drag the cut so that the first clip is lengthened 3 seconds as the second is simultaneously trimmed by 3 seconds – while the combined duration of the two clips remains unchanged in the sequence.

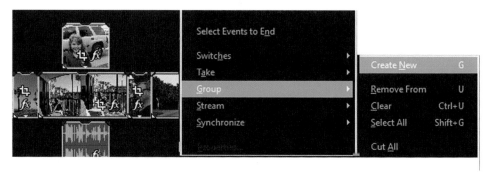

Grouped events on your timeline can be moved, cut, copied and pasted as a single unit.

Group and Ungroup your events

There are times when you want to select several event clips on your timeline and then move or manipulate them as a group.

When you **Group** events, the selected clips lock together into a block. When you move or cut, copy or paste them, they are affected as a single unit.

Events that are **Grouped** remained **Grouped** until they are **Ungrouped**.

Create a Group
To **Group** clips on your timeline:

1   **Select events**

    Select the event clips you want to group, as described in **Select segments or events on your timeline** on page 96.

2   **Group the events**

    Right-click on the selected events and select **Group.** Then, from the sub-menu, select **Make New**.

    Alternatively, you can simply press the **G** key on your keyboard.

Clear a Group
To **Ungroup** your clips, **right-click** on the **Grouped** clips, select **Group** and then, from the sub-menu, select **Clear**. Alternatively, you can simply click **Ctrl+u** on your keyboard.

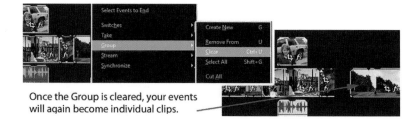

Once the Group is cleared, your events will again become individual clips.

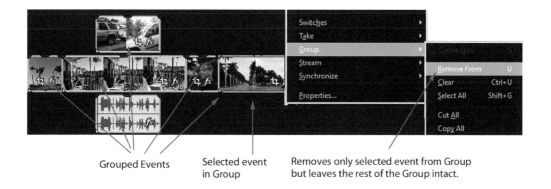

Grouped Events | Selected event in Group | Removes only selected event from Group but leaves the rest of the Group intact.

Remove an individual event from a Group

It's also possible to remove only one event clip from a **Group** and leave the rest of the **Group** intact:

To release one clip from a **Group:**

1 **Select the event clip**

Click to select the single event in the **Group.**

Although the entire **Group** will be highlighted when you select it on the timeline, your selected clip will be highlighted with a slightly heavier color.

2 **Remove From Group**

Right-click on this clip and select **Group.** Then, from the sub-menu, select **Remove From Group.**

Alternatively, you can simply press the **U** key on your keyboard.

When a clip containing both video and audio is added to your timeline, its video and audio are "grouped" to create the single clip.

If you'd like to remove or adjust the independent position of the video or the audio portion of a clip, you can **Ungroup** them as described in **Separate a clip's audio and video** on page 80.

An event clip can only belong to one **Group** at a time.

In other words, if you select both a **Group** and an additional event clip, then select the **Group/Create New** option again, your selected clips will be removed from the old **Group** and a new **Group** will be created.

A smaller **Group** can not exist inside a larger **Group.**

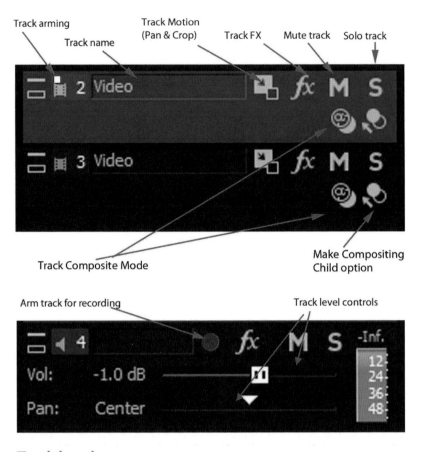

Track arming
Track name
Track Motion (Pan & Crop)
Track FX
Mute track
Solo track
Track Composite Mode
Make Compositing Child option
Arm track for recording
Track level controls

Track headers

To the left of each video and audio track in the **Timeline** window are the **Track Headers**.

These **Track Headers** include customizable names and a number of tools and toggles for affecting how the particular track displays and behaves. (Note that how these **Track Headers** display depends on whether you are in **Simple** or **Advanced** mode, how wide the tracks are and if you are using a **Track Compositing** mode.)

Audio tracks include features for adjusting the **Volume** levels and centering **Pan** (balancing the right and left stereo channels) as well as a toggle for arming the track for accepting live audio recording (such as narration or music). If your project is set up for **5.1 audio**, you'll be able to control the volume level of each of the five main audio channels individually.

We'll discuss many of these toggles and display modes throughout the rest of this chapter.

Note that audio and video effects (including **Pan/Crop Motion**) can be added to individual event clips on your timeline or to entire audio or video tracks, by using the tools on the **Track Headers**. Effects can also be added to media clips and to your project overall.

Add a video or audio track

When you first start a project, the program, by default, will create your **Timeline** with four tracks – two audio tracks (labeled **Audio** and **Music**) and two video tracks (labeled **Video** and **Text**). However, a Vegas Movie Studio Platinum 14 project can include as many as 200 video tracks and a virtually unlimited number of audio tracks.

To add a video or audio track:

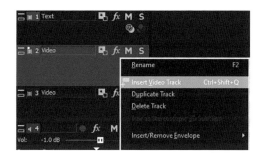

1 **Click on a Track Header**

   Right-click on the **Track Header** for an existing audio or video track. (Click on an audio **Track Header** if you want to create a new audio track or on a video **Track Header** to create a new video track.)

2 **Select the Insert Track option**

   Select the option to **Insert Video Track** or **Insert Audio Track**.

Your new video or audio track will appear directly above the track you've right-clicked on.

Reorder your video and audio tracks

To change the order of your video and/or audio tracks, click on the **Track Header** and drag it to any position above, below or in between any existing tracks.

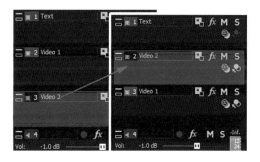

Audio tracks can be stacked in any order – even in between video tracks. However, the order that video tracks are stacked often affects how they interact with each other (see pages 112-122).

Remove a video or audio track

To remove a video or audio track:

1 **Click on the Track Header**

   Right-click on the **Track Header** of the track you'd like removed.

2 **Select Delete Track**

   Select the **Delete Track** option.

If there are any video or audio events on this track, they will be removed from your timeline along with this track.

Rename a track

The default labels on the tracks are merely suggestions. You can put music on the **Sound Effects** track, narration on the **Music** track and video on the **Text** track. Any of the three video tracks can include video, stills or text and any of the three audio tracks can include any forms of audio, from music and narration to the original audio included with your video clips.

To rename a track, **right-click** on the track header and select **Rename**, press the **F2** key on your keyboard or **double-click** on the name box.

New video and audio tracks will be displayed with no names at all. Naming your audio and video tracks can help you manage and keep track of the events on your timeline.

Resize your video and audio tracks

There are a number of ways to control the vertical size (height) of the audio and video tracks in the **Timeline** window:

To resize an individual track, hover your mouse over the bottom seam between the **Track Headers** until you see the **Resize** indicator. Click and drag on the seam to widen or narrow your video or audio track.

To quickly enlarge a track, click on the **Maximize Track Height** button on the left side of the **Track Header.** Click on it again to restore the track to its previous height.

To resize all of your tracks at once, click on the vertical **+** and **−** buttons in the lower right of the **Timeline** window, or hold **Ctrl+Shift** and press the up and down arrows on your keyboard.

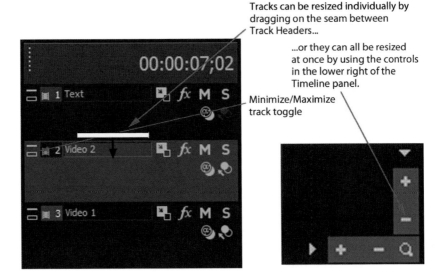

Tracks can be resized individually by dragging on the seam between Track Headers...

...or they can all be resized at once by using the controls in the lower right of the Timeline panel.

Minimize/Maximize track toggle

Your Timeline Grid can be set to display minutes, seconds or even musical beats.

Use the Timeline Grid as a guide

Grids are guides. They appear as dotted vertical lines on the **Timeline**. They can be used to help you time your movie project (dividing the events clips on the **Timeline** into minutes or seconds), or they can be used as guides to snap your events to exact positions.

Grid Spacing is set under the **Options** menu at the top of the interface. (It can also be set via context menu when you **right-click** along the top of the **Timeline** panel.)

In the sub-menu under **Grid Spacing** you'll find options for setting your grid to display time (minutes, seconds, milliseconds or the individual frames on your timeline), to indicate the **Ruler Marks** on your timeline (which varies, according to how closely you're zoomed into your timeline) or to indicate musical beats (measures, quarter notes, 8th notes, etc.).

The grid guides will be most visible on your audio events, appearing as vertical dotted lines (as in the illustration above), but they are also visible along the bottoms of your video events. More importantly, with **Snap to Grid** set (as discussed below) your edits will snap to the divisions of this grid. Your trims, for instance, will snap to divisions of seconds or video frames.

There is no "correct" setting for your **Grid Spacing**. It all depends on what you need at the time. If you are building a project based on precise timing, then one of the time segment spacings would likely be your best choice.

If you are recording music into your movie, or you are timing the cuts in your movie (or slideshow) to match the beats in a music track, then certainly one of the musical beats would be preferred.

For typical video editing work, keeping your **Grid Spacing** set to **Ruler Marks** probably makes the most sense.

Snap clips to the Grid

Your **Grid** is not only a guide for your editing work – but it is also a tool that can be used to "snap" your event clips to precise positions.

When the **Snap to Grid** option is toggled on (also under the **Options** menu), the media clips you position on your timeline will "snap" to the **Grid** whenever you place them near a **Grid** line.

To add several clips as optional Takes to your timeline, right-click and drag the clips to your timeline, then select the Add As Takes option.

By right-clicking on the event on your timeline, you can switch between the Takes that are displayed.

Add multiple Takes of a scene to your timeline

Vegas Movie Studio includes a very advanced feature for adding several **Takes** of a scene to your movie.

When you add **Multiple Takes** to your movie, you are actually adding several clips at once – although only one of these clips will appear as an event on your timeline at a time.

You can then switch between **Takes**, test driving each to see which fits best in your movie.

To add **Multiple Takes** as a single timeline event:

1   **Select media clips**

    By holding down the **Shift** key (to select the first and last in a sequence) or by holding down the **Ctrl** key (to select one media clip at a time), select two or more clips in the **Project Media** panel.

2   **Add as Takes**

    Right-click on the selected clips and drag them to your timeline.

    When you release your mouse button, a pop-up menu will appear.

    On that menu, select **Add as Takes**.

The clips will be added to your timeline as if a single media clip.

To switch between **Takes**:

3   Select a Take

Right-click on the event representing your **Multiple Takes** on your timeline and select **Take**.

From the sub-menu, select which of the **Takes** you would like displayed on your timeline, as illustrated on the facing page.

Note that, because your takes may not be the same length, some takes may be **over-extended**, as discussed on page 80.

Once you've test driven your **Takes**, you can remove the unwanted **Takes** from the event – eventually leaving you with one final, accepted **Take**.

To remove **Takes** from your **Multiple Take** set:

4   Select Takes to delete

Right-click on the event and select **Takes**. Then, from the sub-menu, select **Delete...**

A dialog window will appear, listing all of the clip options you've included as **Takes** in the event, as illustrated below.

By clicking on the **Play** button, you can preview each in the **Trimmer**.

By holding down the **Ctrl** key on your keyboard, you can select any or all of the clips you'd like deleted from the set.

Click **OK** to delete them.

Takes can be previewed a final time in the Trimmer before being selected for deletion from the event.

Edit with J-cuts, L-cuts and multiple tracks of video

The ability to compose your video using several audio and video tracks greatly expands your ability to use interesting and professional-style editing techniques in your video projects.

Multiple tracks of audio merely combine into a single soundtrack for your movie. (For information on how these tracks can be mixed, see **Chapter 9, Edit Audio on Your Timeline**.)

But, with multiple tracks of video, you can combine elements from several video clips at once using a variety of properties and effects.

Think of multiple tracks of video as a stack, like layers of images. In most cases, only the uppermost track in the stack will be visible.

However, if you change the size and position of the clips on the uppermost track – or on several tracks – or if you make portions of video on upper tracks transparent, you can display video on several tracks at once. (We'll show you one powerful method for making areas of your video transparent in **Chroma Key a background** on page 189.)

By using multiple tracks of video and then scaling and positioning your clips on each, you can have any number of video images in your video frame at the same time. (Think of the grid of faces in the opening credits of *The Brady Bunch*.) We'll show you the basic technique for creating these types of compositions in **Create a Picture-in-Picture** effect on page 114.

In addition to editing techniques that combine several layers of video into a second image, multi-track video editing can be used to create popular storytelling techniques called **L-cutting** and **J-cutting.**

L-cuts and **J-cuts** begin or end with an on-screen storyteller. As he or she speaks, the movie cuts away to related video, supplementing the story he or she is telling with visuals.

Think of a TV news report that features video of a reporter shown standing in front of a burned-out building, describing the fire that destroyed it.

As he continues speaking, the video cuts away to footage shot earlier of the fire itself. That's an **L-cut.**

A **J-cut**, on the other hand, would begin with video of the fire and the reporter's voice describing it – then it would cut to the reporter finishing his report.

The techniques are similar and the principle is the same: As audio continues from one scene, the video cuts away to another scene.

L-cuts and **J-cuts** are so named because, back in the "primitive" days of film editing, when a segment of film had to be removed and the audio left in place to allow for the placement of alternate video, the primary video and audio clip resembled an "L" – or a "J," depending on whether the beginning or end of the visual portion was replaced with new footage.

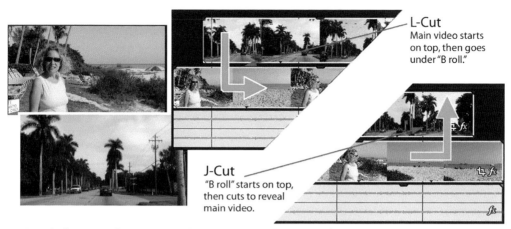

As audio from main clip continues, video cuts away to or from "B roll" footage.

Creating an **L-cut** or a **J-cut** is easy with multi-track editing.

1   Place the main video on a lower video track

This would be the clip of the reporter speaking to the camera or of the person being interviewed.

2   Place the cutaway video on an upper video track

Place the cutaway video – the video illustrating what the reporter or the interviewee is discussing – on a video track above the main video. (You may need to temporarily disable **Auto Ripple** to do this, as described on page 100.)

The cutaway video should overlap the main video slightly, so that we begin or end – or both – with the main video of the reporter speaking.

Voila! Tweak **Clip B**'s position for maximum effect and you're done! We begin with the reporter speaking to the camera and, as he continues to speak, we cut away to the footage of the fire.

L-cuts and **J-cuts** are very effective for news-style reports as well as for interviews, in which you cut away from the person speaking to separately shot footage of what he or she is describing.

It's a great way to reinforce, with images, what's being presented verbally.

By the way, here's some professional vocabulary to impress your friends with. That secondary footage that plays as the main video's audio continues? It's commonly called "**B-roll footage**", a relic from the days when this kind of editing actually did involve pasting in footage from a separate roll of film or video.

Place the video clip that will serve as your Picture-in-Picture on a video track directly above your main video.

Click on the Event Pan/Crop tool.

Create a Picture-in-Picture or Brady Bunch effect

Creating a **Picture-in-Picture** effect is another great way to use multiple tracks of video.

When you create a **Picture-in-Picture** effect, you're essentially stacking one track of video on top of another – then resizing the video on the upper track so that it only takes up a portion of the video frame.

To create a **Picture-in-Picture**

1 **Place your background on a lower video track**

Drag the video you're going to use as your background – the video that's going to dominate your video frame – onto a lower video track.

2 **Place your Picture-in-Picture video on an upper video track**

Place the video you'd like to use as your **Picture-in-Picture (PiP)** inset on a video track directly above your background video. (You may need to temporarily disable **Auto Ripple** to do this, as described on page 100.)

3 **Open Event Pan/Crop**

Click on the **Event Pan/Crop** button on the **PiP** clip.

Pan/Crops can be applied to a single clip or to entire video tracks. In this case, we just want to apply it to a single event clip.

4 **Size and position the PiP clip**

In the **Position** settings in the **Event Pan/Crop** dialog window, set the video frame's **Width** to 2400 and **Height** to 1600 either by typing in the numbers in the settings boxes or by dragging on the corners of the **Selection Box**. (For hi-def video, set **Width** to 4200.)

Making the video frame larger makes the clip appear smaller. These settings will reduce the size of the **PiP** clip to about 25% of the size of your video frame.

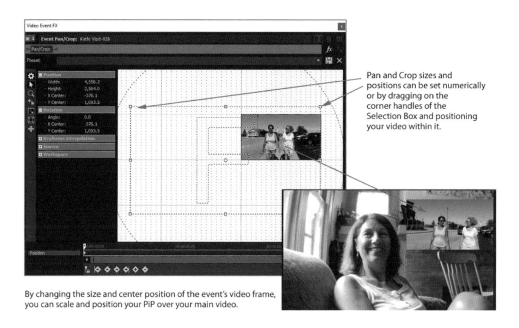

Pan and Crop sizes and positions can be set numerically or by dragging on the corner handles of the Selection Box and positioning your video within it.

By changing the size and center position of the event's video frame, you can scale and position your PiP over your main video.

Set the **Y Center** to 350 and the **X Center** to 500. This will position your **PiP** in the upper left of the video frame. (For hi-def video, set **Y Center** to 1900 and **X Center** to 1070.)

By stacking several layers of video on top of one another and by sizing and positioning each within your video frame, it's possible to create a collage of several videos arranged in a grid.

Below I've taken some old family photos and arranged them into a grid.

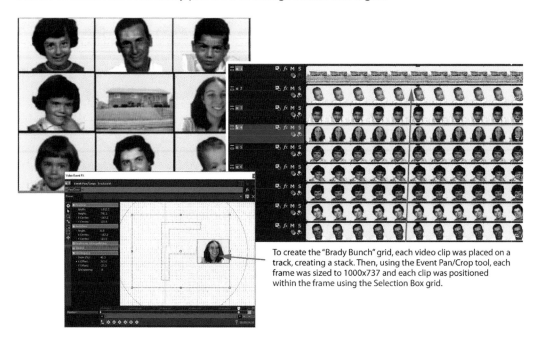

To create the "Brady Bunch" grid, each video clip was placed on a track, creating a stack. Then, using the Event Pan/Crop tool, each frame was sized to 1000x737 and each clip was positioned within the frame using the Selection Box grid.

Parent and Composite your video tracks

The Vegas Movie Studio **Timeline** is capable of some very advanced features. Among these are **Parenting** and **Compositing Modes**.

Parenting and **Compositing Modes** control how two or more tracks of video interact with each other. Using these features, you can, for instance, use a black and white graphic in **Compositing Mode** to create a **Mask** – making areas of a video on another track or tracks transparent. Using **Parenting**, you can affect how this **Mask** affects the one or more tracks of video below it.

In simplest terms, a **Compositing Mode** controls how a graphic or image on an upper video track affects how the track below it is displayed.

Parenting links two or more video tracks together so that they react uniquely to a **Compositing** function.

These are pretty advanced functions, and they can probably be best explained by example.

Mask a composited video

Masking means hiding areas of your video. When a **Mask** is applied to a video, the masked areas become transparent, showing a black background or even an event on a lower video track on your timeline. The area you'll mask is usually defined by a graphic. This graphic can be animated, using keyframes, so that it follows an object in your video, obscuring a moving object.

In my example below, I have some video of a woman bicycling on my **Video 3** track. Above this clip, on the **Video 2** track, I have placed video of a drive down a highway And, on the **Video 1** track, I have placed a **Generated Media** clip of a white circle with a transparent background (created from the **Color Gradient** media generators).

When all tracks are set to standard Source (alpha) Compositing mode, the white circle surrounded by transparency appears over the video of the highway, while the video of the woman bicycling remains hidden below.

Since tracks of video behave as if they were a stack of images, in default mode we can see the white circle over the highway footage, while the footage of the woman bicycling can not be seen at all.

When the track containing the white circle is set to Multiply (Mask) Compositing, the tracks below it are rendered transparent (showing black) except for the area defined by the white circle.

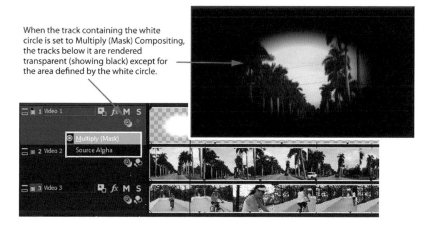

If I switch the **Compositing Mode** of the **Video 1** track to **Multiply (Mask)**, as illustrated on the right, the program uses the white circle and the transparency on **Video 3** to define the areas to be masked in the videos on the tracks below.

In my example, the areas of the **Video 2** and **Video 3** clip defined by the white circle are visible, while the areas outside the circle are masked (appearing as black).

In other words, this masking defined by the white circle goes through the entire movie, and the masked area (outside the white circle) appears as black.

Parenting video tracks

However, when I **Parent** the **Video 1** track to **Video 2** (making the **Video 2** track a "child" of the **Video 1** track), the program treats the composition of **Video 1** and **Video 2** as separate and distinct from any other video tracks.

In this mode, the **Mask** only affects the video on **Video 2!**

The video of the woman bicycling on **Video 3** is revealed through the transparency outside of the white circle **Mask**.

When the video track that includes the clip of the young woman is parented to the track with the white circle on it, the mask effect is limited to those two tracks, and the area outside of the masked video reveals the video of the woman bicycling from the Video 3 track.

Parenting, then, combines two or more video tracks so that they can interact with each other separately from the other video tracks in your project.

Blur a face, as on TV's COPS

Okay, so you've shot your scene, it looks great and you're all ready to include it in your movie. There's just one problem. Somebody in the background has refused to sign a release and won't let you use his face in your movie. Or maybe there's an objectionable word spray-painted on a wall or, worse, *nudity*! How do you hide it?

You've seen this effect, no doubt, if you've watched a reality TV show like "COPS." Among professionals, it's called a spot blur. And, like most effects, there are lots of ways to do it. This is probably the simplest.

To create this effect, we'll create two events of the same media clip – placing one directly above the other on our timeline. We'll apply a **Pixelate** effect to one, blurring it beyond recognition. Then, using the **Cookie Cutter** to hide all but a small area of the blurred clip, we'll reveal the normal video in all but one small, blurred area of our video frame.

1   **Place your video on Video 1 and Video 2**

Drag the clip you want to blur from the **Project Media** window to a lower video track. (We'll call it **Video 1.**)

Then drag the same media clip from the **Project Media** window to the video track directly above the first clip. (We'll call it **Video 2.**) You may need to temporarily turn off **Auto Ripple** (page 100) to keep the clip on **Video 1** from moving down the timeline when you add the new clip to **Video 2**.

Place the same clip on the Video 1 and Video 2 tracks.

Click on Video 2's clip's Event FX button.

Select Pixelate on the Plug-In Chain.

Once the video has been blurred, we'll use the Cookie Cutter mask so that only the blurred video over the man's face will be used and transparency will reveal the video on the Video 1 track around it.

Select the Large Preset for the Pixelate effect to blur the video on the Video 2 track beyond recognition.

2   **Apply a Pixelate effect to Video 2**

Click on the **Event FX** button on the clip on **Video 2**, as illustrated at the bottom of the facing page. Make sure you click on the button on the clip itself – not on the track header.

Hold down the **Ctrl** key and select both the **Magix Pixelate** and the **Magix Cookie Cutter** effects from the **Plug-In Chooser**. Click **OK**.

3   **Set the Pixelation level**

Click on the **Pixelate** listing in the **Plug-In Chain** along the top of the **Video Event FX** dialog window, as illustrated on the facing page.

Select **Large** from **Pixelate's Preset** drop-down menu. This should pixelate your video so much that it's impossible to recognize anyone or anything in it.

This creates our blurred video effect on **Video 2** – the only video we can see in the **Preview** window at this point. We'll now use the **Cookie Cutter** effect to mask all but a small area of this blurred clip. Masking means hiding areas in your video. Usually this masked area will become transparent, revealing the video on the video track or tracks below it.

The **Cookie Cutter** effect masks areas of your video in order to appear to "cut" your video into various shapes. We'll use it to mask the area outside of a small circular area of our blurred clip.

The result will be that the only part of the blurred clip (**Video 2**) we'll see in our final video will be the area within this circle. Outside of this **Cookie Cutter Circle** – in the masked, transparent area – we'll see the video to which no effects have been applied (**Video 1**).

4   **Adjust the Cookie Cutter effect**

Click on the **Cookie Cutter** listing in the **Plug-In Chain** along the top of the **Video Event FX** dialog window.

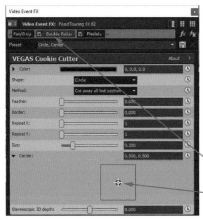

The Cookie Cutter masks all but a defined area of your video, making the surrounding area transparent.
The Center Point control sets the Cookie Cutter shape's location in your frame.

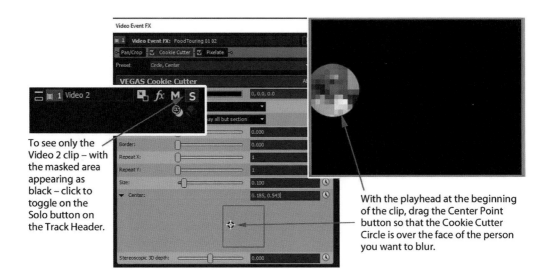

To see only the Video 2 clip – with the masked area appearing as black – click to toggle on the Solo button on the Track Header.

With the playhead at the beginning of the clip, drag the Center Point button so that the Cookie Cutter Circle is over the face of the person you want to blur.

If you have trouble distinguishing the exact location of the blurred area in the **Preview** window, you can temporarily **Solo** your video track so that only your Cookie Cutter Circle is displayed in the **Preview** window, as I've done in the illustration above.

To **Solo** your video track, click on the exclamation point button on the **Track Header** for the video track that includes the **Video 2** clip, as in the illustration.

You should now see only the **Cookie Cutter Circle**, with black around it representing the masked area, as illustrated above.

5   Size and locate the Cookie Cutter for Video 2

Set the **Size** slider for the **Cookie Cutter** to 0.100. (You can, of course, resize it as needed to cover the area you need to cover.)

Drag the **Center Point** definer (inside the white rectangular box) to define the location of the **Cookie Cutter Circle** in your video frame.

This white box represents your video frame, and the little button inside it represents the center of your **Cookie Cutter** shape. If the **Timeline Cursor** (playhead) is positioned over your clip on the timeline, you should see the location of the blurred area of your video moving around the video frame as you drag this button around within the white rectangle.

In fact, I'd recommend, at this point, that you do have the **Timeline Cursor** at the very beginning of this clip on your timeline – since we are now defining the initial location of our blurred area.

6   Turn on Animation

Click the **Animate** button (the clock dial) to the right of the **Center** property. This will open the **Keyframe Controller**, a mini-timeline on which you can create animated effects. (For detailed information on this tool, see **Chapter 15, Create Animation with Keyframes**.)

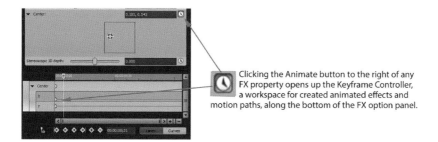

Clicking the Animate button to the right of any FX property opens up the Keyframe Controller, a workspace for created animated effects and motion paths, along the bottom of the FX option panel.

7   **Set your Cookie Cutter's end position**

Now move the playhead on the little timeline that runs along the bottom of the **Video FX** dialog window (called the **Keyframe Controller**) to the end of the clip's timeline.

Drag the **Center Point** definer so that the **Cookie Cutter Circle** is again over the area or the face you want to blur (assuming the person has moved). You can change the **Size** setting also, if you need to.

As you change these settings, a little circular or diamond-shaped keyframe will automatically be created on the **Keyframe Controller** timeline at the position of the playhead.

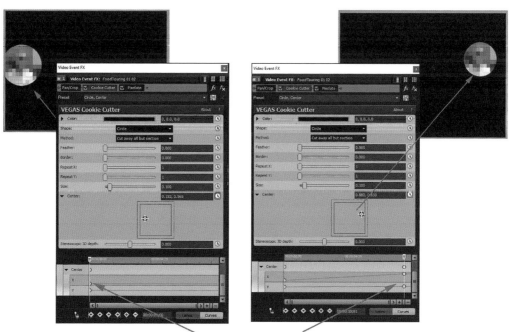

Move the playhead to the end of the Keyframe Controller timeline and reposition and resize the Cookie Cutter Circle as needed. A keyframe will automatically be created at the playhead's position. Add as many keyframes as necessary to follow the face around the video frame throughout the clip.

Play or scrub through your clip, repositioning the **Center Point as** necessary to keep this circle over the person's face. As you do, more keyframes will be created on the **Keyframe Controller** timeline, creating a motion path that keeps the **Cookie Cutter Circle** over the person's face.

If you've got your video track set to **Solo**, click again on the track header's exclamation point to toggle the **Solo** button off so that all of your video tracks will again be visible in the **Preview** window.

The end result should be that, as you play your clip, the area over our unwanted person will remain blurred and follow his face around the video frame while the rest of the video frame remains clear and clean.

Edit Multicam video

An exciting new feature in version 14 – and a feature usually found only in professional video editors – is a workspace for editing multi-camera video.

Multicam video is video shot of a live event (like a wedding, a meeting presentation or a sports event) by up to four cameras from four different locations. Using the Vegas Movie Studio **Multicam Editor,** you'll be able to see all of your video sources at once and then easily select which camera angle is used at any given time. And, once you've created your multicam composition, you can tweak your selections until it's exactly what you'd like.

Add video and audio to your timeline

The first step in editing a multicam editing project is, of course, gathering your clips on your timeline. In Vegas Movie Studio, you can assemble this edit using up to four video sources. You can also include a separate audio source (audio recorded from a lapel microphone, for instance) and even mix a number of audio sources.

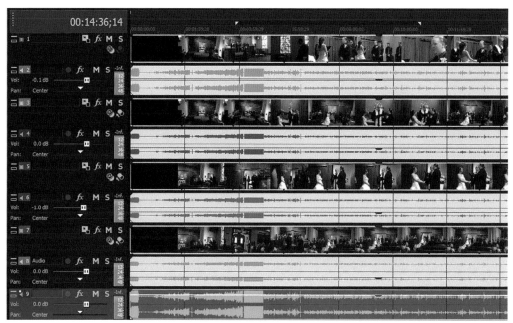

My four camcorder sources plus a master audio track recorded with a remote microphone.

Needless to say, you'll get the best results if all of your video was shot at the same resolution and frame rate. I even try to shoot all of my camera angles with the same brand of camera so that the picture quality from angle to angle is as consistent as possible.

1 Assemble your clips on your timeline

Once you've imported your video and audio clips into your project, place them on the timeline. Stack them one above the other, as in the illustration. Don't worry about synching the clips yet. We'll handle that in the next step.

Synchronizing your clips

This is probably the most challenging step in multicam editing – but it is a vital one, and the more effort you make to get it perfect, the easier things will be later.

There are a number of ways to sync video and audio clips. This is the method I use, and it's served me well.

To use it, you'll need an audio and video sync point. This, in fact, is the purpose of the "clapper" you see in Hollywood movies. ("Steve's movie. Take one." SNAP!) It gives you both a visual and audio cue to line your clips up.

Short of a clapper (or an actor physically clapping once before he or she begins a presentation), you'll need to find some element in your movie you can sync both your audio and video to. A cough. A door slamming or some other action that is recorded as both an action and a sound. You may be able to sync a mouth movement to a voice in a pinch, but the more abrupt the sound – the more of a snap – the better.

2   **Find the sync point**

Right-click on a clip in the **Project Media** panel and select the option to **Open in Trimmer.**

When the **Trimmer** opens, drag the lower right corner to make it bigger, so you can see what you're doing.

Place the playhead on the **Trimmer's** timeline as close as possible to where your visual/ audio cue is located. Tap the **up arrow** on your keyboard to zoom in on this point. Do this several times, adjusting the playhead position as needed.

When you have zoomed into the timeline as much as possible, use the left and right arrow keys on your keyboard to locate the exact frame on which your visual/audio cue appears.

A reader tapping the microphone gave me a fortuitous sync point.

3   **Mark the sync point**

Click the **Insert Marker** button on the **Trimmer** (or press the **M** key on your keyboard) to mark the spot. This marker will appear on both the clip in your **Project Media** panel and on the event clip on your project's timeline.

Continue this process for every audio and video clip you will be using in your multicam editing project, then close the **Trimmer.**

4   **Sync up your clips**

If you've marked your sync point accurately on each clip, this part should be easy.

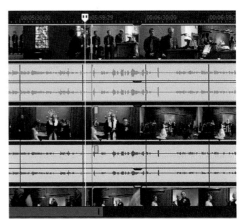

Line up the event clips on your timeline so that all of the markers are in alignment. Zoom in on your timeline (by pressing the up arrow key) and adjust the events' positions.

Aligning the sync point markers on the timeline.

When you've zoomed in all the way and the markers for each event are in direct alignment, you're in sync and we're ready to start editing! (You may want to play your timeline, enabling and disabling tracks, to give it a test drive and ensure you've got everything in sync. If things are off, it's much easier to fix things now than later!)

Enable Multicam Editing

Once your events are synched on your timeline, you can begin the actual editing process.

5 Enable Multicamera Editing

From the **Tools** menu at the top of the program, select **Multicamera**, then **Enable Multicamera Editing**.

6 Create a Multicamera Track

By holding down the **Ctrl** key and clicking to select **Track Headers** of the video tracks you'd like to multicam edit.

From the **Tools** menu, select **Multicamera**, then **Create Multicamera Track**.

Select the video tracks you want to multi-edit, then select the option to Create a Multicamera Track from the Multicamera menu under Tools.

The tool will combine your selected tracks into a single event that includes multiple video takes.

Delete any unwanted audio clips.

Play your movie, selecting your preferred video source or camera angle on the Preview window.

As you make selections, the program will cut your video into segments, each using a "take" from the selected source.

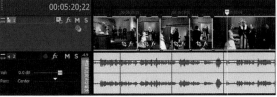

Edit your Multicam video

Your selected video tracks will be combined into one track on your timeline and your **Preview** window will display all of your video sources at once.

The audio from your camcorder video will remain as separate tracks on your timeline. You may want to mute or eliminate (**right-click** and **Delete**) any unwanted audio events so that only your master audio or the audio you want to use in your final video remains.

If your timeline includes audio, you will find the option to **Edit Multicamera Audio with Video** checked by default under the **Tools/ Multicamera** sub-menu. You may, of course, opt not to include the audio in your edit by unchecking this option.

7   **Select your camera angles**

Now the fun begins!

Reset the playhead to the beginning of your timeline (or where you'd like your multicamera editing to begin).

Play your movie.

The selected or "live" video source will appear in the **Preview** window with a blue highlight around it. To switch to another video source or camera angle, click to select it in the **Preview** window.

The program will slice your video into short events, each cut displaying the video source or camera angle you've selected.

If you'd like to preview your cuts full-screen at any point, you can go to the **Tools** menu and, from the **Multicamera** menu, uncheck **Enable Multicamera Editing**. When you're ready to return to multicamera editing mode, just re-check the function.

Don't worry if you miss a shot or if you cut too soon or too late. You can tweak your choices later.

8 Change a take

If you later decide that your cut to Camera 1 should have been a cut to Camera 2, it's easy to fix.

Locate the segment on your timeline that you'd like to change.

Right-click on it and select **Take**.

To swap in a different camera angle, right-click on a segment and select a different Take.

Under the **Take** sub-menu, you'll find each of the video sources listed. Select the one you'd like to swap in.

9 Shorten or lengthen a take

If you've missed a cut or you'd like to lengthen or shorten a video segment, you can easily "slide" a cut to the right or left.

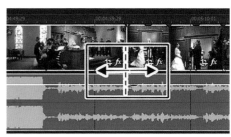

To slide a cut (also known as **Trim Adjacent**), hold down the **Ctrl+Alt** keys and click on the cut you want to change.

To extend or shorten a camera angle, click and drag on the cut between segments while holding down the Ctrl+ Alt keys.

Drag to slide the cut to the right or left. The cut will move, trimming or lengthening the adjacent clips, changing the cut point but not the overall content of your movie.

When you're happy with your cuts, output your finished multicamera composite using **Make Movie** or **Render As**, just as you would any standard movie.

Chapter 8

Work with Photos

Slideshows and motion paths

Photos can make excellent source material for your videos, whether you use them to create a slideshow or you integrate them into your video projects.

Vegas Movie Studio 14 includes a number of tools for making any work you do with photos more interesting.

Project Media tools for working with photos

In addition to the Vegas Movie Studio tools discussed in this chapter, the **Project Media** window includes a couple of quick touch-up tools for your photos.

For more information on them, see **Tools for working with still photos** on page 61.

It's easy to add and use photos in your Vegas Movie Studio projects. For the most part, they can be treated just like video.

But, by using some of these tools, you can make your photos look like more than frozen images. You can add interest and even motion to them, making them seem as alive as your video!

Create a slideshow

You can, of course, create a slideshow simply by dragging your photos from the **Project Media** window to your timeline, trimming them and adding effects as you would any other video clip. But Vegas Movie Studio Platinum includes a tool for automatically creating a slideshow.

A slideshow can be created as a separate project, or can be incorporated into an existing video project.

When you build a slideshow with the **Slideshow Creator**, it's best to have all of your slides in a single folder on your hard drive and have them already optimized in size, per the sidebar at the bottom of this page.

1   Select and arm a video track

Position the **Timeline Cursor** (playhead) on the timeline at the spot you'd like your slideshow to appear.

Arm the track by clicking on the colored button in the upper left of the **Track Header** (as described on page 77).

Optimize your photo sizes

You can load pretty much any size photos into your Vegas Movie Studio project. However, you might be surprised how much the size of the photos affects how the program performs and, even more so, the render times for your video projects.

Using larger, higher-resolution photos won't get you a better, more detailed slideshow. Since Vegas Movie Studio is a *video* editor, whatever you load into it will be reduced to *video* resolution anyway. So adding higher-resolution photos merely forces the program to work harder.

For best results, you should not use a photo larger than 2500x1875 pixels in size (at 72 ppi) in a Vegas Movie Studio project. This will fill the video frame (which is only 1920x1080 pixels) and still leave you room to do some Pan/Crop motion paths if you'd like.

By contrast, a photo taken directly from a 5 megapixel camera is nearly 250% the size of a high-definition video frame. The larger your photo (the higher the resolution) the more time it will take the program to render it as video.

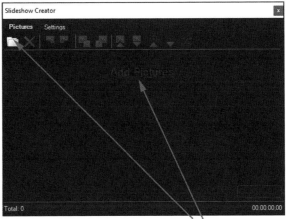

Browse to add pictures.

2   Start the Slideshow Creator

Under the **Insert** drop-down menu at the top of the Vegas Movie Studio Platinum interface, select **Slideshow**.

The **Slideshow Creator** dialog window will open.

3   Add pictures

Add Pictures either by clicking on the link in the middle of the window or by selecting the folder icon in the upper left of the window.

A browse screen will open.

Browse to locate the photos you've prepared as your slides.

Click to select the photos you'd like to add. To select a series of photos, hold down the **Shift** key and click on the first and last in the series. To randomly select several photos, hold down the **Ctrl** key and click on each photo individually.

Click **Open**.

The slides will be added to the **Slideshow Creator** window and will appear as thumbnails.

Rotate slide.   Order by name.   Order by date.
    Move forward/backward one.

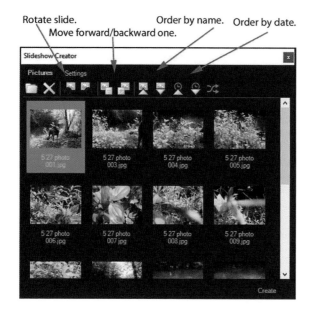

4   Re-arrange your slides

To re-arrange the order of your slides, just drag them around in the **Slideshow Creator** window.

Shortcut buttons along the top of the window will automatically arrange your slides in alpha-numeric order or by date saved.

Other buttons along the top of the panel will move your selected slide's order one position forward or one position back.

A third set of buttons will rotate your slides clockwise or counter-clockwise 90 degrees, if necessary.

5   Customize the slideshow's settings

Click on the **Settings** tab in the **Slideshow Creator** window.

By default, your slides will be added at the current position of the **Timeline Cursor**. However, on this screen, you can set it to begin at any position on your timeline.

The **Duration** of each slide is, by default, 3 seconds (plus one second of transition in and another out). You can customize this **Duration** to any length or set a **Total Length** for your slideshow and let the program average the duration for each slide accordingly.

The **Settings** tab includes options for setting the transitions between each slide (**Effects**). The program offers 15 different transitional effects as well as the option to add **Random** transitions between slides and even **Pans and Zooms** over your photos. You can also set a custom **Length** for your transitional effects.

When you've made your selections, click the **Create** button.

The slideshow will be added to the video track you've armed.

You can leave it as is, or you can further customize it with motion paths.

Create a motion path over your photo

A motion path is a combination of a pan and a zoom across a photo. It's commonly called the Ken Burns effect, named after the great documentary filmmaker who uses it so effectively in his work.

Used well, a motion path can bring focus to specific spots on a photo – or it can make a plain old still photo seem to be moving and alive. (Panning as part of a motion path, by the way, should not be confused with audio panning, which means shifting stereo levels between right and left channels, as discussed on page 142.)

Vegas Movie Studio uses the **Pan/Crop Motion** tool to create motion paths. (When this effect is used on an entire video track, rather than individual events, it is called the **Track Motion** tool – though its function is pretty much the same.)

To create a motion path **Pan/Crop** for a single event:

1 Open an event's Pan/Crop tool

Click on the **Event Pan/Crop** button on the right side of a clip or photo on your timeline.

The clip's **Pan/Crop** dialog window will open.

The Event Pan/Crop tool

A **Pan/Crop** motion path is created using keyframes. Keyframes appear as little diamonds on the **Keyframe Controller**, a timeline representing the duration of the clip along the bottom of the **Pan/Crop** dialog window.

As you re-position the playhead and change the settings for the **Pan/Crop** effect, keyframes will automatically be created on this timeline. The program will then create the animated movement between these keyframes.

2 Set a Pan/Crop opening position

Ensure that the **Keyframe Controller** playhead at the bottom of the **Pan/Crop** window is at the beginning of the clip's timeline.

Set an opening **Pan/Crop** setting by either changing the numbers listed on the left side of the window or by dragging on the **Selection Box** in the workspace window. The results of your new settings will be reflected in the program's **Preview** window. (If not, ensure that the program's **Timeline Cursor** (playhead) is positioned over the clip you are working on.)

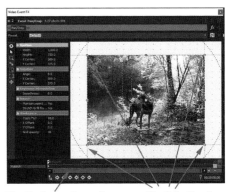

The Keyframe Controller   The Selection Box

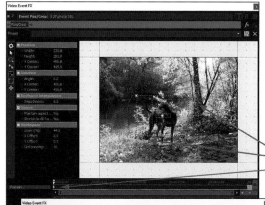

With the Selection Box sized and positioned over the center of the photo, the Preview window shows a close-up of the dog.

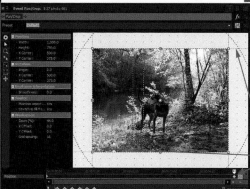

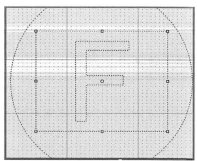

With the playhead at the end of the clip's timeline and the Selection Box set to default, we pan back to show the entire photo and a keyframe is added to the timeline.

The **Selection Box** (the dotted-line rectangle with the "F" in the middle) represents your video frame. It can be dragged into position, resized and even rotated by dragging on its corner handles.

By dragging on the grid behind the **Selection Box,** you can adjust your view of the workspace. And you can zoom in and out of this workspace by using the roller on

The Selection Box

your mouse or by changing the **Zoom (%)** level in the **Workspace** settings on the left side of the window.

Because this **Selection Box** represents the size and position of the video frame over your clip, you have to think a little bit backwards when using this tool.

- The *larger* you make the **Selection Box**, the *smaller* your clip will appear in your video frame.

- The *smaller* you make the **Selection Box**, the more you will appear to have *zoomed in* on your clip.

3   Set a Pan/Crop closing position

Move the playhead in the **Pan/Crop** dialog window to the end of the clip's **Keyframe Controller** timeline.

Reposition the **Selection Box** over your clip to determine the end position of your motion path. (Your changes should, again, be reflected in the program's **Preview** window.) As you do, a new keyframe will automatically be created on the clip's timeline.

By the way, you can quickly set your **Selection Box** to its default position– with your photo centered in and filling your video frame – just select **Default** from the **Preset** drop-down at the top of the **Pan/Crop** dialog window.

When you play your clip, you should see a smooth movement from the first keyframed position to the last.

You can add just about as many keyframes as you want to a clip and the program will create the movements to each. Keyframes can also be easily edited, repositioned and revised. They can even be customized in order to control how the program moves from one to another.

We'll discuss keyframes in more detail in **Chapter 15, Create Animations with Keyframes**.

Lengthen or shorten your slideshow

Once you've created your slideshow, you may want to tweak the length of the slideshow a bit by lengthening or shortening the duration of the slides.

While, technically, there is no simple way to change the length of all of your slides at once, there is a trick that can essentially accomplish the same thing.

1   Select your slides

To select your slides, click to select the first slide in your slideshow on your timeline, then, holding down the **Shift** key, click on the last. This will select the first, last and every slide in between.

2   Create a Group

Right-click on the selected slides and select **Group**, then **Create New** (as discussed on page 104).

Once your slides have been grouped, the entire set will move as one unit.

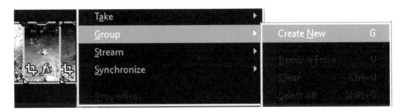

When grouped, your slideshow can be lenghtened or shortened using the Time Stretch tool.

3   Time Stretch the slideshow

Holding down the **Ctrl** key, hover your mouse over the end of the slideshow until you see the **Time Stretch** indicator, as illustrated above.

Drag on the end of the slideshow group to stretch it longer or shorter.

Technically, what this does is speed up or slow down the group of clips. This means that any motion paths or transitions you've added to your slideshow will also slow down or speed up.

But, since we're working with still photos, the audience won't see it as a **Time Stretch**. Rather, they'll just see the longer or shorter slideshow you've created.

For more information on using **Time Stretch**, see **Speed up or slow down an event clip** on page 81.

Reduce Interlace Flicker

If you add photos to your timeline using **Insert/Slideshow**, as described on page 130, the program will automatically apply flicker reduction to your stills. Flicker reduction can reduce the flickering or trembling that sometimes appears in photos when they are added to video.

When you add photos directly to your timeline, you may get better, cleaner looking slides if you manually turn on this feature.

To turn on this feature, **right-click** on the photo or photos on your timeline, select **Switches** and then, from the sub-menu, check the **Reduce Interlace Flicker** option.

Adding Audio Media to Your Timeline

Fading In and Fading Out Audio

Adjusting Gain Level and Normalizing

Controlling Volume with Audio Envelopes

Filling Left or Right Audio Channels

Adding Narration

Pacing Your Recording with a Metronome

Chapter 9

Edit Audio on the Timeline

Adding and mixing your movie's sound

As it does with video, Vegas Movie Studio includes a wealth of tools for editing, mixing and enhancing your audio.

The program even includes tools for recording narration or live music directly to your movie's timeline!

As with your video, your audio clips can be trimmed and sliced on the timeline. Vegas Movie Studio also includes a wealth of effects that can be added to them.

As with video, these effects can be added to the original media, to individual event clips on the timeline or to entire audio tracks.

Likewise, audio levels can be adjusted for individual events or for the entire audio track. Or, using **Audio Envelopes**, you can set the volume levels for an audio track at specific points so that, for instance, you can lower the volume level of a music track so that the narration track can dominate a sequence.

Add audio media clips to your timeline

There are a number of ways to add audio media to your timeline:

Drag a clip from the Project Media window. Far and away the most common way to add a media clip to a timeline is to simply drag it into position from the **Project Media** panel.

Double-click a clip in Project Media. By default, double-clicking a clip in the **Project Media** panel adds it to the armed track (see page 77) on your timeline, at the position of the **Timeline Cursor** (playhead). (However, many people prefer to use double-clicking to open the clip in the **Trimmer** instead, as discussed on page 65.)

Drag a clip from Windows Explorer. A clip can be added to the timeline directly from a Windows Explorer browse screen. When a clip is added using this method it is also added automatically to your **Project Media** panel.

Drag a clip from the Trimmer timeline. If you've trimmed a clip in the **Trimmer** or you'd like to add only its video or only its audio to your timeline, you can drag it to your timeline from the **Trimmer** timeline. For more information on adding media clips directly from the **Trimmer**, see **Chapter 5, Prepare Your Media in the Trimmer**.

How your movie behaves as clips are added to it is determined by the **Auto Ripple** mode it is in, as discussed on pages 100 and 101.

Add Audio Only or Video Only from Project Media

To add the audio portion only or the video portion only of a media clip from the **Project Media** panel, drag the clip to a track on your timeline with a **right-click** rather than a left-click.

When you release the mouse button, a pop-up menu will appear, offering you the option of adding the **Video Only** or **Audio Only** portion of the media clip to your movie.

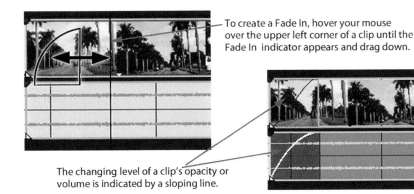

To create a Fade In, hover your mouse over the upper left corner of a clip until the Fade In indicator appears and drag down.

The changing level of a clip's opacity or volume is indicated by a sloping line.

Add a Fade In or Fade Out to an audio event clip

A **Fade In** or **Fade Out** at the beginning or end of an event is added to both video and audio clips in essentially the same way.

To add a **Fade In** to a clip:

1 **Hover over the beginning of a clip**

   Hover your mouse over the upper left corner of a clip until the **Fade Offset** indicator appears, as illustrated above.

2 **Create your Fade In**

   Click and drag down from the corner to create the **Fade in**.

Your **Fade In** will be indicated by a curved line, representing the fading in of the volume level from the beginning of the clip. The longer this slope is, the longer your **Fade In** will last.

A **Fade Out** is created exactly the same way, except over the end of a clip.

Basic audio event editing

Most of the same tools that can be used to edit video clips on the timeline can also be used to edit audio clips.

Arming an audio track makes it the default track for adding new audio clips to the timeline, as discussed on page 77.

Trimming a clip removes footage from its beginning or end, as discussed on page 78.

Splitting a clip slices it into two or more segments, which can be edited separately or removed from the timeline, as discussed on page 79.

As with video clips, audio clips can be pre-trimmed in the **Trimmer**, as discussed in **Chapter 5, Prepare Your Media in the Trimmer Window**.

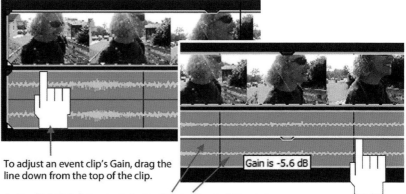

To adjust an event clip's Gain, drag the line down from the top of the clip.

Gain is -5.6 dB

As the clip's Gain is lowered, the audio waveform will narrow.

Adjust the Gain level for an audio event

The audio level of your movie can be raised or lowered for an entire audio track by adjusting the **Volume** level (as discussed in **Adjust Volume or Pan for an audio track** on page 142) – or for an individual audio event by adjusting its **Gain** level.

By definition, **Volume** is the level of sound that is heard in your movie. **Gain** refers to the level of the *audio on the event clip itself*. There's a subtle difference, but the main distinction, for our purposes, is that **Volume** refers to the level of the final sound output while **Gain** refers to the sound level on the media clip itself.

Monitor your movie's audio levels

It's best not to trust your ears or you computer's speakers when setting your movie's **Gain** and **Volume** levels.

To the right of the **Preview** window in the program's interface is the **Master Audio Control**, a tool for monitoring and adjusting your movie's audio levels.

You'll also find little meters (and control sliders) on each of the audio track headers.

For best results, you should always ensure that your audio levels register as full – but never so full that they peak beyond the range of the meter (indicated by red warnings at the tops of the meters). Overloading your audio levels can cause over-modulation, which will result in poor or distorted audio.

Raising and lowering the slider next to the meters raises or lowers the audio level of your entire movie or all audio on an audio track with a single adjustment.

To adjust the **Gain** level for an audio event:

1   **Locate the Gain level adjustment line**

    Hover your mouse over the top of an audio event clip until your cursor becomes a hand, as illustrated on the facing page.

2   **Drag the Gain level**

    As you click and drag down, you'll see a line appear over the clip. This line represents the clip's **Gain** level. And, as you drag down, a pop-up will indicate the level you are raising or lowering it to.

As you raise or lower this line, the waveform on the clip (representing the clip's audio level) should indicate the change by increasing or decreasing in size.

Normalize a clip's Gain level

A great feature for quickly adjusting the **Gain** level of a clip is the **Normalize** tool.

When a clip is **Normalized**, its **Gain** is automatically set to a "normal" level. This makes it great for automatically raising the **Gain** level of audio that was recorded at too low of a level (such as a conversation that was recorded from too far away).

To **Normalize** an event's audio, **right-click** on the event clip and select **Switches.** Then, from the sub-menu, select **Normalize.** (You should immediately see a change in the strength of the audio clip's waveform.)

Normalizing isn't magic, of course. So, if your audio clip includes a combination of loud and soft sounds, the automatic **Gain** level will be based on the louder sounds in the clip. Also, if your clip has a lot of background noise, **Normalizing** will increase the undesirable as well as the desirable sounds' levels.

But it is a great first-step in improving a clip's sound levels.

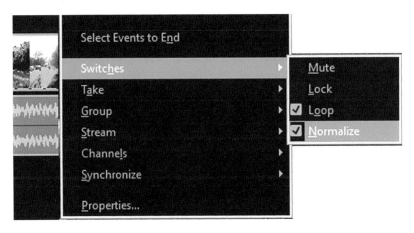

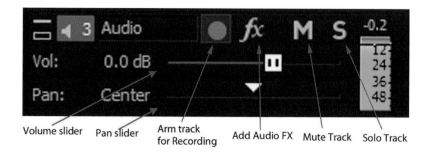

Volume slider   Pan slider   Arm track   Add Audio FX   Mute Track   Solo Track
for Recording

Adjust Volume or Pan for an entire audio track

On the audio **Track Headers** (on the left side of the **Timeline)** there are two sliders: One adjusts the track's **Volume**, the other adjusts the track's **Pan**. (How these sliders appear depends on how wide your track is.)

Volume is, of course, the loudness of an audio track.

(If your project is set up for **5.1 Audio** rather than **Stereo**, your main audio will appear as five separate audio tracks – each with its own separate **Volume** control.)

The Pan is the *balance* between the right and left stereo channels on an audio track.

Both the **Volume** level and the **Pan** level can be set overall, for an entire audio track, or they can be set at specific levels at specific points on your audio track using **Audio Envelopes**.

Use Audio Envelopes to adjust audio levels at specific points

An **Audio Envelope** controls the **Volume** or **Pan** levels for an audio track. However, unlike the overall slider adjustments made on the **Track Header**, **Audio Envelopes** can also be keyframed so that, say, the **Volume** levels of a particular audio track can be raised and lowered at specific points on the track.

This feature will, for instance, allow you to raise the **Volume** of one half of a conversation in a clip that was recorded at too low a level to match the level of the other half of the conversation that was recorded at a higher level.

It can also be used to mix audio tracks so that, for instance, the **Volume** level of a music track can be temporarily lowered to allow narration on another audio source to dominate your movie.

To create and use a **Volume Audio Envelope**:

1   **Add an Envelope to an audio track**

    Right-click on an audio **Track Header** and select **Insert/Remove Envelope**. Then, from the sub-menu, select **Volume** – or click to select an audio track's **Track Header** and, from the **Insert** menu at the top of the program's interface, select the **Audio Envelope** option.

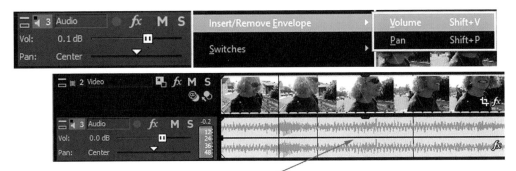

Once an Envelope has been added to a track, a heavy, blue line representing the Envelope levels will appear, running horizontally through the track.

A heavy, blue horizontal line, representing the **Volume Level** will appear through your audio track. This line is the **Volume Envelope**.

2   Add a keyframe

Hover your mouse over the **Volume Envelope** line until your cursor turns into a little white hand, as illustrated below.

Double-click on the **Envelope** line. A little blue square will appear. This is a keyframe.

3   Add another keyframe

Double-click on another spot on the **Volume Envelope**. Another keyframe will appear.

4   Position your keyframes

Raise or lower the keyframes to increase or decrease the **Volume**.

The **Volume Envelope** represents the loudness of the audio track. The higher a keyframe is positioned, the louder your clip will play.

You can add as many keyframes as you need to control your **Volume** on a track, and you can adjust the keyframe positions at any time. To remove a keyframe, just **right-click** on it and select **Delete**.

For best results, use the **Mixer** meter to monitor your movie's audio levels, as discussed in the sidebar on page 140.

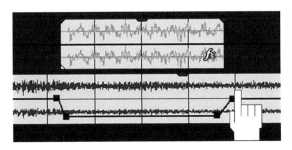

Double-click to create a keyframe.

Keyframes can be used to raise and lower the Volume levels on the Envelope at specific points – as when a music's Volume needs to be temporarily lowered to allow for narration to be heard.

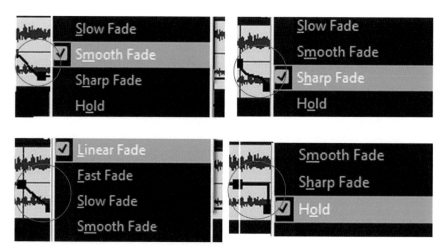

Interpolation determines how the audio levels transition from keyframe setting to keyframe setting. These Interpolations can be smooth and gradual or (as in Hold) abrupt.

Interpolate audio keyframes

Adding keyframes to an **Audio Envelope** (as discussed on page 143) sets an audio track's volume levels at specific points.

By default, the transition between these keyframed points is set to **Smooth Fade**. This means that, between a low volume level keyframe and a high volume level keyframe is (as you can see on the timeline and in the illustration above) a slightly curved line. This **Smooth Fade** creates a nice, natural transition between your levels. But it's not your only option.

If you **right-click** on any keyframe point in an **Audio Envelope**, you'll see a list of six options, called **Interpolations**. **Interpolations** affect how your audio levels behave between your keyframes.

If you **right-click** on a keyframe and select **Sharp Fade**, you'll notice that the line between this keyframe and the next changes shape. The **Envelope** line is more S-shaped, representing a sharp drop-off or sharp rise in audio level between keyframes.

Linear Fade gives you a direct line, representing a steady change in volume level between keyframes – while **Fast Fade** gives you a line with a very slight curve.

Hold maintains the current volume level, then abruptly changes levels at the next keyframe point.

There is no "right" setting for your **Audio Envelope** keyframe interpolation. It all depends on the effect you're trying to create.

Though, for a nice, natural transition between audio keyframes, the default **Smooth Fade** usually works best.

Edit or delete a keyframe or Audio Envelope

Keyframes can be adjusted or repositioned at any time. Naturally, the closer your keyframes are together, the faster the transition between them.

To delete a keyframe, just **right-click** on it and select **Delete**.

To remove an **Audio Envelope** completely from your audio track, click to select your audio track and then go to the **Insert** menu at the top of the program's interface. From the **Insert** menu, select **Audio Envelopes** and, on the sub-menu, uncheck **Volume**.

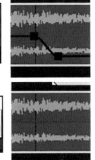

Unchecking the Audio Envelopes Volume toggle deletes all keyframes and returns the audio track to its default state.

The heavy, blue **Audio Envelope** line will be removed from the audio track as well as any keyframes added to it.

Adjust an audio track's Pan Audio Envelope

Adjust Pan for an entire audio track

As discussed on page 142, the **Pan** slider on the **Track Header** adjusts the levels of the right and left channels of your stereo audio relative to each other.

In other words, the farther left you move the slider, the more your stereo audio will be shifted to the left channel. The farther right you move the slider, the more your audio will be shifted to the right.

As with **Volume**, when you adjust these levels using the sliders on the **Track Header**, this adjustment will be made for the entire audio track.

Adjust Pan at specific points on your timeline

Just as an **Audio Envelope** can be used to control your volume levels at specific points on your timeline, an **Audio Envelope** can also be used to control your audio track's **Pan** levels at specific points.

To create a **Pan Audio Envelope, right-click** on an audio **Track Header** and select **Insert/Remove Envelope.** Then, from the sub-menu, select **Pan** – or click to select an audio track and, from the **Insert** menu at the top of the program's interface, select the **Audio Envelope** option.

A heavy, orange-colored horizontal line (the **Pan Audio Envelope**) will appear running through the middle of your audio track.

Keyframes are added to and adjusted for your **Pan Audio Envelope** exactly the same way as they are added to your **Volume Audio Envelope**, as discussed on page 142. These keyframes can also be **Interpolated**, as discussed on the facing page.

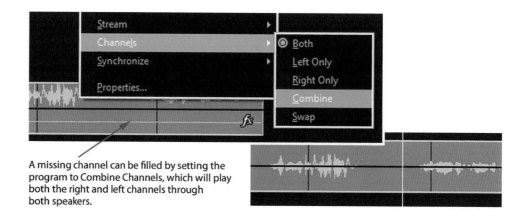

A missing channel can be filled by setting the program to Combine Channels, which will play both the right and left channels through both speakers.

Fill in a missing right or left audio channel

Occasionally, you may find that an audio clip includes only a right or only a left channel. This often happens when you record your audio into your computer with a monaural microphone.

When this happens, your audio will sound weak for that clip and the waveform on your timeline will only show one channel of audio.

Fortunately, Vegas Movie Studio includes an easy fix for this.

Right-click your audio clip and select **Channels.** Then, from the sub-menu, select **Combine**.

The program will combine your right and left channels into a single channel, which fills both your right and left stereo channels.

As an alternative, you can select the option to play only the track's right channel or only the track's left channel through both speakers.

Edit your audio in another program

It's easy to send an audio clip or the audio portion of a video clip – even one already added to your timeline – to an audio editing program (such as Magix's Sound Forge) for some sweetening.

To do so, **right-click** on the audio portion of your clip on the **Timeline** or in the **Trimmer** and select the option to **Open in Sound Forge**.

The audio clip will open in the program you have set as your **Preferred Audio Editor** in your **Options/Preferences/Audio.**

Record narration into your project

Built into Vegas Movie Studio is a tool that allows you to record narration right into your movie project.

Naturally, your recording doesn't need to be voice. You can also record live music into the program. It even includes a metronome for keeping the beat (as discussed on page 149).

An audio track armed for recording.

Microphone level Input Meter.

Needless to say, you'll need to have a microphone or other electronic audio source (such as a guitar) plugged into your computer. The program will work with microphones plugged into your computer's audio card as well as those connected via USB. (Though you may need to restart the program after plugging in the mic.)

To record into your Vegas Movie Studio project:

1   **Arm your track for recording**

Position the **Timeline Cursor** (playhead) at the point on your timeline you'd like your narration to begin.

Click on the red **Arm for Record** button on the **Track Header** for the audio track you'd like your narration recorded to, as illustrated above.

An **Input Meter** will appear on the track header.

If your microphone isn't recognized...

Sometimes, particularly if your microphone is connected via USB, the program may not recognize your microphone or may not use it as your default recording device.

To set up a USB microphone for recording narration in Vegas Movie Studio, go to the **Options** menu and select **Preferences**.

Under the **Audio Device** tab, ensure that **Audio Device Type** is set to **Windows Classic Wave Driver.** Then set **Default Audio Recording Device** to **Generic USB Audio Device.**

If this doesn't work, you may need to check Windows to ensure it is recognizing your USB device.

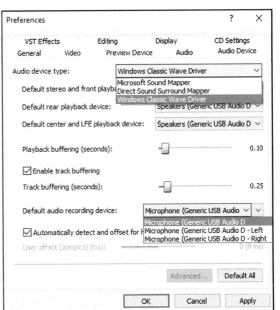

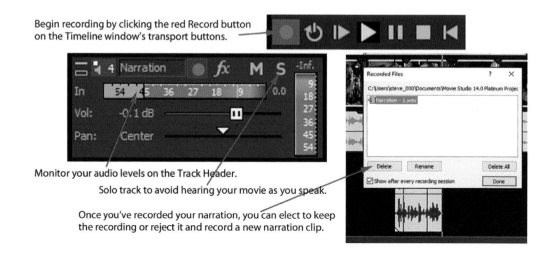

Begin recording by clicking the red Record button on the Timeline window's transport buttons.

Monitor your audio levels on the Track Header.

Solo track to avoid hearing your movie as you speak.

Once you've recorded your narration, you can elect to keep the recording or reject it and record a new narration clip.

You have the option of playing the audio from your movie as you record your narration or muting it.

If you play it, you of course will want to ensure that your computer's sound is low enough or that your microphone is far enough from your speakers that you don't pick up the movie's sound on your narration. (Or you can wear headphones as your record your narration.)

To mute the movie's sound while you record your narration, click the **Solo** button (the exclamation point) on the **Track Header**, as illustrated above.

2   Record your narration

To begin recording, click on the red **Record** button on the transport controls along the bottom of the **Timeline** window. The program will begin recording immediately.

As you record, be sure to monitor your microphone input levels on the meter on the **Track Header**. Ensure that your microphone input levels don't peak in the "red." Over-modulated audio can sound overly-loud or distorted and fuzzy.

To stop recording, click the **Stop** button on the **Timeline's** transport controls.

3   Save or reject your recording

Once you've finished recording, your narration will appear in a **Recorded Files** dialog window.

At this point, you can click **Done** to save the file and add it to your movie, or click **Delete** to reject and delete the audio clip and record it again.

By the way, you don't have to record your narration to the audio track labeled **Narration**. Any audio track can be armed for recording – whether what you are recording into your movie is voice, music or a combination of the two. The labels on the audio and video tracks are merely for your reference.

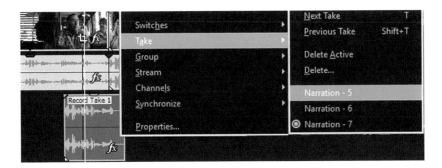

Record alternate narration Takes

If you'd like, you can record several **Takes** of the same narration to an audio track and then test drive each in your project.

To record more than one **Take**, record and save your narration clip, as discussed in the previous section of this chapter.

When you click **Done**, your audio clip will be saved to your timeline and the **Timeline Cursor** (playhead) will be positioned at the beginning of the clip.

Click the **Record** button at the bottom of the **Timeline** window to record another **Take**, clicking **Done** in the **Recorded Files** dialog **window** to save it as another media clip. You may record as many **Takes** as you'd like.

Although only one audio event will display on your timeline, this event will include all of the **Takes** you have recorded.

To switch between **Takes**, **right-click** on the event clip, select **Take** and then, from the sub-menu, select your alternate recording.

Takes can also be removed completely from an event, as discussed on page 111.

Pace your recording with the Metronome

If you're recording live music into your Vegas Movie Studio project, the program can provide you with a **Metronome** to help you keep the beat!

To activate the program's **Metronome**:

1   **Activate the Metronome**

    On the **Options** menu at the top of the program's interface, click to activate the **Metronome**.

2   **Set your tempo**

    Go to the **Project** menu at the top of the program's interface and select **Properties**.

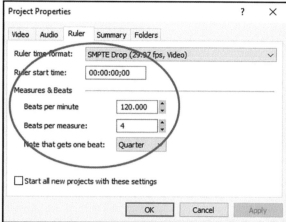

Under the **Ruler** tab on the **Project Properties** window, set **Measures & Beats** to the tempo you'd like your **Metronome** to keep.

Click **OK**.

3   Record your audio

Set up your audio input and record your audio as described in **Record narration into your project**, on page 147.

The **Metronome** will provide you with a steady beat at the tempo you've set.

The actual **Metronome** sound will not be included in your final recording.

If you'd like to customize the sound of the **Metronome**, you can do so by going to the **Options** menu and selecting **Preferences**. The option to select a custom sound for your **Metronome** can be found under the **Audio** tab.

Adjusting Preview Size and Quality

Using Safe Margins

Understanding Interlacing

Grabbing a Snapshot of Your Video

Viewing Your Video on an External Monitor

Chapter 10

Preview Window Tools

Test driving your video

The Preview window shows you what your movie-in-progress looks like.

But, like every window, it also includes some useful tools for creating your video project.

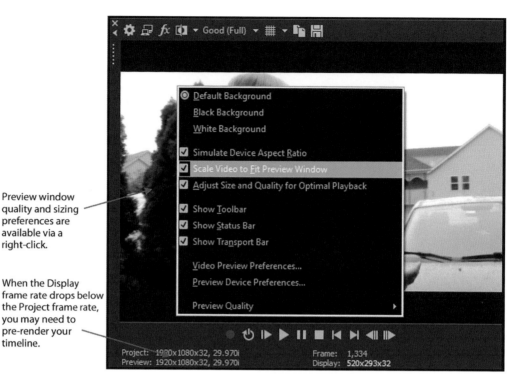

Preview window quality and sizing preferences are available via a right-click.

When the Display frame rate drops below the Project frame rate, you may need to pre-render your timeline.

The primary purpose of the **Preview** window is, of course, to preview the movie you've assembled on the **Timeline**. Yet, like the other windows in Vegas Movie Studio, it also includes a number of tools for building, enhancing and maintaining your movie project.

Adjust your Preview window's size and quality

The **Preview** windows includes a set of preferences for controlling how – and how large – your movie project playback is displayed.

These preferences are most easily accessed by **right-clicking** on the **Preview's** display, as illustrated above. They are:

Simulate Device Aspect Ratio. This setting should probably always be toggled on. A frame of video, as you may or may not know, is composed of non-square pixels. These pixels can vary in width and, without getting into a deep discussion, they account for the fact that both a 4:3 video and a 16:9 widescreen video are created using the same number of pixels. This setting interprets your video image's non-square pixels so that your movie will appear in the **Preview** window as it will when played on TV or your other playback device.

Scale Video to Fit Preview Window. With this setting toggled on, the **Preview** display will grow larger or smaller as you resize the window in the program's interface. With this toggled off, the **Preview** will remain locked at one of several fixed sizes.

Adjust Size and Quality for Optimal Playback. If you've selected the option to **Scale Video to Fit Preview Window**, you should also leave this toggle switched on. When activated, the program will automatically adjust your **Preview** window display's quality to the best that your system can handle, given the current timeline load.

Additionally, there is some valuable information displayed along the bottom of the **Preview** window.

Project displays the actual size and frame rate of your movie project.

Preview displays the size and frame rate of your preview video.

Frame displays the number of frames in your movie up to the playhead's current position.

Display shows the size of your actual **Preview** window's video. This size has been optimized, based on the settings you've selected, and will likely be different than the **Preview** number. The **Display** number will also include (when your video is paused) the color depth of your video. When your timeline is playing, your playback's frame rate will be displayed.

The **Display** frame rate can be an important indicator of how much your computer is struggling with your current timeline load. If your frame rate is significantly lower than that of your actual project – or your timeline is playing erratically and skipping lots of frames – you may need to pre-render some of your project, as discussed on page 88.

Your project's preview quality levels are set by selecting them from the drop-down menu at the top of the **Preview** window.

The quality and size of your video that is displayed in the **Preview** window can be set manually or automatically. In fact, there is not just one but *several* automatic quality settings, based on how much you're willing to compromise the program's performance to see a good preview.

For most purposes, you'll likely find that setting your display quality to **Preview** or, on a slower machine, **Draft/Auto** will give you the best balance of quality and performance.

Your Preview display can be set to a number of specified or automatic levels, based on your system's performance with its current timeline load.

Display the Safe Area overlays

Overlays are dotted-line guides that appears over your **Preview** window.

The **Safe Area** overlays are guides for positioning your titles and other vital visual information in your video frame.

The reason why it's important for you to indicate the **Safe Area** on your **Preview** playback is because all TVs cut off some of the sides of your video picture to some extent. Some TVs cut off more than others – but even modern LCD and flat-screen TVs can cut off as much as 10% from around the sides of your video frame!

Safe Area overlays are a way of ensuring that your vital information will not be lost due to this cut-off (technically called "overscan").

The **Safe Area** overlay, which is activated via a drop-down menu at the top of the **Preview** window, consists of two concentric rectangles.

Interlacing and Progressive Scan

Traditional television images – and, by nature, much of the video created to be displayed on TV – have been created using a process called interlacing. This means that every frame of the video is created in two passes, each pass creating every other line of pixels.

Some video formats (MPEGs and VOBs, for instance) create these frames by drawing odd-numbered lines of pixels first, while other formats (DV-AVIs) create their frames by drawing even-numbered lines of pixels first.

Computers and many newer TVs create their video using a system called progressive scan – meaning that each video frame is drawn in a single pass rather than two interlaced passes.

You will often see these systems indicated with an "i" or "p" in their format names. For instance, "1080p" means that the video creates its 1,080 lines of pixels for each frame in a single pass, using progressive scan. A video that lists its format at "29.97i" means that it creates each of its 29.97 frames per second in two *interlaced* passes.

An interlaced 29.97 fps video is also sometimes referred to as "60i", since the 60 interlaced passes create approximately 30 frames of video every second. In the PAL video system, "50i" video creates its standard 25 interlaced frames per second.

50p and 60p are more advanced video frame rates that are available on some camcorders.

Vegas Movie Studio 14 includes project presets for 50p and 60p at 1280x720 only.

If you've shot your video in full HD 1920x1080 at 50p or 60p, it's best to customize the project properties just a bit, as discussed in the sidebar on page 30.

And, for best results when mixing media using different interlacing formats and frame rates, we recommend that your **Project/Preferences**, under the **Video** tab, are set to the **Interpolate Fields Deinterlace Method**, as discussed on page 261.

Content Safe Area   Title Safe Area

The outer rectangle defines the **Content Safe Area**. Any important visual information you want included in your video should fit within this area.

This doesn't mean, of course, that you should resize your entire video to fit within this area! However, if, for instance, your video includes a photo of a family posed for a group photo, you *will* want to ensure that everyone in the picture is within this outer rectangular overlay – otherwise, Uncle Frank, who was on the edge of the picture, may not show up at all on some TVs!

The inner rectangular overlay is the **Title Safe Area**. All text you include in your videos – whether titles or sub-titles – *must* stay within this **Safe Area** in order for you to be assured that it will appear on every TV! Otherwise, your title "Gone With the Wind" may appear on some TVs as "one With the Win."

Whether or not you do all of your editing with these **Safe Area** overlays turned on is a matter of preference. But you should definitely turn them on regularly and spot check your movie – especially your titles. Doing so can save you from getting an unpleasant surprise after you distribute your final piece!

Project Properties

The button in the upper left corner of the **Preview** window is a short-cut to your **Video Project Properties** (also available under the **Project** menu).

Unlike **Preferences** (under the **Options** menu), which affect how the entire program performs, **Project Properties** are unique to the settings of your current video project.

Save Snapshot
to Clipboard

Grab a "snapshot" of your video

Saving a snapshot – or grabbing a freeze frame – from your movie is easy, using the tools on the **Preview** window.

The snapshot can then be pasted into another program or saved as a graphics file and used in your current movie project.

Grab and paste your snapshot
To grab and save a snapshot from your video:

1 Copy your snapshot to your clipboard

Position your **Timeline Cursor** (playhead) so that the frame you want to grab appears in the **Preview** window.

Click the **Save Snapshot to Clipboard** button at the top of the **Preview** window, as illustrated above.

Vegas Movie Studio will create a snapshot of the frame as it is displayed in the **Preview** window. This snapshot will include any effects or titles you've added to your original media.

Note that the size and quality of this snapshot will be based on the **Preview** quality you currently have set for your preview display (as discussed on pages 152 and 153). So, even if only temporarily, be sure to set your Preview quality to **Best/Full** before you take your snapshot!

2 Paste your snapshot into an open graphics file

Paste your snapshot into the open file of a graphics editing program.

You can paste your snapshot into pretty much any program that will accept graphics – from a photo editing program, like Photoshop Elements or Photo to Go, to a graphics-capable program, like Microsoft Word or PowerPoint.

Photoshop Elements includes a **New/Image from Clipboard** feature that will automatically create a file the same size as your snapshot.

Your image can be pasted from your clipboard into any graphics editing program.

Note that snapshots taken from video are relatively low resolution images. A snapshot from a standard definition video, for instance, is a mere 720x480 pixels – barely large enough to print out as a 3½" x 2½" picture.

High-definition video (1920x1080 pixels) can produce a relatively clean 9½" x 5" printed photo.

Save your snapshot to a file

As an alternative to pasting your snapshot into another program, you can elect to save your frame grab as a still photo file right in your Vegas Movie Studio project.

To save your snapshot as a file:

1 **Save your snapshot as a file**

   Position your **Timeline Cursor** (playhead) so that the frame you want to grab appears in the Preview window.

   Click the **Save Snapshot to File** button at the top of the **Preview** window.

Vegas Movie Studio will create a snapshot of the frame displayed in the **Preview** window. This snapshot will include any effects or titles you've added to your original media.

Note that the size and quality of this snapshot will be based on the **Preview** quality you currently have set for your preview display (as discussed on pages 152 and 153).

Save Snapshot to File

157

Your saved snapshot is automatically added to your Project Media.

So, even if only temporarily, set your **Preview** quality to **Best/Full** before you save your snapshot!

2   Save your photo file

When you click on the **Save Snapshot to File** button, a dialog window will open.

Select a location to save your photo file.

You also have the option of saving your file as a JPG or a PNG (pronounced "ping").

When you save your photo file, it will be automatically added to your **Project Media** window.

You may then add this still photo to your movie project's timeline, if you'd like.

Play your video on an external monitor

There are times when you'd like to see your video **Preview** in much more detail. You may even want to preview your video on an actual television, so you can judge how it will look in its final media form.

The **Preview** window includes a toggle switch for playing your video on an external monitor.

To use this feature, you must have the external monitor plugged into your computer's video card's second monitor port or connected through a camcorder via FireWire.

In addition to a standard VGA port, many computer video cards include an output for at least one additional monitor. This output may be a DVI

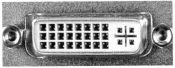

A DVI port, an S-Video port and an HDMI port.

port, an S-video port and/or an HDMI port. (You may need an adapter to connect some TVs to your available jack.)

If you are using your DVI jack as an output to a second computer monitor on a dual-monitor computer system, your second monitor can also be used to play a full-screen preview of your video.

As an alternative, you can connect a DV camcorder to a FireWire/IEEE-1394 jack on your computer and then connect the camcorder's AV plugs to your TV monitor.

Once your device is plugged in, you will need to set it as your preview device in your preferences.

Go to the **Options** menu at the top of the program and select **Preferences**.

On the **Preferences** dialog window, go to the **Preview Device** tab. Select your **Device** connection from the drop-down menu at the top of the panel.

Once your device is plugged in and configured, you'll be able to play a preview of your video on this device at any time by clicking on the **Video Preview on External Monitor** button along the top of the **Preview** window.

Video Preview on External Monitor

Creating Generated Media Titles

Setting a Title's Length

Building a Credit Roll

Inserting Text Media

Animating a Title

Saving a Custom Title Preset

Chapter 11

Add and Customize Your Titles

Putting text in your movie

Text can play a very important role in your video storytelling – whether it's in the form of titles, subtitles or call-outs.

Vegas Movie Studio 14 includes a number of great tools for creating text and titles for your movies as well as a number of tools for controlling how it looks and behaves on-screen.

Text – whether in the form of titles, subtitles, call-outs or other indicators on-screen – can be added to your Vegas Movie Studio project in a couple of ways:

Text can be added to your movie as Generated Media, using pre-created and sometimes pre-animated templates; or

Text can be added directly to your project, simply by selecting the option to add it to a video track (as discussed on page 170).

However you elect to add text to your project's timeline, it will appear in the form of **Generated Video Media**, and any of a number of templates or pre-created animations can be applied to it. You also have the option of creating your own animated effects using keyframes.

Once added to your timeline, your text behaves as any other video event. You can apply video effects, fade ins/outs or **Pan/Crop** motion paths to it.

By the way, by default, your timeline automatically may include a video track labeled **Text**, although text clips can be placed on *any* video track.

If your text clip includes areas of transparency, the video on the video tracks below it will show through.

Create a title using Generated Media template

The **Generated Media** panel is part of the tabbed window set that includes **Project Media**, the **Explorer, Transitions** and **Video FX.** Click on the **Media Generator** tab to view this panel.

Animated and stationary text templates from both Magix and from third-party titles and effects companies can be found in the Media Generator.

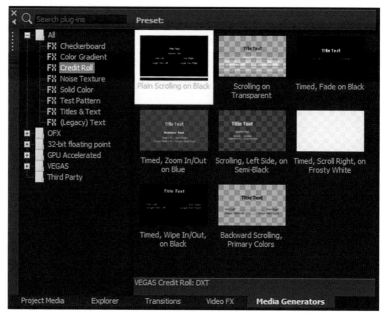

There are three categories of **Generated Media** text templates, as illustrated on the facing page. A preview of any animated media preset can be viewed by clicking on the preset's thumbnail on this panel.

> **Credit Roll** templates include nine variations of scrolling text, including credit scrolls up, across and over as well as opaque, semi-opaque and transparent backgrounds.

> **Titles & Text** includes 25 animated text templates. These templates include a variety of colors, backgrounds and effects. When you select the option to **Insert Text Media into your timeline** (see page 164), your title will be the **Default** template from this set.

> **(Legacy) Text** (so named because the templates were created for earlier versions of the program) include a variety of basic text templates.

To use any of these templates in your project, simply drag it to your timeline.

When a title template is added to the timeline, the Video Media Generator window opens.

Customize a Generated Media title

Generated Media templates can be used as is (You simply add your custom text), or they can also be easily modified and customized.

When a **Generated Media** title is added to your timeline, the **Video Media Generators** dialog window will automatically open.

If your **Timeline Cursor** (playhead) is positioned over this clip on your timeline, any changes you make will be displayed in the **Preview** window.

Create a title from a (Legacy) Text template

If you've selected one of the **(Legacy) Text** templates:

1 **Select an optional Preset**

> If you'd like, you can select a preset look from the **Preset** drop-down menu along the top of the window, as illustrated on the following page.

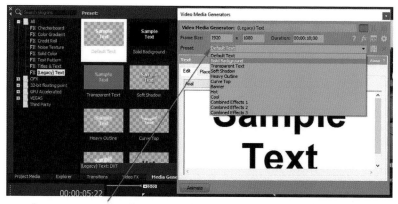

As with most Generated Media, Text templates include a set of Preset designs. The preset designs listed under this drop-down menu correspond to the templates listed on the Media Generators window.

2　**Customize your text**

Under the **Edit** tab, type your title over the **Sample Text** placeholder text.

Select a font, style, size and alignment for your title.

(If you're going to use one of the presets, it's important that you apply your preset *before you* add your custom text. This is because, when a new preset is selected from the drop-down menu, it not only changes the colors of your title but it also replaces the text itself with generic text in the process.)

3　**Position your text**

Under the **Placement** tab, drag your text into position within your video frame. The red outline indicates the **Title Safe Zone** (as discussed on page 155).

The **Text Placement** drop-down menu will automatically align your title within this **Title Safe Zone**.

Your text can be dragged into place within the Safe Zone or positioned by a preset.

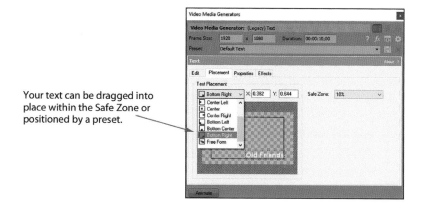

4 Set your Text and Background Properties

Under the **Properties** tab, use the sliders to define the color and opacity (transparency) of your text and background.

Under this tab, you can also set your text's **Tracking**, **Scaling** and **Leading**.

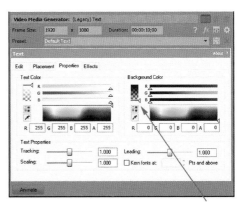

Title properties not only include color but opacity – the transparency level of the text or background.

5 Create Effects

Under the **Effects** tab, you will find options for creating **Outline** and **Shadow** for your title. To create an **Outline** or **Shadow**, click the checkbox, select a color and define its properties with the sliders.

Also under the **Effects** tab is a tool for warping and shaping your text. To enable it, click the **Enable Deformation** checkbox.

As illustrated below, the drop-down menu lists 14 warp effects, including **Shears, Squishes, Compresses, Curves** and **Bends**. Once you select a **Deformation**, you can control its intensity with the **Amount** slider.

As with all title properties, your **Deformation**, colors and other effects can be animated using keyframes, as discussed on page 165.

6 Set the title's duration

By default, **Media Generator** title events are 10 seconds long.

For information on changing the duration of your title, see the sidebar on page 166.

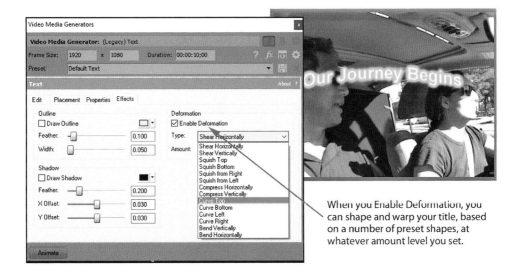

When you Enable Deformation, you can shape and warp your title, based on a number of preset shapes, at whatever amount level you set.

Create a title from a Titles & Text template

If you've selected a **Titles & Text** template, in addition to text and background color properties, you will find 24 pre-created animations for your text.

1   Select an Animation

Animations are optional, of course. But because they overwrite your text with generic text, if you are going to animate your text, you should do so *before* you add your custom text.

Titles & Text templates come pre-loaded with 24 text animations. An animation can be applied either by selecting it from the **Preset** drop-down menu at the top of the **Video Media Generators** dialog window or by selecting it from the **Animations** drop-down menu, located under **Text Color**.

These animations include **Action Flip, Bounce, Coming At You, Double Flash Glow, Drop Split, Dropping Words, Earthquake, Fall Down, Float and Pop, Fly In, Fly In From Right, Jump, Menace, Popup, Rolling Glow and Enlarge, Rough Day, Scroll, Slide, Slide Down, Slide Up, Slide Left, Slide Right, Speedy** and **Twist In**.

Text animations can be selected from the Preset drop-down or Animation drop-down menu.

By the way, these animations are timed to the length of your title event. So you can slow down or speed up any animation by changing the title's duration, as discussed below.

Set a title's duration

By default, **Media Generator** title events are 10 seconds long.

You can manually change a title's length by typing over the numbers in the **Duration** box at the top of the **Media Generators** dialog window. (The number is displayed as hours: minutes: seconds: video frames. A second of NTSC video is approximately 30 frames in length. A second of PAL video is 25 frames.)

Alternatively, you can manually stretch or trim the title to a preferred length on your timeline. Then, to set the title to match the length of the event clip on your timeline, click on the **Match Event Length** button at the top right of the **Video Media Generators** dialog window.

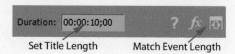

Set Title Length   Match Event Length

2 Add your custom text

Select the **Sample Text** displayed in the **Video Media Generators** dialog window and overwrite it with your custom text.

3 Set text attributes

Select the font, size, style, alignment and color for your text and background.

Color is represented with levels of red, green, blue and alpha (or transparency). When alpha is set to 1.0, it is 100% opaque. When it is set to 0.0, it is completely transparent.

4 Set advanced characteristics

Further title characteristics can be set by toggling the little black triangles:

Text scale. The number represents a percentage of the actual size, e.g., 1.000 represents 100% size.

Location/position of text in video frame. These numbers represent a percentage distance across the frame, e.g., 0.50, 0.50 represents the center of the video frame.

Background color and alpha. The four colors represent levels of red, green, blue and alpha (opacity or transparency).

Text tracking and line spacing.

Text outline color and width.

Shadow, color, blur, location (offset) relative to the text and distance from the text.

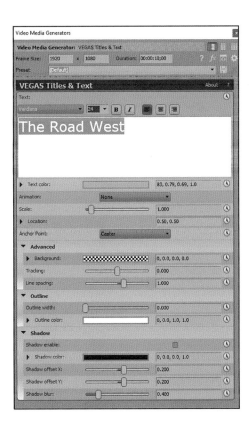

 The clock icons that appear to the far right of each setting are for creating keyframed animations. We show you how to use keyframing to create your own custom animated titles on page 171.

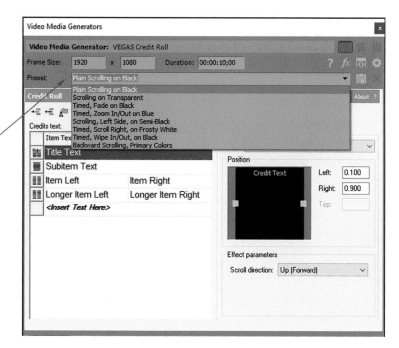

Credit Roll templates include a number of preset scrolling and timed sequence animation presets.

Create a title from a Credit Roll template

If you've selected a **Credit Roll** text template:

1 **Select an animation preset**

The **Preset** drop-down menu along the top of the **Video Media Generators** dialog window offers a number of optional pre-created scrolling and timed sequence animations.

Once you have applied one of these presets to your title, you can further customize the text and animation, as described in **Step 4.**

2 **Add your custom text**

Credit Roll templates include several levels of text, including **Header/Title Text, Subitem Text, Item Left/Item Right** and an undefined line labeled **<Insert Text Here>.** To add your title's text, just type right over the placeholder text in the **Credits Text** box.

Each of these placeholders is optional, and you can remove the lines you don't want to use by **right-clicking** on them and selecting **Delete Row**, as illustrated at the top of the facing page.

Likewise, you can add more lines of text by **right-clicking** on any line and selecting **Insert Row.**

You can also change the text level for any line by clicking on the line definition button to the left of any line of text. As you click and hold on this button, you will see the option to set up the line as a **Header, Subitem Text** or **Item Left/Item Right.**

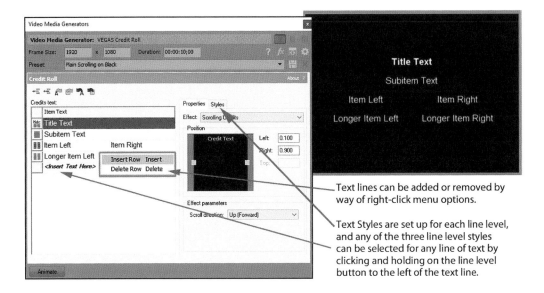

Text lines can be added or removed by way of right-click menu options.

Text Styles are set up for each line level, and any of the three line level styles can be selected for any line of text by clicking and holding on the line level button to the left of the text line.

3   Set your Text Styles

Click the **Styles** tab on the **Video Media Generators** dialog window.

On this panel, you can set the font, size, style and color of your text as well as its **Tracking, Space Above, Space Below** and **Left, Right** or **Center Justification**.

The **Styles** you set are applied to each line level. In other words, you can set one text style for **Header/Title Text,** another for **Subitem Text** and another for **Item Left/Item Right**.

These styles will be applied to your text, based on the line level in which it appears.

On this panel you may also set the alpha (opacity/transparency) level and color of your title's background.

4   Select the title's Scroll Properties

On the **Properties** tab, you have the option of setting the **Effect** to **Scrolling Credits** or a **Timed Sequence**, as illustrated on the following page.

When you select **Scrolling Credits**, you will have the option on this panel of setting your scroll to go **Up (Forward)** or **Down (Backward)**.

When you select the **Timed Sequence** animation option, you will have the option of setting your title to begin or end with a number of transitional **Effects** including **Fade In/Out, Enter/Exit Right/Left/Top/Bottom**, **Zoom In/Out** or any of a number of **Wipes**.

The speed that your title scrolls and the speed of your timed sequence's animation are based on how long your title clip is on your timeline, as discussed in **Step 5**.

The longer your clip, the more slowly your title will scroll.

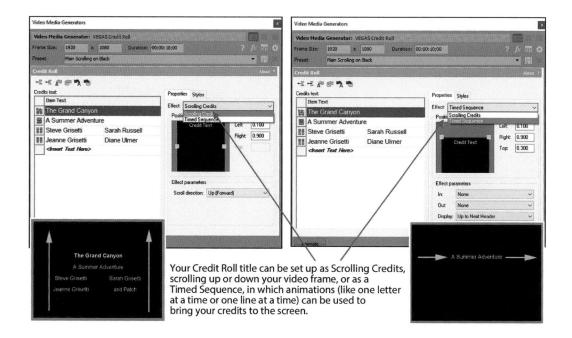

Your Credit Roll title can be set up as Scrolling Credits, scrolling up or down your video frame, or as a Timed Sequence, in which animations (like one letter at a time or one line at a time) can be used to bring your credits to the screen.

The **Display** drop-down menu allows you to set whether your title comes in all at once or as individual elements.

How long each element appears on-screen before transitioning to the next is based on how long your title clip is, as discussed below.

5   **Set the title's length**

By default, **Media Generator** title events are 10 seconds long.

For information on changing the length of your title, see the sidebar on page 160.

Insert Text Media into your project's timeline

In addition to using a **Generated Media** template to create a title, you can add a title directly to your project's timeline using the **Insert Text Media** command.

Although it is created directly on your timeline, this **Text Media** will still be a **Generated Media** clip. And like any **Generated Media**, it can be customized in the **Video Media Generators** dialog window.

In fact, when you select the option to **Insert Text Media** to your timeline, the **Video Media Generators** dialog window will automatically open.

This **Video Media Generators** dialog window will be the same dialog that appears when you add a **Titles & Text** template, as discussed on page 166.

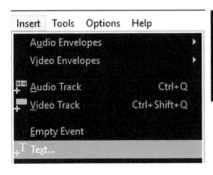

A 5-second title can be added directly to your timeline by selecting the Text Media option from the program's Insert menu or by right-clicking on a video track and selecting Insert Text Media.

There are two ways to **Insert Text Media** directly to your timeline:

From the **Insert** drop-down menu at the top of the interface, select the **Text Media** option. Your title will be added to your **armed video track** (see page 77) at the position of the **Timeline Cursor** (playhead).

Right-click on any video track on your timeline and select the option to **Insert Text Media** from the context menu. Your title will be added to the video track you've right-clicked on, at the position of the **Timeline Cursor** (playhead).

Whichever option you select, a 5-second title will be added to your timeline and the **Video Media Generators** dialog window for this **Text** clip will open.

To add your custom text, position it in your video frame and apply colors and other attributes to it, follow the steps in **Customize a Titles & Text template** on page 166.

Animate your title's properties with keyframes

A title's properties – including its shape, size, colors and position – need not remain the same throughout the entire duration of the clip. As with any effect, these properties can be set to vary or animate over the clip's duration using keyframes.

In other words, you can animate your title to change shape or color or create a movement of your text within your video frame.

To create an animation, a keyframe is on a **Keyframe Controller** timeline. This keyframe defines your title's characteristics at a given point. When a new keyframe is added later on this timeline, defining changed characteristics, the program will automatically generate the transition or animated movement between these two keyframes.

In the example on the following page, I am using keyframes to create an animation of the text's position within a video frame on a **(Legacy) Text** template (although the principles of animation are the same in any dialog window, for any characteristic or property).

Virtually any number of keyframes can be added to a media clip, and virtually any of a clip's properties can be animated.

Clicking the Animate button at the bottom of a Media Generator dialog window or clicking on the clock icon on the Titles & Text dialog opens the Keyframe Controller along the bottom of the window.

1 Open the Keyframe Controller

Open the **Keyframe Controller** (the mini-timeline that runs along the bottom of a **Video Media Generators** dialog window) by clicking the **Animate** button (or the **clock icon** to the right of any **Titles & Text** property).

Similar timelines appear along the bottoms of the **Video FX, Audio FX** and **Pan/Crop Motion** dialog windows.

2 Position the playhead on the Keyframe Controller

The playhead should be at the beginning of the **Keyframe Controller** mini-timeline. If necessary, drag it to the position on this timeline at which you'd like your animation to begin.

3 Set the initial Placement for your text

Under the **Placement** tab, place your text in the top left of the video frame. This position is indicated on the **Keyframe Controller** with a diamond-shaped keyframe point.

4 Change the text Placement

Move the playhead on the **Keyframe Controller** to the point in your clip you'd like your animation to end.

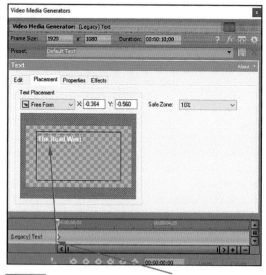

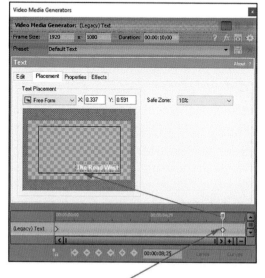

When the playhead is repositioned on the Keyframe Controller timeline and a change is made to any characteristic of your media clip or title, a keyframe is automatically generated at the playhead's position. The program creates the animation or transition between the settings represented by the keyframes.

Drag the text on the **Placement** panel to a new position. A new diamond-shaped keyframe will automatically appear on the **Keyframe Controller mini**-timeline at the position of the playhead.

And that's all there is to it! You've created an animation! As you play the clip, the text will move from one position in the video frame to the other.

But keyframed animation is not limited to creating motion paths.

By adding keyframes to your **Keyframe Controller** timeline, you can create titles that shift through colors as they play. You can create a title animation in which your text changes size as it plays. And, if you've enabled **Deformation** under the **Effects** tab, you can even use keyframes to create a shape-shifting animation for your text!

The speed of your animation is determined by how close your keyframes are to each other. The nearer they are to each other, the faster the transition or animation between them.

Keyframes can also be easily moved – by clicking and dragging on them – and can also be modified and even deleted with a right-click.

Keyframes are a very powerful tool for creating effects and animations. We discuss them in much greater detail in **Chapter 15, Create Animation with Keyframes**.

Use special characters for a professional look

Many word processing programs include "smart" features for automatically creating special text characters as you type. Vegas Movie Studio does not.

If, for instance, you type quotation marks into the **Edit** panel of a title, rather than getting real quotes (") you will get tick marks ("). Type an apostrophe (') and you will get a single tick (').

That may not make much of a difference to a non-discriminating viewer. However, you can certainly add a more professional look to your titles by using the *actual* text characters rather than their generic counterparts. This can be accomplished in Windows by using **Alt key** combinations.

To create an **Alt key** combination character, hold down the **Alt** key as you type the **Alt number** combination. When you release the **Alt** key, the special text character will appear.

Here are a couple of common **Alt key** combination characters:

Open quotation marks (") – **Alt+0147**   Close quotation marks (") – **Alt+0148**
Apostrophe (') – **Alt+0146**   Bullet (•) – **Alt+0149**

Many more **Alt key** combinations can be found online, including support for different monetary signs and for text characters with accent marks and umlauts.

Edit a title event

You can re-open a title's **Video Media Generator** dialog window and edit your title or any of its properties by clicking on the **Generated Media** (filmstrip) icon on the right side of the clip on your timeline.

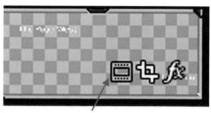

Re-open a Generated Media title for editing.

Any changes you make to your title in the **Video Media Generators** dialog will be made in real time to your event. If your **Timeline Cursor** (playhead) is positioned over this clip, your changes will be displayed in the **Preview** window.

Add effects to a title event

Once a title has been added to a timeline, it behaves just like any other video clip.

- As with any video clip, video effects can be added to your title. (For more information on working with video effects, see **Chapter 12, Add and Adjust Video Effects**.)

- **Fade Ins** and **Fade Outs** can be added to your titles. (For more information on adding fades, see **Add a Fade In or Fade Out to an event clip** on page 84.)

- **Pan/Crops** can be added to a title event. (For more information on using the **Pan/Crop** tool, see **Create an animated Pan/Crop motion path** on page 222.)

- Transitions can be added between titles or between titles and any other video events. (For more information on using transitions, see **Chapter 14, Add and Customize Transitions**.)

Save a custom look as a preset

If you like a look you've created for a title, you can save it as a preset and then re-use it in you current project or in any future Vegas Movie Studio projects.

There are, however, a couple of things to understand about title presets:

- These presets will only appear as options in similar title types. In other words, if you create a **Credit Roll** title preset, it will appear as a **Preset** option in **Credit Roll** titles. It will not be available for **Text, (Legacy) Text** – each of which have their own unique sets of presets.

- The text displayed in your **Edit** box when you create your preset will become part of your preset! In other words, if you've created a title that includes the text "Wedding Day," when you save this title's look as a preset, the words "Wedding Day" will be saved as part of this look.

This can be a bit frustrating because, when you apply this preset to a future title, the words "Wedding Day" automatically overwrite whatever text you've previously added.

- Presets are for the properties of the title only (text, font, size, colors, placement, etc.) and do *not* include any keyframed animations. If you've keyframed animation for a title and you save the title's look as a preset, only the properties represented by the *first keyframe* in your animation will be saved. Not the entire animation.

- **Credit Roll** titles include their animation as one of their title properties – so any non-keyframed **Scroll** or **Timed Sequence** you create for a **Credit Roll** title *will* be saved as part of that preset.

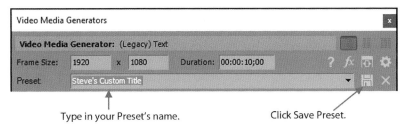

Type in your Preset's name.   Click Save Preset.

Save a custom preset

To save a title's look as a preset:

1   Name your preset

Click to select the current preset displayed in the **Preset** box and *type over it with the name you want to give your new preset.*

2   Save the preset

Click on the **Save Preset** (floppy disk) icon to the right of the **Preset** drop-down menu.

The program will warn you if the name you've chosen is already in use.

Until this preset is removed by you, it will remain a permanent part of your program's library.

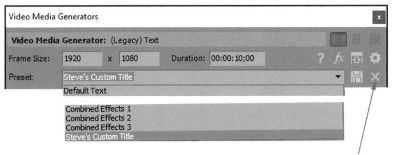

Your preset will become a permanent part the program's library – until you remove it.

Apply a preset look

To apply a preset look to a title, simply select it from the **Preset** drop-down menu in that title's **Video Media Generators** dialog window.

In addition to applying font, size and color properties to your title, a preset will also add default text – overwriting whatever you've already typed into the **Edit** panel. For this reason, it's probably best to apply a preset *before* you begin any other work on your title.

Delete a custom preset from the Preset library

To remove a custom preset from your list of preset options, select it from the **Preset** drop-down menu and then click the **Delete** (red X) button, as illustrated on page 175.

Only presets that you've created can be removed from the program's library. Default presets are locked to the program.

To restore your title to a default look, select **Default Text** from the **Preset** drop-down menu.

Applying Video FX

Video FX Defined

Adding Video FX in a Chain

Using the Chroma Keyer

Adding More VST Effects

Chapter 12

Add and Adjust Video Effects

Adding magic to your movies

Vegas Movie Studio comes loaded with
a wealth of tools for giving your movies
a Hollywood look.

Some effects are fixes for making a good
movie look great.

Others are tools for creating some
amazing visual magic!

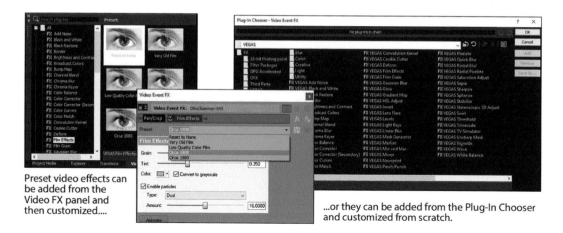

Preset video effects can be added from the Video FX panel and then customized....

...or they can be added from the Plug-In Chooser and customized from scratch.

Magix has included a great bundle of video effects with Vegas Movie Studio and Vegas Movie Studio Platinum.

These effects are in the form of **Plug-ins** – which means that technically they aren't a part of the program itself but are, rather, *add-ons* to the program. The advantage of using a plug-in system is that it gives you, the user, the option of adding even more plug-ins – increasing the number of effects available in your program! (We show you how to add plug-in effects in **Load additional VST effects into your program** on page 192.)

Add FX to your video

There are five ways to apply a video effect in Vegas Movie Studio:

A preset effect can be added to an event clip from the **Video FX** window (page 180), the window that shares the tabbed interface with the **Project Media**, the **Explorer, Transitions** and **Media Generators** windows. This is often the most intuitive way to apply an effect to your project because the **Video FX** window displays thumbnail image previews of each of the effects. When you apply a preset effect from the **Video FX** window to an event clip on your timeline, the **Video Event FX** dialog window for your clip will open. We discuss this dialog window's options in more detail on page 187.

A video effect can be applied to a **media** clip in the **Project Media** window.

A video effect can be applied to an **event** clip in your timeline.

A video effect can be applied to an entire **video track** at once.

A video effect can be applied to your **entire movie**.

When a plug-in effect is applied to a media clip, event, track or movie, the **Plug-In Chooser** dialog window will open (page 182). This dialog window lists all of the video effects plug-ins installed in your program.

Once you have selected your plug-in effect and clicked **OK**, you will be able to adjust and customize the effect. How this effect changes your video clip(s) depends on how it is applied to your movie.

Event vs. Track vs. Media vs. Video Output FX

There are actually four ways to apply a video effect **Plug-In** to a clip or clips in your movie. And how this effect functions depends on which form of the clip or clips you've applied this effect to.

Media refers to clips in your **Project Media** window. Essentially, a clip is considered "media" when you're working with it *outside of the timeline*.

Video effects can be applied to a media clip via a right-click context menu.

> **Media FX** are effects applied by **right-clicking** on a clip in your **Project Media** or on your timeline and selecting the **Media FX** option.

> When an effect is applied to a media clip, the effect essentially becomes a part of the clip itself. In other words, any time you use that clip in your current project, the effect will be included with it.

> In most cases, then, you'll be using **Media FX** to correct color or to apply a visual effect that you'll want to appear throughout your movie.

Effects can also be applied to individual event clips on your timeline...

> **Event FX** are effects that have been added to an individual clip on your timeline. The original media is not affected and no other clips in your movie are affected unless similar effects have been added to them.

> This is far and away the most common way to add an effect to your movie. An effect is applied as needed, and only to a particular clip or clips on your timeline.

...or to entire video tracks...

> **Event FX** are applied by clicking on the **Event FX** button in the lower right of a clip on your timeline.

> **Track FX**, as the name implies, are applied to entire video tracks at once. The effect, then, is applied equally to every event clip on that particular video track.

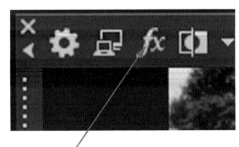

...or even to your entire movie.

> This method of applying effects might be used, for instance, if you wanted to apply a certain visual style to an entire sequence in your movie.

The Event FX, Track FX and Video Output FX buttons launch the Effects Plug-In Chooser.

> **Track FX** are applied by clicking on the **Track FX** button on the **Track Header.**

Video Output FX are less often used, but available if you need it. **Video Output FX** are applied to your *entire movie* at once by clicking on the button at the top of the program's **Preview** window.

> Using **Video Output FX**, for instance, you can output your entire movie as black & white or apply ragged **Film Effects** to your entire movie project as a single, overall effect.

Once Video FX have been applied to an event, track or movie, they can be customized in the Video FX dialog window.

Apply an effect from the Video FX window

The **Video FX window** shares the tabbed interface with the **Project Media**, the **Explorer, Transitions** and **Media Generators** windows in the upper left of the program's interface.

Applying effects from this window to the clips on your timeline is often the most intuitive way to add effects because the window displays previews for each of the effects.

The effects in this window, however, are merely presets (pre-applied settings) of the same effects available through the **Plug-In Chooser** – the effects dialog window that launches when you apply an effect to an event, track or video output, as described on the facing page. In fact, each of the effects categories listed on the left side of the panel is actually one of these plug-in effects.

For instance, although the **Pinch/Punch** category of **Video FX** displays seven effects, these effects are actually just pre-applied settings of the **Magix Pinch/Punch** effect plug-in.

> To apply **Video FX** from this window to an event clip, drag the thumbnail preview of the effect to the clip on your timeline.

> To apply **Video FX** from this window to a video track, drag the thumbnail preview of the effect onto the video track's **Track Header**.

> To apply **Video FX** from this window to your entire movie, drag the thumbnail preview of this effect onto the movie's display on the **Preview** window.

Once you have applied an effect to an event, track or to your entire movie, a **Video FX** dialog window will open.

Customize your effect as discussed in **Adjust a video effect**, on page 187.

When you click the Event FX, Track FX or Video Output FX button, the Plug-In Chooser will open.

After an effect has been applied, this button will display as blue, and clicking it will launch the Video FX dialog window.

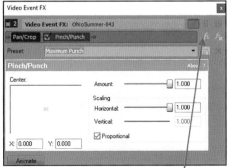

The Plug-In Chooser can be relaunched from the Video FX window by clicking the Plug-In Chain button.

Select an effect from the Plug-In Chooser

When you click on the **Event FX, Track FX** or **Video Output FX** button on a clip, **Track Header** or on the **Preview** window, the program will launch the **Plug-In Chooser** dialog window.

If an effect has already been applied to your event, track or video output, the **Event FX, Track FX** or **Video Output FX** button will display as light blue rather than white, as illustrated above.

If an effect has already been applied to your clip, track or movie, clicking this button will take you directly to the **Video FX** dialog window for that effect.

To return to the **Plug-In Chooser** from the **Video FX** dialog window, click the **Plug-In Chain** button at the top right of the window, as illustrated.

The **Plug-In Chooser** dialog window lists all of the effects that have been "plugged-in," or loaded into Vegas Movie Studio.

There are over 50 Magix effects included with Vegas Movie Studio 14.

Brief descriptions of each of the program's basic set of **Plug-In** effects can be found in the next section of this chapter (page 182).

To apply an effect, select it from the list of plug-ins and click **OK**.

By holding down the **Ctrl** key and selecting several effects, more than one effect can be applied to a clip or sequence in a **Plug-In Chain**. How these effects are managed and how they interact is discussed in greater detail in **Multiply effects in a chain** on page 188.

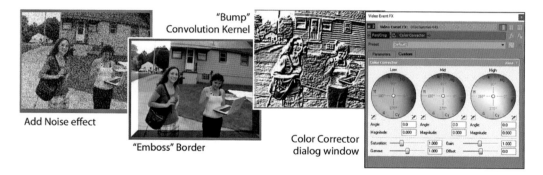

"Bump" Convolution Kernel

Add Noise effect

"Emboss" Border

Color Corrector dialog window

Video FX Plug-Ins defined

Magix includes nearly 50 plug-in video effects with Vegas Movie Studio Platinum (in addition to some bonus plug-ins). Here's a brief description of each.

Add Noise. This effect adds grainy video noise to your movie. This noise can remain stationary or be set to random, static-like animation.

Black and White. Removes the color from your video to various degrees.

Black Restore. This effects sets the black level for your video. The higher you set the **Threshold**, the more blackness in your video.

Border. This effect creates a blurred, beveled or solid color border for your video frame.

Brightness and Contrast. As you would expect, this effect allows you to adjust the brightness and contrast levels of your video.

Broadcast Colors. Computers display a much wider range of colors than televisions can reproduce.

Bump Map. There are actually two ways to use the **Bump Map** effect. When used on a video clip on a **Parented** track set to **(Multiply) Mask** (see page 116), it uses the lightness of the video on the **Child** track to create its texture. When used on a non-composited track, it can be used to create spotlight effects over a clip.

Channel Blend. This effect is used to display, balance or unbalance the individual red, green and blue (or hue, saturation and lightness) color channels that make up your clip.

Chroma Blur. This effect blurs the color values of the pixels in your image without affecting their brightness. It's sometimes used in a chain with the **Chroma Keyer** to soften the edges of a key effect.

Chroma Keyer. This is the powerful tool that's used to take a video of a person standing in front of a green or blue screen and then make him or her appear to be standing in front of any real or imaginary background you provide. It's such a powerful tool, in fact, that we show you how to use it in detail on pages 183-185.

Color Balance. As the name would imply, this effect is used to correct color and balance the red, green and blue highlights and midtones in your video image.

Color Corrector. Like the **Color Balance** effect, the primary use of the **Color Corrector** is to tweak and balance the colors in your video image. However, the **Color Corrector** is a very sophisticated tool with a very intuitive interface.

"Sharpen Edges"
Convolution Kernel

"Squeeze" Deform

"Emboss"
Convolution Kernel

"Pop-Up" Cookie Cutter

By dragging the point in the center of each Scope (or selecting from the list of Presets), you can adjust hue, saturation and lightness of the low, mid and high color tones

Color Corrector (Secondary). This even more advanced **Color Corrector** gives you the option of focusing on a single color or element in your video (selected on your **Preview** monitor with the eye dropper) and then adjusting the video's color based on it.

Color Curves. **Color Curves** is a very high level method of adjusting your video's colors individually or all together. By creating adjustment points on a line representing your color levels and then raising and lowering them individually, you can set your color's intensity at specific levels. As I've said, it's a pretty high-level tool, so you may find that the **Presets** can get you most of where you need to be.

Color Match. The **Color Match** tool allows you to match the color tint and tone of an existing clip or photograph. We'll show you how to use this cool new tool on page 180.

Convolution Kernel. With this very artsy effect you can blur, emboss, add bumps, find edges and overly sharpen edges in your video.

Cookie Cutter. As the name would imply, this effect allows you to "cut" your video into any of a number of basic shapes, with hard or soft edges. If you use this effect on an upper video track, the lower video tracks will show through the areas outside the **Cookie Cutter** shape.

Deform. This effect warps your video by shearing, squeezing, curving, bending and compressing your video at whatever level you set.

Film Effects. One of my favorite effects, this one makes your video look like an old, damaged movie. It comes with a number of effect levels, making your movie look like a 30-year-old home movie or a 100-year-old relic.

Film Grain. Another effect for making your video look like an old, worn movie, this one adds various levels of granularity and damaged color.

Gaussian Blur. This effect can add a softness to your video – or make it an incomprehensible blob, depending on the levels you set.

Glow. This effect adds a soft, dream-like quality to your video by making lighter areas in your video glow in whatever color you designate.

Gradient Map. This effect reduces the colors of your video to a gradation of the colors you define.

Film Grain

Lens Flare

Film Effects

Glow

HSL Adjust. Another color correction tool, this effect allows you to adjust the colors of your video based on settings for hue, saturation and lightness.

Invert. An inversion swaps the colors in your video with their complementary colors, creating a sort of negative film effect.

Lens Flare. This effect generates a bright flare in your video as if a bright light were shining back toward your camera.

Levels. Another color adjustment tool, this effect allows you to adjust the amount of dark, light and mid-range for the individual red, green and blue color channels.

Light Rays. This effect creates the look of a light shining over or onto your video. With it, you can create the look of beams of light coming toward the camera, or you can create a spotlight in a variety of colors and sizes.

Linear Blur. As you might expect, this effect creates a horizontal, vertical or diagonal motion blur across your video.

Mask Generator. This effect masks areas in a video clip based on a color, luminance setting or alpha channel you designate on a video clip or graphic. When used on a **Parented** video track, it will use a designated color or channel to create transparency in the video clip on the **Child** track, revealing video on the track(s) below through the transparent areas. (For more information on using masks with composited video tracks, see **Parent and Composite your video tracks** on page 116.)

Median. This filter reduces pixel contrast, softening your video image to reduce video noise or to create a watercolor-like effect.

Min and Max. This effect creates a sort of boxy look by reducing your video image to large blocks of color.

Mirror. As you might expect, this effect creates a reflection of your video, based on a center point you define.

News Print. Adding this effect gives your video the look of a low-resolution image created with dots of ink, as in a newspaper or a comic book.

Pinch/Punch. Applying this effect warps your video image by rounding it out or sucking it in around a center point you define.

Pixelate. This effect reduces your video image to sort of a mosaic by pixelating it. We use it to **Blur a face, as on TV's COPS**, on page 118.)

Quick Blur. A simple tool for blurring your video.

Light Rays

Linear Blur

News Print

Radial Blur

Radial Blur. This effect creates a blur as if you are quickly zooming into a point on your video.

Radial Pixelate. This effect creates rounded pixelation radiating from your video's center or any defined point in your video frame.

Saturation Adjust. The saturation level is the amount of color in your video. This effect can be used to reduce the amount of color in your video image all the way to black & white or to reduce color noise.

Sepia. As you would expect, this effect gives your video an old photo look by reducing its colors to a faded yellow or other color.

Sharpen. This effect increases the contrast between pixels, giving it a sharper look. It won't, of course, bring out of focus video into focus – but it can sharpen your video's look.

Spherize. An effect for warping your video by rounding it out from a center point you define.

Stabilize. A great tool for taking the extra movement from a hand-held shot. We use this effect to pre-stabilize a media clip on page 59.

Stereoscopic 3D Adjust. This tool is used to adjust the alignment of the right and left channels of a 3D video, correcting out of alignment issues or, as we show you on page 88, to create a 3D effect with a standard 2D title.

Swirl. As the name implies, this effect swirls your video around a point you define.

Threshold. This effect reduces your video to extremes of light and dark. A common use for this effect is to reduce a clip to pure black and pure white so that it can be used more effectively as a mask.

Timecode. This tool overlays a running timecode onto your video.

TV Simulator. This effect creates the look of a video shot from a TV screen by adding exaggerated scan lines. It includes settings for making the video look as if it's showing on a very bad TV!

Unsharp Mask. Like **Sharpen**, this effect sharpens the look of your video by increasing the contrast between pixels. Most professionals consider this the better way to add sharpness to your work.

Vignette. Vignetting adds a fade around the edges of your video frame to create a cool, dream-like look, as illustrated to the right.

The Color Match Effect

Vegas Movie Studio 14 includes an easy-to-use tool for matching the color temperature, tint and tone of a given video clip to another video clip or photo – or for matching your video's color tone to any of several color tone presets.

The **Color Match Video FX** panel is by far the largest of all of the FX option panels. You may need to toggle the little triangles to open and close each section or use the scroll bar to access all of the panel's options.

To match your clip to a preset tone, select a preset from the drop-down list at the top of the panel.

Or select the image you want to use as your color **Source** Image. This can be a media file that is displayed in the **Trimmer**, a video or still copied to your **Clipboard**, or it can be a video or still browsed to on your hard drive (**File**). Your color tone can also be based on area you drag across on your computer **Screen** or it can be the video that is currently displayed in your **Preview** window.

In the **Target Image** panel, select the video you want to apply this color tone to. This can be a video displayed in the **Trimmer**, a video on your **Clipboard** or a video file that you browse to. In most cases, if the **Timeline** playhead is over the clip you want to affect, you will select the video displayed in the **Preview** window.

The result of your **Color Match** will be displayed in the bottom panel.

You can control the intensity of this effect by adjusting the **Strength** slider at the top of the panel and/or by selecting the option to **Match Brightness**.

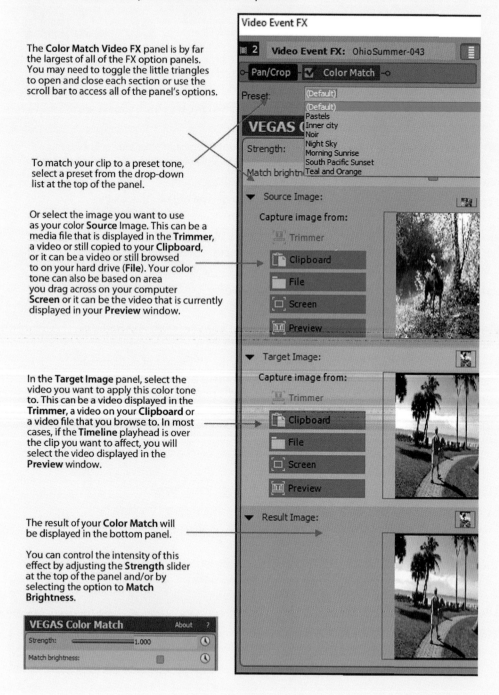

Wave. As the name implies, this effect adds ripples to your video image.

White Balance. This is a powerful tool for correcting the colors in your video. When you select the eye dropper on the **Video FX** dialog window and then sample the whitest spot in your video in the **Preview** window, this tool will automatically adjust all of your video's color levels so that this white spot becomes *pure* white – often automatically correcting all of your video's color levels in the process.

All effects can be animated or set up so the effect's settings change over time. For more information on creating animated effects, see page 226 in **Chapter 15, Create Animations with Keyframes**.

Adjust a video effect

Once you've added a video effect to a media clip, event clip, video track or video output (as described on pages 179-179), you have the option of adjusting or customizing the effect's settings in the **Video FX** dialog window.

Video FX dialog windows vary from effect to effect, but they all include:

- A map of the **Plug-In Chain**, listing all of the effects applied to a particular media clip, event, track or video output in the order that they have been applied. For more information on the **Plug-In Chain**, see the sidebar **Multiply effects in a chain** on page 188.

- Buttons for launching the **Plug-In Chooser** and removing an effect from the **Video FX Plug-In Chain** (see page 181).

- A drop-down list of **Presets** for the effect as well as buttons for saving and deleting customized presets. (For more information on creating presets, see **Save a custom look as a preset** on page 178.)

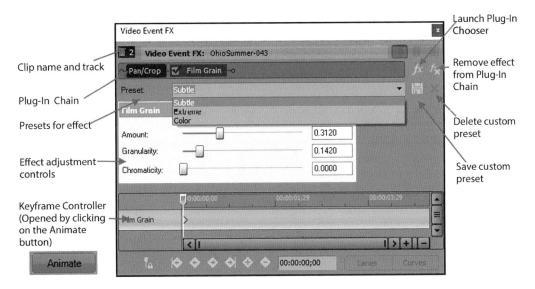

- A control panel for customizing the effect selected in the **Plug-In Chain**.

- A **Keyframe Controller** timeline for creating animated effects. (For more information, see **Chapter 15, Create Animation with Keyframes**.)

If your **Timeline Cursor** (playhead) is positioned over the clip or sequence of events that you're adding the effect(s) to, any changes you make in the **Video FX** dialog window will be displayed in the **Preview** window.

Your video effect changes are made in real time, and you do not have to save your changes or close the **Video FX** dialog window in order for your changes to take effect.

Multiply effects in a chain

Multiple effects can be added to a single clip, video track or video output. And often the order they appear in a "chain" can affect how they change your video.

For instance, if you add both **Film Effects** and **Sepia** effects to the same clip, they become part of the clip's **Plug-In Chain**. And you will get slightly different results if **Sepia** appears first in this **Plug-In Chain** than if **Film Effects** is listed first.

(The order that the effects are listed in any clip's **Plug-In Chain** can be easily rearranged simply by dragging them into new positions at the top of the **Video FX** or **Audio FX** dialog window or at the top of the **Plug-In Chooser**.)

Another important thing to note about using **Plug-In** effects in a chain is that each effect has its own separate timeline on the **Keyframe Controller** along the bottom of the **Video FX** or **Audio FX** dialog window, as illustrated below. This feature allows you to animate each effect separately, as discussed in **Chapter 15, Create Animations with Keyframes**.

A Plug-In Chain can produce slightly different effects if the order of the Plug-In Effects is changed.

Each effect has its own separate timeline in the Keyframe Controller, allowing separate animations for each.

Chroma key a background

To "key" something in video means to make it transparent. There are a number of ways to key a video, as well as a number of reasons for doing it.

A popular method of keying an area of a video is called **Chroma Keying**. "Chroma" essentially means a color's value or definition – and when you **Chroma Key a** video, you designate areas of a video to be made transparent based on their *color*. Usually, this "key" color is blue or green, because these colors don't appear in human skin tones.

A common use for chroma key in movies and television is in the creation of a scene in which a character, shot in one location, is made to appear in another location. It's the essential special effect, in other words, in all fantasy and science fiction movies. Using chroma key, you can make a person filmed in a studio appear to be in any real or imagined place in the universe!

The use of this effect doesn't always need to be in such an elaborate setting, of course. You can see this effect used every night on local news broadcasts, as the weather person, standing in front of a bright green screen, is made to appear to be standing in front of animated weather maps, scenery and various other computer-generated backgrounds.

And now, thanks to Vegas Movie Studio's **Chroma Keyer** effect, this same special effect is available to you!

Remove a video effect

Open the
Video FX
dialog
window.

Remove an effect in the Plug-In Chain by clicking the Remove Selected Plug-In button.

A **Plug-In** effect can be removed from a clip, event, track or movie in the **Video FX** dialog window, opened by clicking on the green **Event FX, Track FX** or **Video Output FX** button – or by **right-clicking** on a media clip and selecting **Media FX** – depending on how the effect was applied. For more information on the difference between each of the methods of adding effects, see **Event vs. Track vs. Media vs. Video Output FX** on page 179.

To remove an effect from a clip, track or movie in the **Video FX** dialog window, click to select it in the **Plug-In Chain** along the top of the window and then click the **Remove Selected Plug-In** button, as in the illustration above. **You may also remove an effect by right-clicking** on the effect's listing on the **Plug-In Chain** and selecting **Remove**. (See also **Bypass or disable an effect** on page 192.)

Add your background to a lower video track and your foreground to a track directly above it.

To swap in a new background using the **Chroma Keyer** effect, you will need two clips:

- A video of someone standing in front of a smooth, evenly-lit blue or green screen. We'll call this our foreground video.
- A video or still image of a background scene.

Although you can use a smooth, wrinkle-free sheet, blanket or even a wall as your background, blue and green backdrop screens work best if they are very vivid in color. Bright, professional-style green or blue screens can be found online at sites like greenscreenoutlet.com for surprisingly little cost.

Good lighting is also crucial to creating a good key. Make sure your green or blue screen is well lit and without any shadows or hot spots – and make sure your foreground actor is lit separately and equally well.

Once you've got the parts, the rest comes pretty easy:

1   Add your background to a lower video track

Place the video or still image that will serve as your new background on a lower video track, as illustrated above.

2   Add your foreground video to an upper track

Place your foreground video on a video track directly above your background video clip. Ensure that the videos on both tracks are of equal length.

3   Apply the Chroma Keyer

Apply the **Chroma Keyer Plug-In** effect to the foreground clip, as described in **Select an effect from the Plug-In Chooser** on page 181.

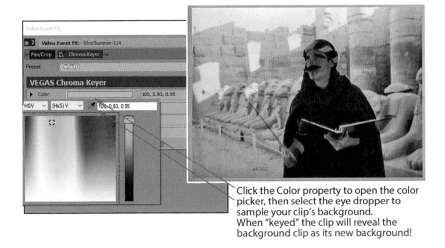

Click the Color property to open the color picker, then select the eye dropper to sample your clip's background.
When "keyed" the clip will reveal the background clip as its new background!

4 Set the key color

Often, if you've got a good, rich, evenly-lit green or blue backdrop for your foreground clip, you'll be able to apply the key simply by selecting the appropriate setting from the **Video FX** dialog window's **Preset** drop-down menu.

If this doesn't work, clear the preset by setting the H, S and L sliders all to zero. (This will set the key color to black – essentially making your green or blue screen completely visible.)

Then click the **Color** property and, on the color picker that opens, select the eye dropper and click your green or blue backdrop in the **Preview** display of your foreground video to "sample" its color. This will automatically set your key color to perfectly match the color of the clip's green or blue screen.

Movie Studio's **Chroma Keyer** is a very nicely designed tool, and it usually does a great job of applying a key. But, if your key effect needs some additional fine tuning, you can do so by adjusting the **Low Threshold, High Threshold** and **Blur Amount** sliders.

If you check the **Show Mask Only** box, the non-keyed elements will display as white silhouettes. This is often makes it much easier to see how your adjustments are affecting your key's quality.

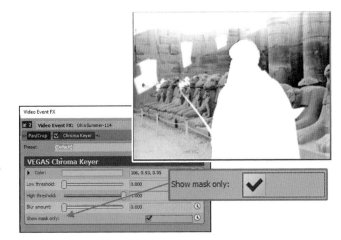

Load additional VST effects into your program

The effects in Vegas Movie Studio are in the form of plug-ins. This means that they are separate from the program itself and are loaded into the program whenever the program launches.

One of the chief advantages of using a plug-in system, rather than having the effects integrated into the program's core, is that it makes it a relatively simple process to add more effects.

These effects needn't be created by Magix. Any third-party **VST** (Virtual Studio Technology) video or audio effect plug-in can be added to your program – including those designed for Vegas Pro.

(www.NewBlueFX.com is an excellent resource for professional-style effects, including a number of great free ones!)

Loading new plug-in effects into your program is relatively easy.

1   **Install the effect**

Download the VST plug-in effect(s) and/or install them per the manufacturer's instructions.

Take note of the folder that these effects install to.

Bypass or disable an effect

An effect applied to an event clip, to an audio or video track or to your project overall can be disabled without actually being removed.

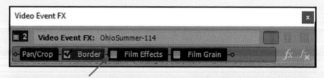

Effects can be turned off or temporarily disabled by unchecking their listing in the Plug-In Chain along the top of the FX dialog window.

Disabling or bypassing off the other effects allows you to focus on the effect you're currently adjusting.

To disable or bypass an effect that's been applied to an event, track or your entire project, open the **Video FX** dialog window (or, for an audio effect, the **Take** or **Audio Plug-In** dialog window) by clicking on the **Event FX, Track FX, Master FX** or **Video Output FX** button.

Uncheck the plug-in effect you'd like to disable, as illustrated above.

This feature can be very helpful if you're working with several effects in a **Plug-In Chain**. (See **Multiply effects in a chain** on page 188.)

Temporarily disabling all of the effects except for the one you're adjusting the settings for allows you to see the results of that single effect's settings exclusively.

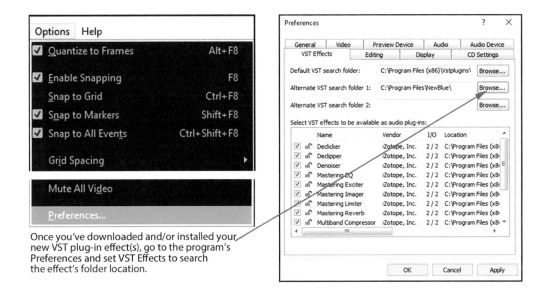

Once you've downloaded and/or installed your new VST plug-in effect(s), go to the program's Preferences and set VST Effects to search the effect's folder location.

2   **Set your program's preferences to locate the new plug-ins**

Go to the **Options** menu at the top of the interface and select **Preferences**.

In the **Preferences** dialog window, go to the **VST Effects** tab.

Click on the **Browse** button for either the **Default VST Search Folder, Alternate VST Search Folder 1** or **Alternate VST Search Folder 2** (whichever is available) and locate the folder that your new effect(s) have been installed to.

As an alternative, you can simply place the new effect(s) in one of the **VST Search Folders** listed already on this panel.

Click **OK**, and that's pretty much it!

What are OFX effects?

OFX is an open standard for Video FX. When effects providers adhere to this standard, their effects can be used as plug-ins in any program built to that standard.

In other words, any effects, transitions or other software developed by companies that adhere to the OFX standard can be used as plug-ins in both Vegas Pro and Vegas Movie Studio.

Effects companies that comply with the OFX standard include BorisFX, NewBlue, GenArts, ProDAD, Red Giant and Re:Vision.

When you next open the **Plug-In Chooser** (as discussed on page 181), for a media clip, event, track or video output, your new effect(s) will be listed among the available plug-ins, and it/they can be applied and customized just like any of the default effects.

Pre-render your video effects

Vegas Movie Studio will do its best to play a soft preview of any clips you've added effects to in real time. However, you may find at some point that this process creates a load so great that the playback in your **Preview** window is sluggish and at a greatly reduced frame rate.

When this happens, it's best to pre-render your timeline or even render a complicated sequence as a new clip on an upper video track. For information on pre-rendering options, see **Render and pre-render your video project** on pages 89-94.

Chapter 13

Add and Adjust Audio Effects

Shaping your movie's sound

As with video effects, audio effects can be used to improve the sound of your movie or to add an unusual tone or special effect to your project's sound.

Vegas Movie Studio includes a full toolkit of audio effects for shaping the sound of your movie.

Vegas Movie Studio includes a large library of audio effects. As with video effects, these audio effects are in the form of plug-ins – and more can be easily loaded into the program's library of audio effects.

Like video effects, several audio effects can be added to a single event clip or audio track in a chain. Each effect in this chain can then be customized using presets or by using the **Audio FX** dialog window's control panel.

When an effect is added to an audio clip on your timeline, the program can either add the effect to the event in "real time," changing it immediately, or it can create a new audio clip based on the effect(s) applied. This new audio clip will then automatically replace your event clip's existing audio. However the original, un-effected audio will remain available as an alternative **Take** – so you have the option of switching your event back to your original audio if you'd like, as discussed in **Swap between alternate audio Takes** on page 204.

An effect that is added to an audio clip on your timeline and generates a new audio clip is referred to as a **Non-Real-Time Event FX**.

Apply an audio effect

There are four ways to apply an audio effect **Plug-In** to a clip or clips in your movie. And how this effect functions depends on which form of the clip or clips you've applied this effect to.

> **An audio effect can be pre-added to a file** in the **Project Media** window.
>
> **An audio effect can be applied to an individual event clip** on your timeline.
>
> **An audio effect can be applied to an audio track**, affecting all of the audio on that track.
>
> **An audio effect can be applied to your entire movie** (**Master FX**).

As an alternative to using one of the effects in Vegas Movie Studio to change or sweeten your movie's audio, you can opt to port your audio to an external audio editing program. For more information on this process, see **Edit your audio in another program** on page 146.

Add an audio effect to an event on your timeline

FX applied to audio clips on your timeline can either be applied in "real time," by applying **Audio Event FX**, or used to create a new, *alternate* audio clip (or **Take**) by applying **Non-Real-Time Event FX**.

To apply **Audio Event FX** or **Non-Real-Time Audio FX** to a clip on your timeline:

1   **Select an Audio Event FX option**

Select an audio clip on your timeline (or the audio portion of a clip that includes both a video and an audio track) and, from the **Tools** menu at the top of the interface, select **Audio**. Then, from the sub-menu, select either **Audio Event FX** or **Non-Real-Time Event FX**.

As an alternative, you can **right-click** on an audio clip on your timeline and select either **Apply Audio Event FX** or **Apply Non-Real-Time Event FX**.

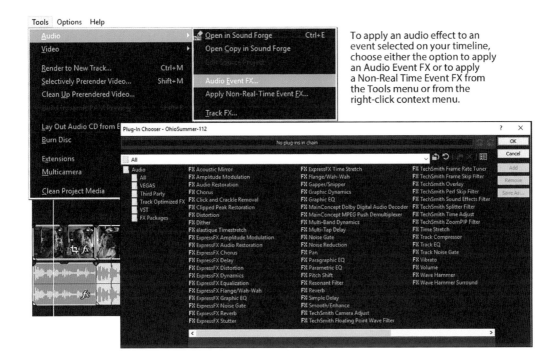

To apply an audio effect to an event selected on your timeline, choose either the option to apply an Audio Event FX or to apply a Non-Real Time Event FX from the Tools menu or from the right-click context menu.

The **Plug-In Chooser** will open, as illustrated above.

2   **Select a Plug-In**

Select an audio effect (or several effects) from the **Plug-In Chooser**.

Click **OK**.

The **Plug-In Chooser** window will close, and the **Take** or **Audio FX** dialog window will open.

3   **Customize your effect**

Adjust your effect's settings as needed, per **Adjust an audio effect** on page 196.

Click **OK**.

If you are applying a **Non-Real-Time Event FX**, you will be prompted to render your new audio clip.

Select a **Render As** template (usually a default WAV).

Click **Render** to save your audio clip.

Your audio clip, with the effect(s) applied, will automatically be saved as an alternative **Take** to your event clip's current audio. (For information on switching between alternative audio clips, see **Swap between alternate audio Takes** on page 204.)

To apply an effect to all of the audio on a particular audio track, click on the Track FX button on the Track Header.

To open the Audio FX Plug-in Chooser, click the Plug-in Chain button on the Audio FX dialog window.

Add an effect to an audio track

Track FX are applied to an entire audio track. To apply **Audio Track FX**:

1   **Click the Track FX button**

Click on the **Track FX** button on the **Track Header**.

The **Audio Track FX** dialog window will open. By default, the **Track Noise Gate, Track EQ** and **Track Compressor FX** are applied to every audio track and may be adjusted, as described on page 202.

2   **To apply another audio effect, open the Plug-In Chooser**

Click the **Plug-In Chain** button. The **Plug-In Chooser** will open.

Select an audio effect (or several effects) from the **Plug-In Chooser**.

Click **OK**.

The **Plug-In Chooser** window will close, and the **Audio Plug-In** (Audio FX) dialog window will open.

3   **Customize your effect**

Adjust your effect's settings as needed, per **Adjust an audio effect** on page 202.

Add an effect to your entire movie's audio

Master FX are applied to your entire movie project. To apply **Master Audio FX**:

1   **Click the Master FX button**

Click on the **Master FX** button on the **Master Audio Mixer** window.

The **Plug-In Chooser** will open.

To apply an audio effect to your entire movie at once, click on the Master FX button on the Mixer window.

2 **Select a Plug-In**

Select an audio effect (or several effects) from the **Plug-In Chooser**.

Click **OK**.

The **Plug-In Chooser** window will close, and the **Audio Plug-In** (Audio FX) dialog window will open.

3 **Customize your effect**

Adjust your effect as needed, per **Adjust an audio effect** on page 202.

Audio FX plug-ins defined

Magix has included a full toolkit of plug-in audio effects with Vegas Movie Studio, including some effects created by third-party effects companies

Depending on the plug-ins already installed on your computer by other software, your specific list of effects may vary. Many are "borrowed" from Magix' Sound Forge Pro.

Here are brief descriptions of the program's key effects:

Acoustic Mirror. The **Acoustic Mirror** effect can be used to mimic the sound qualities of any environment, from a theater or church to a small room, often based on "impulse file" presets (available from Sony) representing these environments.

Amplitude Modulation. This effect adjusts the gain (sound level) of your audio at specific frequencies, often creating a wavering or trembling sound pattern.

Audio Restoration. Advanced tools for cleaning up noise in your recordings.

Chorus. This effect adds feedback or flanging to your music or audio to create the illusion of more instruments playing or voices singing.

Click and Crackle Removal. More tools for cleaning up noisy recordings, specifically pops and crackles on recordings made from vinyl record albums.

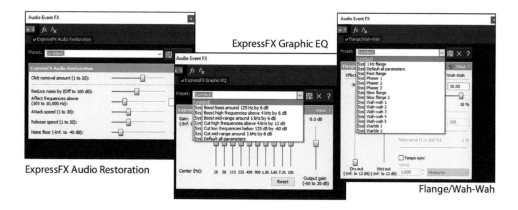

ExpressFX Graphic EQ

ExpressFX Audio Restoration

Flange/Wah-Wah

Distortion. As you might expect, this effect adds distortion and a tinny sound to your audio, creating, for instance, the effect of your audio being played on a tiny or overloaded speaker.

Dither. Dithering adds white noise to your audio to mask quality reduction when a clip's quantization depth is reduced.

ExpressFX Amplitude Modulation. This effect modulates your audio levels to better highlight drums, musical instruments or speech.

ExpressFX Audio Restoration. A tool that can sometimes be effective for removing clicking or other noise in your audio by filtering sound at different levels.

ExpressFX Chorus. An effect that uses reverberation to add depth and lushness to your sound.

ExpressFX Delay. This tool creates a simple delay effect for creating echoes.

ExpressFX Distortion. A tool for adding fuzzy distortion to your audio.

ExpressFX Dynamics. This effect narrows the range between the loudest and quietest parts of your audio.

ExpressFX Equalization A simple three-band graphic equalizer for boosting or reducing your audio's bass, mid-range and treble.

ExpressFX Flange/Wah-Wah. This effect adds a strange phase shift to your audio so that its frequency levels waver in and out.

ExpressFX Graphic EQ. This 10-band graphic equalizer can be used to boost or reduce your audio's low, mid and high frequency sounds.

ExpressFX Noise Gate. A tool for reducing noise and hum.

ExpressFX Reverb. A tool for creating echo effects, with presets for simulating the sounds of various sizes of rooms.

ExpressFX Stutter. An effect that adds trembling distortion to your audio.

ExpressFX Time Stretch. As the name implies, this effect slows down or speeds up your audio.

Flange/Wah-Wah. This effect adds a phase shift to your audio so that its frequency levels waver in and out.

Gapper/Snipper. A tremolo effect that gives your audio a distorted and choppy sound by feeding brief gaps into it.

Graphic Dynamics. A tool for compressing your audio's sound by limiting its loudest and/or quietest sounds.

Reverb

Noise Gate

PitchShift

Graphic EQ. A high-level tool for setting the levels of your audio at various frequencies based on a curve pattern you create.

Multi-Band Dynamics. A tool for limiting low and high audio levels in order to, for instance, reduce hissing "s" and popping "p" sounds.

Multi-Tap Delay. A high-level tool for creating echo effects or reverberation.

Noise Gate. A tool for reducing noise and hum by trimming sounds below a given audio level threshold.

Pan. Controls the balance of audio on your right and left stereo channels.

Paragraphic EQ. A graphic tool for adjusting the levels of your audio's various low, mid and high frequencies.

Parametric EQ. A tool for trimming the high or low frequencies from your audio to produce, for instance, the effect of someone talking on a telephone.

Pitch Shift. An effect for raising and lowering the pitch of your audio to create the effect of sped up or slowed down sound.

Resonant Filter. An effect that filters or exaggerates your audio at certain levels – making for some rather extreme audio distortions!

Reverb. A more advanced tool for creating a variety of echo effects.

Simple Delay. A simplified tool for creating echo effects.

Smooth/Enhance. A tool for smoothly enhancing and enlivening the upper end of your audio.

Time Stretch. An effect that speeds up or slows down your audio, often with an echoey effect.

Track Compressor. A tool for increasing the output gain (loudness) of your audio with minimal loss of dynamics.

Track EQ. A powerful tool for boosting or cutting bass or rumble and reducing hiss.

Track Noise Gate. A filter for eliminating sounds above and below certain thresholds.

Vibrato. An effect that adds a slow or fast pitch modulation to your audio, often distorting it in very strange ways.

Volume. A tool for increasing your audio's sound level. By adding several of these effects in a chain and setting each to its peak level, you can often rescue a very quiet clip.

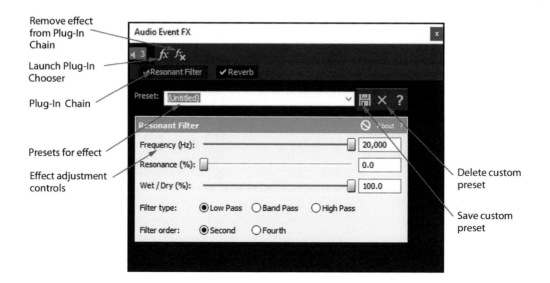

Remove effect
from Plug-In
Chain

Launch Plug-In
Chooser

Plug-In Chain

Presets for effect

Effect adjustment
controls

Delete custom
preset

Save custom
preset

Adjust an audio effect

Once you've added an audio effect to an event clip, video track or your master audio (as described on pages 196-199), you have the option of adjusting or customizing the effect's settings. Which **Audio FX** control panel you use to adjust your effect(s) depends on where you are adding your effect:

- **If you are adding a Non-Real-Time effect(s) to an event clip on your timeline**, you will adjust the effect in the **Take** dialog window.

- **If you are adding your effect(s) to an audio track or to your master audio**, you will adjust the effect in the **Audio Plug-In** dialog window.

These dialog windows vary from effect to effect, but they all include (as illustrated above):

- A map of the **Plug-In Chain**, listing all of the effects applied to this particular media clip, event, track or video output in the order they have been applied. For more information on the **Plug-In Chain**, see the sidebar **Multiply effects in a chain** on page 188.

- A button for launching the **Plug-In Chooser.**

- A **Preview** button for test driving your audio effect. (This button is only available when you are applying a **Non-Real Time Event FX** to a clip on your timeline. Audio effects applied to an audio track or to your project's master audio are applied in real time and can be tested simply by playing your timeline.)

- A drop-down list of **Presets** for the effect as well as buttons for saving and deleting custom presets. (For more information on creating presets, see **Save a custom look as a preset** on page 168.)

- A control panel for customizing the effect selected in the **Plug-In Chain**.

To apply several effects at once in a chain (see page 182), first remove the current effects, as described in the next section of this chapter.

Launch the **Plug-In Chooser**, as described on pages 196-199.

In the **Plug-In Chooser**, hold down the **Ctrl** key and click to select all of the effects you would like to add. When you click **OK** on the **Plug-In Chooser** window, the selected effects will appear in the **Plug-In Chain** on the **Take** or **Audio Plug-In** dialog window.

Remove an audio effect

Audio effects are removed from a clip in one of two ways, depending on whether these effects have been applied to an event, track or to your movie's master audio. (Also see **Bypass or disable an effect** on page 192.)

Remove a Non-Real-Time effect from an audio event

Because **Non-Real Time Event FX** are not really added to an audio clip until you generate a new audio clip (see page 196), you can remove an effect (or all effects) that you've just added to an audio clip on your timeline simply by clicking the **Cancel** button on the **Take** (Audio FX) dialog window.

Once **Non-Real Time Event FX** have been added to an audio clip – a process that creates an alternate audio clip – you have the option of going back to the original, unaltered audio file or of removing the effected audio completely, as described in **Swap between alternative audio Takes** on page 204.

Remove an effect from an audio event, track or master audio

A **Plug-In audio** effect can be removed from a clip by opening the **Audio Plug-In** dialog window by clicking on the green **Event FX, Track FX** or **Master FX** button (depending on whether the effect was applied to an audio event, track or to the master audio).

To remove an effect, select it in the **Plug-In Chain** along the top of the **Audio Plug-In** dialog window and then click the **Remove Selected Plug-In** button, as in the illustration below.

Open the Audio Plug-In dialog window.

Remove the effect selected in the Plug-In Chain from a clip by clicking the Remove button.

When Non-Real Event FX are applied to a clip on your timeline, the effected audio is saved as an alternative Take, and this Take – as well as the original audio – can be swapped into the event via the right-click menu.

Swap between alternative audio Takes

When you add an audio effect to an event (an audio clip on your timeline), the effect is not so much applied to the clip as much as a new audio clip is generated that combines this effect with your original audio. In fact, whenever you add **Non-Real Time Event FX**, you are prompted to save the effected audio as a new clip (as discussed on pages 196-197).

When you save this new audio clip, it is automatically swapped in as a replacement for your current audio event.

However, this new clip does not *permanently* replace the audio in your clip. In reality, this new clip is merely saved as a **Take.**

A **Take** is alternative audio or video for an event. (For information on working with video **Takes**, see **Add Multiple Takes of a scene to your timeline** on page 110.)

You can easily switch between the event's existing audio and any alternative takes – or between the audio with effects applied to it and your original audio –by **right-clicking** on the event clip on your timeline.

To switch between an event's audio **Takes**:

1 **Right-click on an event**

   Right-click on an event clip on your timeline to which you've added **Non-Real Time Event FX**.

2 **Select a Take**

   From the right-click menu, select **Take.**

   From the **Take** sub-menu, select the audio clip you'd like to swap in for this event.

To remove **Takes** from this list of alternatives, follow **Step 4** on page 111.

Chapter 14

Add and Customize Transitions

Smooth moves from clip to clip

It's fun to add interesting transitions between your event clips!

Some transitions are showy and obvious.

Others are so subtle your audience will hardly notice them at all.

It's all about creating a mood and style for your movie.

Transitions are interesting ways to get your audience from one scene or sequence to another. Whether your transitions are fun and showy, fast and exciting or subtle and simple is entirely up to you. But the transitions you choose can do a lot to define the style and mood of your movie.

Vegas Movie Studio includes 30 basic transitions (each with several variations) in addition to a simple **Cross-Fade**, the simplest and least intrusive of all transitions.

Like effects, transitions can be customized in a number of ways. And, once you've created a custom transition, you can even save it as a preset for later use!

Because of the way transitions work, they require a bit of extra footage beyond the end or beginning of your event clips. Understanding why this extra footage (technically called "head" and "tail" material) is needed and how it is used can help you understand why your transitions behave the way they do. We show you how transitions use "head" and "tail" material in **How transitions work** on page 213.

Create a simple audio or video Cross-Fade

A **Cross-Fade** is a simple, smooth transition between event clips.

Vegas Movie Studio allows you to create a **Cross-Fade** by simply overlapping your clips on the timeline.

To use this feature, the **Automatic Cross-Fade** button must be toggled on along the bottom of the **Timeline**, as illustrated below.

To create an **Automatic Cross-Fade**, you simply drag one clip until it partially overlaps the event clip before it.

As you create this overlap, the program will indicate the length of the **Cross-Fade** transition. (If this figure does not show, you can activate it by going to the **View** menu and checking the **Event Fade Lengths** option.)

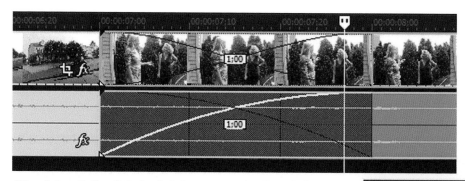

When Automatic Crossfades is selected, you can create a Cross-Fade between audio and video events by dragging them to overlap on the timeline.

As you overlap the clips, the program will indicate the Cross-Fade duration.

This method works for creating audio as well as video **Cross-Fades**. In fact, if your clips include audio and video, they will both automatically create a **Cross-Fade** together.

This **Cross-Fade** is indicated by crossed blue lines over a darkened area between the clips. These blue lines, in a video transition, represent the dropping opacity level of the outgoing clip and the rising opacity level of the incoming clip.

In an audio transition, these lines represent the falling and rising volume levels of the clips.

Convert a Cross-Fade to another transition

Replacing a **Cross-Fade** – or any transition, for that matter – with another transition is pretty much as simple as dragging a new transition from the **Transitions** window onto the transitional segment on your timeline.

It can also be done, however, via a right-click menu.

Right-click on the video **Cross-Fade** or other transition and select **Transition** from the context menu.

You'll be presented with a number of options. Selecting **Insert Other** gives you access to the program's entire **Transitions plug-in** library.

Interpolate your transition

A standard transition smoothly replaces one clip with another in a relatively linear, gently curved manner.

However, if you'd like, you can **interpolate** your transition so that, for instance, one clip is removed quickly and then is quickly replaced by the next.

To change how a **Cross-Fade** or any transition interpolates, **right-click** on the transitional segment on your timeline and select **Fade Type**.

The various patterns illustrate how the program smoothly, gradually or abruptly transitions between these event clips.

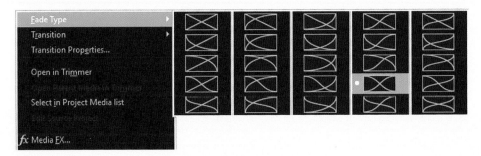

Add a video transition to your timeline

Like effects, transitions are actually plug-ins to the program, and more can be added using the method described in **Load additional VST effects into your program** on page 192.

There are two ways to add a transition to your timeline. A transition may be selected from the library of transition plug-ins – or it may be added from the presets listed on the **Transitions** window.

Note, by the way, that nearly all transitions available in the program are for transitioning between *video* events. The only audio transition is the **Cross-Fade**, which is created using the method on page 206.

Transition preferences

The preferences for the transitions in your project are set in the **Preferences** dialog window, launched from the **Options** drop-down menu at the top of the interface. Transition preferences are listed under the **Editing** tab.

Alignment sets the default location for your transition. In most cases, the ideal setting is **Centered on Cut** – which places your transitions evenly on the cut between events. However, if one of your clips lacks sufficient "head" or "tail" material (as discussed below) you may want to change this setting to favor its position over one clip or the other.

The **Cut-To-Overlap Conversion** (seconds) sets the **default length** of any transition you add to your timeline. However, the actual length of the transition may be affected by the presence of "head" or "tail" material.

"Head" and "tail" material is the extra few frames beyond the end of one clip and beyond the beginning of the other that the program uses to create the transitional segment. For more information on how the presence of "head" and "tail" material can affect how your transition behaves, see **How transitions work** on page 213.

By the way, in case you're wondering, the **Automatically Overlap Multiple Selected Media When Added** preference will automatically add **Cross-Fades** between your events when you add more than one media clip at once to your timeline if **Automatic Crossfades** is selected on the **Config** menu along the bottom of the **Timeline**.

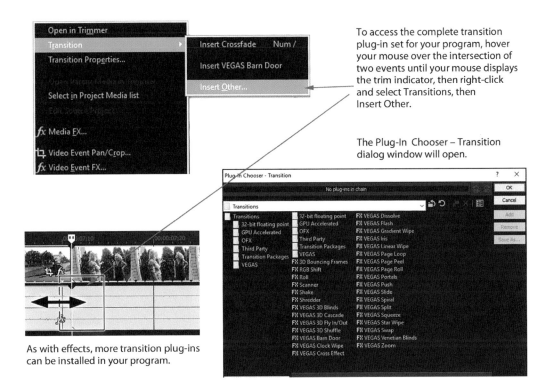

To access the complete transition plug-in set for your program, hover your mouse over the intersection of two events until your mouse displays the trim indicator, then right-click and select Transitions, then Insert Other.

The Plug-In Chooser – Transition dialog window will open.

As with effects, more transition plug-ins can be installed in your program.

Add a transition from the plug-in library

To access the library of "raw" transition plug-ins, hover your mouse over the end or beginning of an event clip on your timeline until you see the **trim** indicator, as illustrated above. **Right-click** and select **Transitions** and then, from the sub-menu, select **Insert Other.**

The **Plug-In Chooser – Transition** window lists all of the transition plug-ins that have been installed in the program.

Once you select a transition plug-in and click **OK**, you will have the option of adjusting or customizing it in the **Video FX** dialog window. For more information on how to use the tools in this window, see **Customize your transition** on page 214.

Add a preset transition from the Transitions window

The more intuitive (and the more popular way) to add transitions to a movie is to add them from the **Transitions** window.

The **Transitions** window, by default, shares the tabbed window space with the **Project Media, Explorer, Video FX** and **Media Generators** windows in the upper left of the program's interface. Click on the tab to access the **Transitions** window.

These thumbnails are presets of the default transition plug-ins that have been installed in your program. In other words, the **Simple, Left to Right, Slot Machine**, and **Spin** transitions that appear under the **3D Blinds Transition** category are actually just pre-created customizations of the **3D Blinds** transition plug-in.

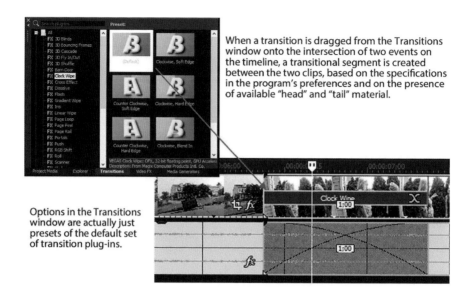

When a transition is dragged from the Transitions window onto the intersection of two events on the timeline, a transitional segment is created between the two clips, based on the specifications in the program's preferences and on the presence of available "head" and "tail" material.

Options in the Transitions window are actually just presets of the default set of transition plug-ins.

In fact, if you were to add the **Simple 3D Blinds** transition to your timeline, you would find, under the **Presets** drop-down in the **Video Event FX** dialog window (page 214), each of the other effects displayed with it in the **Transitions** window.

To preview any of these transitions, hover your mouse over the transition's thumbnail in the **Transitions** window.

An animation will display the transitional effect in action. (The "A" panel in the transition animation represents the outgoing clip and the "B" panel represents the incoming clip.)

To apply a transition between two events, simply drag it from this panel onto the intersection of the clips on your timeline.

If both clips include adequate "head" and "tail" material, the transition will position itself according to the preferences you set up (on page 208). For more information on "head" and "tail" material, see **How transitions work** on page 213.

When you add a transition to events on your timeline, the **Video Event FX** dialog window will open, allowing for customization of your new transition. For more information on how to use the tools in this window, see **Customize a transition** on page 214.

Transitions defined

Here are brief descriptions of the transition included with Vegas Movie Studio 14.

3D Blinds. Transitions from one event to the next as if opening the slats on Venetian blinds.

3D Bouncing Frames. Very animated transitions with crazy descriptive names like **Migraine** and **Photon Torpedo**.

3D Cascade. The new event replaces the old in a series of 3D strips.

3D Fly In/Out. The new event flies or tumbles in to replace the old with a 3D animation.

3D Shuffle. One event replaces the other as if being shuffled like cards.

Barn Door. One event parts (like barn doors) to reveal the next.

3D Fly-In

Page Roll

3D Blinds

Clock Wipe

Clock Wipe. One event replaces the other through an animation like a clock's hand sweeping in a circle.

Cross Effect. Animated transitions in this set include blurs, zooms and pixelations.

Dissolve. Dissolves from one event to the next through various colors or fade out/in effects.

Flash. Dissolves from one event to the next through a camera-like flash.

Gradient Wipe. A powerful tool for creating transitions through various shapes – including custom grayscale patterns that you create!

Iris. Reveals the new event through a variety of basic shape animations.

Linear Wipe. Transitions from one event to the next with a simple hard- or soft-edged wipe.

Page Loop. One event replaces another through a 3D animation that resembles one page curling over another.

Page Peel. One event replaces another through a 3D animation that resembles a page turning.

Page Roll. One event replaces another through a 3D animation that resembles a page curling back to reveal the next.

Portals. One event is introduced over another as a series of random rectangles.

Push. One event replaces another by sliding over it or pushing it aside.

RGB Shift. Transitions that break your videos into red, green and blue channels.

Roll. Cool, motion-blurred rolling and spinning transitions.

Scanner. Wipes and pushes with a surreal feel.

Shake. Bouncy, highly kinetic ways to transition from one event to another.

Slide. One event slides in over another.

Spiral. The new event slides in over the old in a circular pattern.

Split. One event clip splits into parts to reveal the next.

Squeeze. The events are squeezed and distorted as one replaces the other.

Star Wipe. This effect transitions your clips between any of 18 preset shapes, from stars to diamonds to an opening eye.

Swap. A 2D version of the 3D shuffle, with the new event shuffled in, card-like, to replace the old.

Venetian Blinds. A 2D version of 3D blinds, the new event is introduced through a series of slats animated through the old.

Zoom. The new event zooms in and/or the old event zooms out.

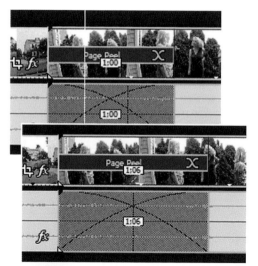

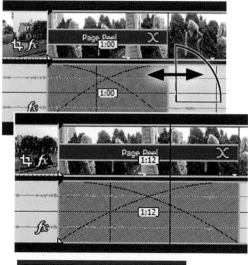

When the Automatic Cross-Fades switch is toggled on, you can extend the length of a transition by dragging one clip further onto the other.

The length of a transition can also be extended by toggling off Auto Ripple and then dragging on either end of the transition.

Change the duration of a transition

The speed at which your transition transitions is based on how long your transition lasts. In other words, the longer your transition on the timeline, the slower the transitional animation from one event clip to another.

There are two ways to change the length of a transition on your timeline.

(If the **Event Fade Lengths** option is checked (under the **View** menu), the program will display the length of your transition as you make these changes, as illustrated above.)

Change the length of the overlap

In order to use this method of increasing the length of your transition, the **Automatic Cross-Fades** button must be toggled on, as discussed in **Create a simple audio or video Cross-Fade** on page 206.

To change the length of the transition, drag one event or extend the length of one clip so that the overlap that represents their transitional segment is longer or shorter.

Stretch the transition

You can also change the length of the transitional segment without changing the positions of the events on your timeline.

To do this, ensure **Auto Ripple** is toggled off and hover your mouse over one end of your transition segment until you see the **Fade Offset** indicator (as illustrated above). Drag the end of the transition to extend or shorten its length.

Note that there must be adequate "head" and "tail" material on your clips to support the length of your transitional segment. For more information, see **How transitions work** on the facing page.

How transitions work

In order to understand why transitions behave certain ways at certain times, you must understand how transitions work.

A cut is the point at which one event clip ends and the next begins.

When a transition is added to a clip, there is no longer a hard cut, but rather a period (usually a second long) at which both clips are on-screen at the same time, transitioning through some fade or animation as one gives way to the other.

In other words, when you replace a cut with a one-second transition centered on a cut, your out-going clip must use an extra *half a second of footage* beyond its end point and your incoming clip must use *half a second of footage beyond its beginning*. Officially, these extra half-seconds of video are called "tail" and "head" material, respectively.

If you **right-click** on a video track's **Track Header** and select **Expand Track Layers** (as I've done in the illustration below), you'll be able to see a more graphic representation of how the program uses footage beyond each clip's cut to create the transitional segment.

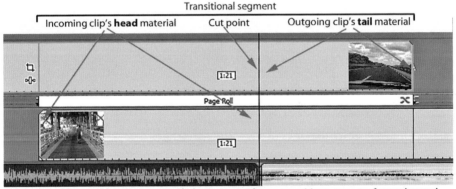

When your video track layers are expanded, you can see how a transition uses extra frames beyond each clip's cut to create the effect segment in which one event is giving way to the next.

So what happens if one or both of your clips have no available "head" or "tail" material?

In that case, the program will use a freeze frame of the last available frame in your video – or, depending on how your preferences are set, possibly even frames from another part of your clip! And that's not likely an effect you'd like added to your transition.

Additionally, when you add a transition between two clips and the program sees that there is not enough head or tail footage, it may automatically position the transition so that it favors one clip over the other rather than resting directly between the two.

The wisest move, then, is to always allow yourself adequate head and tail material wherever you add a transition. You can do this by trimming back half a second or so of footage from the beginning or end of any clips you plan to add a transition between (see page 78).

Customize a transition

Whenever you add a transition to your timeline – either by selecting it from the **Plug-In Chooser** or by dragging it from the **Transitions** window (page 209) – a **Video Event FX** dialog window will automatically open, allowing you to customize the transitional effect.

As with any video effect, the control panels for each transition vary from transition to transition, based on the effects and animations available.

However, there are certainly elements common to all transition **Video Event FX** dialog windows:

- A button for launching the **Plug-In Chooser** in order to replace the current transition. (A transition can also be replaced by simply dragging a new transition preset onto it from the **Transitions** window, as described on pages 207.)

- A button for removing the transition completely. (When a video transition is removed, the transitional segment on your timeline will default to a **Cross-Fade**.)

- A drop-down list of **Presets** for the effect as well as buttons for saving and deleting customized presets. The default presets in this list correspond to the presets that appear in the Transitions window.

- A control panel for customizing your **transitional** effect.

- A **Keyframe Controller** timeline for creating animated effects. Although this function is rarely used for transitions, you can use it to change your transition's control panel settings over the course of the transition. (For more information on using the **Keyframe Controller**, see **Chapter 15, Create Animation with Keyframes**.)

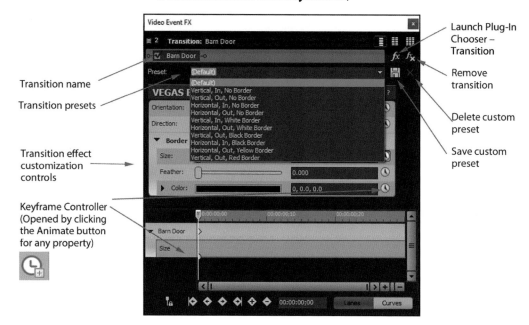

Transition name

Transition presets

Transition effect customization controls

Keyframe Controller (Opened by clicking the Animate button for any property)

Launch Plug-In Chooser – Transition

Remove transition

Delete custom preset

Save custom preset

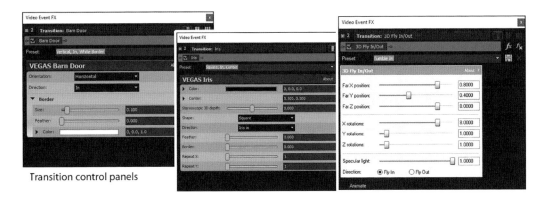

Transition control panels

 A transition can be re-opened for further editing or customization by clicking on the **Transition Properties** button that appears on the right side of the transition on your timeline.

Some common control panel settings include:

Orientation. Controls if the effect is moving horizontally or vertically.

Direction. Sets the direction of the transition – as in whether it moves from left to right or right to left or top to bottom, etc.

Feather. Defines how soft or hard the line between your clips is in a wipe or how soft the edges of a shape are in an iris-style transition.

Border. An optional line between the incoming and outgoing clip. If there's an option for a border, there is usually a color picker for setting the color of this border as well as a slider for setting its width.

Repeat X/Repeat Y. If you have the option of using a shape as your transition, this control sets the number of times a basic shape is repeated horizontally or vertically in the transition's final shape.

Center Point. This graphical control often determines the center location of a shape during a transition (as in the **Iris** transition above). Drag the **Center Point** to any position to define its location within a video frame.

Specular. In 3D effects, a **Specular** simulates a light source reflecting off a moving or rotating image or clip.

Save a custom transition preset

If you're especially happy with your settings for a transition, you can save it as a custom preset, just as you can a custom effects or title preset (see page 175).

To save your control panel settings as a custom preset for a transition, type the name you'd like to give your preset over the text in the **Preset** drop-down box, then click the floppy disc icon to the right of this box, as illustrated on the facing page.

Add transitions to several events at once

There are two ways to add a transition to several clips at once – depending on whether this transition is being added to clips already on your timeline or it is being added to the timeline simultaneously with your clips. (Additionally, the Vegas Movie Studio **Slideshow Creator** includes a feature for automatically adding transitions between still photos, as discussed on page 132.)

Add transitions between selected clips

If you'd like to add transitions between clips that have already been added as events on your timeline:

1   **Select a sequence of events**

    Select a series of clips on your timeline by either:

    Dragging over the event clips with the **Selection Edit Tool** (see page 96);

    Holding down the Shift key as you click to select the first and last clip in a series; or

    Using Ctrl+a to select all of the clips on your timeline.

2   **Add a transition from the Transitions window**

    Drag a transition preset onto the intersection between any two of your selected clips.

    When you release your mouse button, this transition will be added between *all* of the selected events.

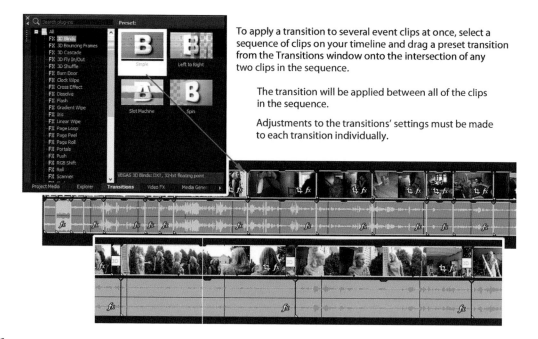

To apply a transition to several event clips at once, select a sequence of clips on your timeline and drag a preset transition from the Transitions window onto the intersection of any two clips in the sequence.

The transition will be applied between all of the clips in the sequence.

Adjustments to the transitions' settings must be made to each transition individually.

3 Customize the transition

The presets you select and the customizations you make to the transitions (page 214) will be applied to one transition at a time.

Select each transition on your timeline and customize it as needed.

Automatically add Cross-Fades as you add your clips

By changing a preference, you can set the program up to automatically add a **Cross-Fade** between your clips when you add more than one media clip at a time to your timeline.

1 Set up your Editing preference

Go to the **Options** menu at the top of the interface and select **Preferences**.

In the **Preferences** dialog window, select the **Editing** tab.

Check the option to **Automatically Overlap Multiple Selected Media When Added**.

Click **OK**.

2 Add several media clips from Project Media

Hold down the **Ctrl** key as you select a group of individual clips in the **Project Media** window – or hold down the **Shift** key and select the first and last in a series of clips.

Drag these clips to your timeline.

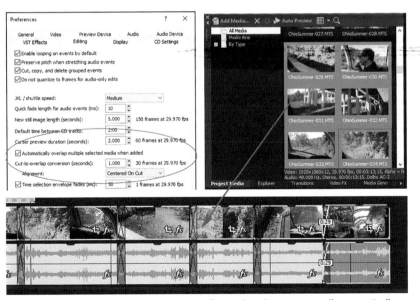

With the Editing preferences set to automatically overlap, the program will automatically add Cross-Fades between events when a group of clips is added to the timeline.

When you release your mouse, the clips will appear on your timeline with **Cross-Fades** between them.

To convert these **Cross-Fades** to transitions, use one of the methods described on page 207.

Use an effect as a transition

In addition to the transitions included with Vegas Movie Studio – and any other VST or OFX plug-ins you've loaded into the program – you can create your own transitions by using keyframes to animate the program's effects.

For more information, see **Keyframe a Video FX animation** on page 226.

Animation and Keyframe Basics
Animating a Pan/Crop Motion
Animating Video FX
Animating Generated Media
Animating Titles and Text
Keyframing and Video Envelopes

Chapter 15
Create Animations with Keyframes
Adding motion to your effects

Keyframes take your simple effects to a whole other level.

Using keyframes, you can make a basic effect into an animated effect.

Keyframes can also create motion paths over photos – making still pictures come alive!

You can even use keyframes to create your own custom transitions!

Keyframes are tools for creating custom effects and movements in Vegas Movie Studio.

The principle is a simple one: You use keyframes to set an effect's various settings, audio track's volume levels or video's **Pan/Crop** positions at specific points and the program will create the animated movements or transitions between them.

You can, for instance, keyframe a motion path over a photo so that your view of the picture begins as a close-up on someone's face, then zooms back and pans across the photo to reveal the rest of the picture (as on page 133).

You can use keyframes to animate a video effect, like **Film Effects,** so that your movie dissolves from looking clean and new to looking old and weathered.

You can even use keyframes on an audio track to raise and lower the volume at specific points so that your background music quiets while your narrator is speaking. When this type of keyframed animation is applied to an entire audio or video track rather than to an individual clip, it is called an **Audio or Video Envelope** (see pages 142 and 235) since its settings and keyframes affect the clips that are within it.

Magix has done an excellent job of making working with keyframes as intuitive as possible. And, once you understand how keyframes work, you'll likely see many applications for this great and powerful tool throughout the program.

Keyframe and video animation basics

Running along the bottom of every **Video FX, Media Generator** and **Pan/Crop** dialog window (including those for customizing titles and transitions) is a workspace called the **Keyframe Controller.** (For a close-up, see page 222.)

This workspace is hidden on the **Video FX, Audio FX** and **Media Generators** dialog windows until you click on the **Animate** button.

The **Keyframe Controller** is actually a mini-timeline representing the duration of your video clip, video track, movie or transition. (Even though titles and still photos may not technically be "video," they behave like video when added to your timeline and, as media clips, have frames and duration.)

Keyframe Controllers – the timelines for creating keyframed animation – can be opened on the Media Generators, Pan/Crop and FX panels by clicking on the Animate or clock buttons.

When the playhead on the Keyframe Controller timeline is repositioned and the settings in the control panel are changed, new keyframes are generated and the program animates the transition between them.

In a Media Generator dialog window, the **Keyframe Controller** will indicate the graphic or title whose properties are set in the window's control panel.

In a Pan/Crop dialog window, the **Keyframe Controller** will indicate the position of the **Selection Box** (see pages 223-225), which defines the view and scale of the video or still in the **Preview** window.

In a Video FX dialog window, the **Keyframe Controller** will list the effects applied to the **Plug-In Chain** for the selected event clip, video track or video output (see **Multiply effects in a chain** on page 188).

In a **Video FX dialog** window, each effect listed in the **Keyframe Controller** can have its own keyframed animation.

Regardless of the dialog window, media or effect, the **Keyframe Controller** timeline will include an initial keyframe by default. (That's the little diamond that appears at the beginning of the mini-timeline.)

If no other keyframes are added to your **Keyframe Controller** timeline, this single keyframe will remain the single effect setting, **Pan/Crop** position or **Media Generator** properties setting for your clip. In other words, there will be no animation.

Once the playhead on this mini-timeline is moved to a new position and changes are made to any of the settings in the control panel for that particular effect, media or position, a new diamond-shaped keyframe point will appear at the position of the playhead.

When two or more keyframes appear on a **Keyframe Controller** timeline, the program will automatically generate the transition or animated motion path between these settings, properties or positions.

In other words, you set the "waypoints" – and the program will create the animations between them!

Create an animated Pan/Crop motion path

A **Pan/Crop** motion path is an animation that begins with one view of video clip or still photo, then pans and/or zooms in or out to another view or views.

This effect is also commonly called the Ken Burns effect, named for the legendary filmmaker who uses it so effectively to make still photos seem to come to life in his brilliant documentaries on baseball, jazz and the American Civil War.

Although this animation effect can be used on any visual media, including video, stills and titles, it is used most effectively on still photos whose sizes have been optimized for video resolution (page 130).

One challenge with using this effect on video is that your video's resolution is likely the same as your video project's. This means that, as you zoom into a video clip, you'll be blowing it up beyond its actual resolution – and your results will often look fuzzy or pixelated.

Likewise, you can also use the **Pan/Crop** to animate a title on your timeline. However, you may find you get the cleanest results when you do your size and motion animations right in the **Media Generators** dialog window (see page 165), where you'll be generating animation with raw media rather than working with a pre-generated media clip.

Get to know the Keyframe Controller

The **Keyframe Controller** is the workspace that runs along the bottoms of the **Media Generators, Pan/Crop** and **Video FX** dialog windows.

This workspace includes a number of tools for creating keyframes and navigating its timeline.

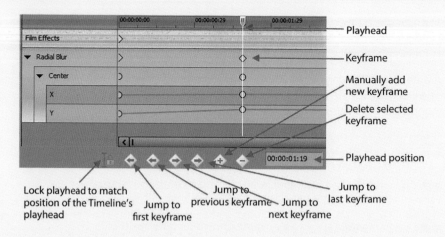

Keyframe points can be easily added, copied, deleted and even moved.

To change a keyframe's position, simply drag it up or down this mini-timeline. The closer your keyframes are together, the faster your animation between them.

Photos, however, make the ideal media for creating motion paths over. If a photo is, say, 2500x1875 pixels in size – and it's being used in a project with 1920x1080 pixel video frame, you'll have enough extra resolution that you will be able to zoom at least a third of the way into a picture before your photo will begin to look fuzzy.

The **Pan/Crop** motion path is the most basic of animations – and perhaps the best effect to use to demonstrate how keyframing animation works. (This animation is also discussed in **Create a motion path over your photo on page 133.**)

1 Open the Pan/Crop tool

Click on the **Event Pan/Crop** button on the right side of a video clip or photo on your timeline.

Note that this tool also appears on the **Track Header**, where it is called the **Track Motion** tool. It's function is similar – but it is applied there to an entire video track rather than an individual event clip. A common use for **Track Motion** might be to resize an entire video sequence at once in order to crop a side.

2 Set an initial position for your view

There are a number of ways to define the area that will appear in your video frame, including numerically (using the properties panel along the left side of the **Pan/Crop** dialog window). But the most intuitive way is to drag the **Selection Box** (the dotted line rectangle with the "F" in the middle) so that it frames the area you'd like to fill your video frame.

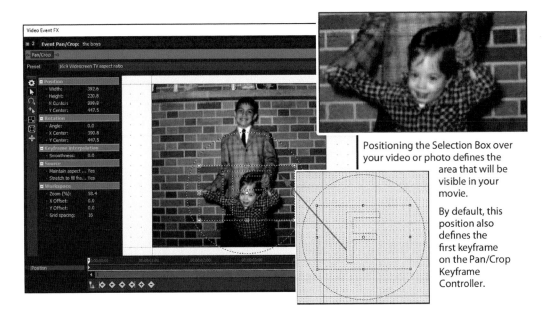

Positioning the Selection Box over your video or photo defines the area that will be visible in your movie.

By default, this position also defines the first keyframe on the Pan/Crop Keyframe Controller.

The program transitions between the two keyframe settings to create an animated pan and zoom motion path.

Drag on the **Selection Box** and its corner handles to create the initial view of your video clip or still photo.

If your **Timeline Cursor** (playhead) is positioned over your clip on your timeline, the results of your settings will be displayed in the program's **Preview** window.

Using the **Selection Box** to create a view position can be a little challenging at first. It seems to function a little counter-intuitively, since the *smaller* the **Selection Box** in the **Pan/Crop** dialog window the *larger* your video or still will appear in your **Preview** window.

It's often easiest to think of the **Selection Box** as a framing box for what will appear in your movie's video frame. Framing a smaller area of your video or still causes that small area to fill your video frame.

The **Selection Box** can be repositioned, resized and/or rotated.

> **To reposition the Selection Box**, click and drag on it.
>
> **To resize the Selection Box**, click and drag in or out on the box's corner handles.
>
> **To rotate the Selection Box**, click and drag within the circular area outside the box's rectangular frame.

The **Preset** drop-down menu at the top of the dialog window includes a number of pre-set positions for the **Selection Box**. The **(Default)** preset will set the **Selection Box's** position so that your video or still fills, and is centered within, your video frame.

By setting the **Zoom** percent listed in the **Workspace** properties, you can get a closer or wider view of the area you're working with. You can also click to select the **Magnifying Glass** tool along the upper left of the dialog window or zoom in and out using the roller on your mouse.

The **Zoom** setting does not in any way affect the actual *position* of the **Pan/Crop**, of course. It merely changes your view of the workspace.

You can also move this workspace up, down, left or right by clicking on and dragging the grid background outside the **Selection Box**.

3   Define a second position for the Selection Box

Drag the **Keyframe Controller** playhead to a new position or to the end of the clip's mini-timeline.

Change the view of your video clip or still by changing the size and/or position of the **Selection Box** – either numerically, in the properties listings, or by dragging on the **Selection Box**, as in **Step 2**.

A new, diamond-shaped keyframe point will automatically be generated at the playhead's position on the mini-timeline adjacent to your effect's listing in the **Keyframe Controller**. This keyframe represents your new **Pan/Crop** settings.

And *voila*! You've created a simple **Pan/Crop** motion path. The program will now create the transitional animation between your defined views.

You can add as many keyframes as needed to your **Keyframe Controller** timeline – and you can reposition those keyframes closer to or further from each other by dragging on them.

As illustrated in the sidebar on page 225, the closer your keyframes are to each other, the faster the animation between them.

Interpolate your keyframes

Interpolation defines how your transition or animation moves from keyframe to keyframe. A keyframe's interpolation can be set by **right-clicking** on the keyframe.

By default, this interpolation is set to **Linear**, a direct movement from one keyframe setting to the next. Other options include:

Fast begins as a fast animation, then eases in as it approaches the next keyframe.

Slow eases out, then speeds up as it approaches the next keyframe.

Smooth eases out, then speeds up, then slows and eases in as it approaches the next keyframe.

Sharp begins as a fast animation, then slows, then speeds up again as it approaches the next keyframe.

Hold maintains the current keyframe's setting right up to the next keyframe – then abruptly changes.

Some interpolations can also be manually set using **Curves**, as discussed on page 234.

Keyframe a Video FX animation

The **Keyframe Controller** that runs along the bottom of the **Video FX** dialog window provides the tools for you to create animations from your video effects. It is opened by clicking on the **Animate** button in the lower left corner of the dialog window.

These animations can be based on any of the effect's properties. In other words, not only can you animate the size and shape of the elements in your effect, but you can also animate your effect to change intensity, color, size, rotation, center, etc.

These animations can be applied to individual media clips, event clips on your timeline, a video track or even to your entire movie. (See page 179.)

If more than one effect has been added to the event, track or movie's **Plug-In Chain** (see **Multiply effects in a chain** on page 188), you will animate each effect separately on the **Keyframe Controller**.

To animate an effect to change settings over time:

1 **Open the Video FX dialog window**

   When you first apply an effect or effects to a media clip, event, track or movie, the **Video FX** dialog window automatically opens.

   If it is not open, you can open the **Video FX** dialog for an event, track or movie by clicking on the appropriate **FX** button. (When an effect has been added to one of these clips or sequences, this button will be light blue.) To open the **Video FX** dialog for a media clip, **right-click** on the clip in your **Project Media** panel and select **Media FX**.

2 **Create the initial settings for your effect**

   Adjust and customize your video effect, as on described on page 187. (If you have more than one effect in a **Plug-In Chain**, click to select the effect you want to create the animation for in the **Plug-In Chain** listing along the top of the **Video FX** dialog window.)

   Click the **Animate** button to open the **Keyframe Controller** timeline.

To open the Keyframe Controller timeline for an effect, click the Animate button for an individual property or,

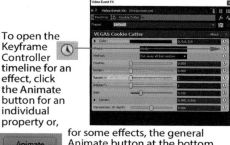

for some effects, the general Animate button at the bottom left of the FX panel.

The **Preset** drop-down menu at the top of the dialog window includes a number of pre-set looks for your effect. Your settings will automatically serve as the initial keyframe for your animation.

3 **Define a second keyframe**

   Drag the **Keyframe Controller** playhead to a new position on the clip's mini-timeline.

   Change your effect's settings. A new, diamond-shaped keyframe point will automatically be generated at the playhead's position on the mini-timeline adjacent to your effect's listing in the **Keyframe Controller**. This keyframe represents your new effect settings.

When you play this clip or sequence on your timeline, you should see a smooth transition from your first set of effect settings to the next.

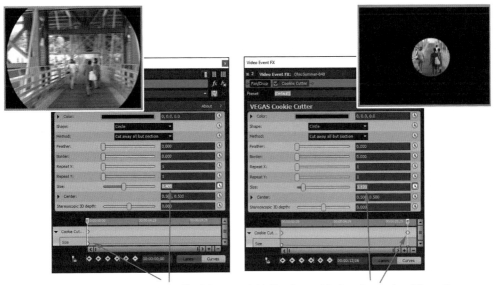

Your initial Video FX settings automatically define your initial keyframe. Moving the playhead down the Keyframe Controller timeline and then changing any settings (in my case, changing the size and center point location of the Cookie Cutter Circle effect) automatically generates a new keyframe.

You can add as many keyframes as needed to your **Keyframe Controller** timeline – and you can reposition those keyframes closer to or further from each other by dragging on them.

As discussed in the sidebar on page 216, the closer your keyframes are to each other, the faster the animation between them.

Create an animated transition

Using keyframes to create an animated effect, you can change virtually any video effect into a custom-designed transition.

For instance, apply the **Magix Swirl** effect to an event clip. Then, from the **Preset** drop-down menu, you select **Reset to None**. The effect will show no change on the clip.

Then go to approximately a second from the beginning or end of your clip on the **Keyframe Controller** timeline and manually create a keyframe (as described in **Get to know the Keyframe Controller** on page 222). This keyframe will lock the "**None**" effect's setting up to that point and will mark the beginning of your transition segment.

Now go all the way to the beginning or end of your clip and set the **Amount** and **Scaling** sliders to 1.00. This will give you a full-on **Swirl** – and it will create a swirling transition between your keyframes. Apply the opposite animation to the adjacent event clip and your video will seem to swirl out from one clip and then swirl in from the next!

Other effects that can produce custom transitions include the **Cookie Cutter, Deform, Gaussian Blur** and **Pixelate**.

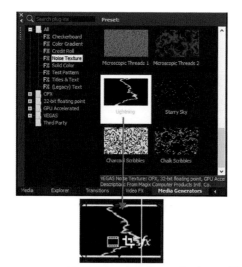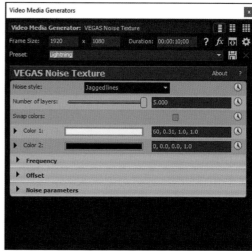

Media Generator clips can be dragged from the Media Generators preset window to your timeline, where they can be modified and customized in the Video Media Generators dialog window.

Keyframe a Generated Media animation

The **Media Generators** window shares the tabbed windows in the upper left of the program's interface with the **Project Media, Explorer, Transitions** and **Video FX** windows.

When a **Media Generators** template is dragged from this window to your timeline, a **Video Media Generators** dialog window will open, in which you can customize virtually every element of the text or design. (For more information on using **Media Generators** templates to create titles, see **Customize a Generated Media title** on page 163.)

Every property of a **Video Media Generators** clip can be animated with keyframes.

This means you can use keyframes to transition your **Generated Media** clip to animate between positions in a video frame or you can use keyframes to create a transition in size, color, background, shape, etc.

Any settings you make in a **Generated Media** clip's control panel can be keyframed to create a motion or transition in the clip's settings!

For instance, if you were to drag the **Large Tiles** template from the **Media Generators** window to your timeline, you could use keyframes to create an animation in which this design of approximately 10 squares by 8 squares morphs into a design of four square by three squares – and you can even morph this design from black and white squares to green and blue squares in the process!

You can also create animations in which, for instance, a title changes size, position and even color over the course of the clip.

Media Generator clips are customized and their animations are keyframed in the **Video Media Generators** dialog window:

> **The Video Media Generators dialog window opens automatically** when you first add a Media Generator clip to your timeline.

> **The window can be re-opened** by clicking on the **Generated Media** button on the right side of the event/clip on your timeline.

Create a Generated Media graphic animation

To demonstrate how to create a graphic animation from a **Generated Media** clip, we'll create a lightning bolt that appears briefly then disappears.

1 **Add the Lightning Bolt Noise Texture to your timeline**

From the **Noise Texture** category on the **Media Generators** window, select the **Lightning Bolt** preset and drag it to your timeline.

It will appear, by default, as a 10-second event clip, and the **Video Media Generators** dialog window will open.

2 **Set Noise Style to Smooth**

From the **Noise Style** drop-down menu along the top of the control panel, select **Fractal - Smooth**.

If your **Timeline Cursor** (playhead) is positioned over the event clip on your timeline, you should see only the black background and no lightning in the program's **Preview** window.

3 **Create an initial keyframe for your effect**

Click the **Animate** button to open the **Video Media Generator's Keyframe Controller** mini-timeline.

Select the Noise Style Preset to Smooth (which means no lightning, at this point), and then click the Animate button to open the Keyframe Controller mini-timeline.

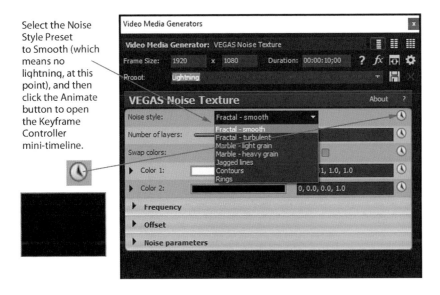

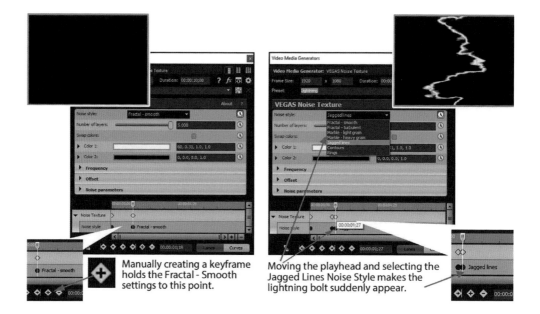

Manually creating a keyframe holds the Fractal - Smooth settings to this point.

Moving the playhead and selecting the Jagged Lines Noise Style makes the lightning bolt suddenly appear.

4   Create a keyframe to start the lightning bolt

Move the playhead on the **Keyframe Controller** timeline along the bottom of the **Video Media Generators** dialog window until it is at the point at which you'd like your lightning bolt to begin.

Click the button along the bottom of the **Keyframe Controller** to manually create a diamond-shaped keyframe at the position of the playhead.

This keyframe represents the end of the **Fractal - Smooth** settings for the effect.

5   Add lightning bolt

Move the playhead on the **Keyframe Controller** about half a second to the right.

Select **Jagged Lines** from **Noise Style** drop-down menu.

A lightning bolt will appear in the **Preview** window, and a little diamond-shaped keyframe will be added to the **Keyframe Controller** timeline.

6   Create lightning bolt movement

Move the playhead on the **Keyframe Controller** just a bit more to the right.

Click the **Animation** button to the right of the **Progress (in Degrees)** slider to add movement to the lightning bolt and adjust the slider to about 9 degrees. A new keyframe will be added to the **Keyframe Controller** timeline.

7   End lightning bolt

Move the playhead on the **Keyframe Controller** just a bit more to the right.

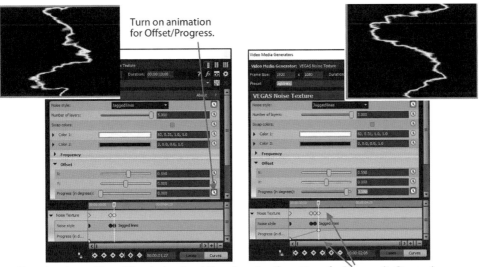

Turn on animation for Offset/Progress.

Changing the position of the playhead and then changing the settings for Progress (in Degrees) adds animated movement (and another keyframe) to the lightning bolt effect.

Set the **Noise Style** drop-down back to **Fractal - Smooth**. A new keyframe will be added to the **Keyframe Controller** timeline representing the end of the lightning animation.

When you play your clip on the timeline, you should see a lightning bolt that suddenly appears, wiggles, then vanishes – like a real lightning bolt! (By the way, if you set **Color 2** to 0% opacity, the background of this clip will be transparent, so you can overlay it onto another video.)

To speed up or slow down the animation, you can drag the keyframe positions farther from or closer to each other. You can also interpolate the keyframe animations, as discussed in the sidebar on page 225.

Naturally, this effect is much more effective with a good, loud sound effect!

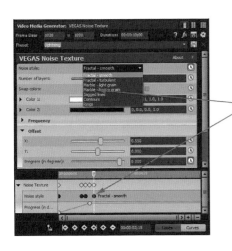

Finally, finish the lightning bolt animation by moving the playhead a few frames further to the right and selecting the Fractal-Smooth (no lightning) Noise Style to create an end keyframe.

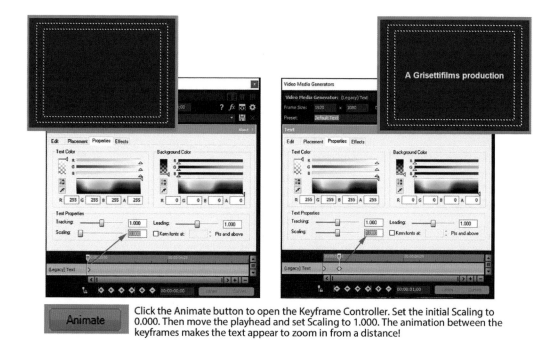

Click the Animate button to open the Keyframe Controller. Set the initial Scaling to 0.000. Then move the playhead and set Scaling to 1.000. The animation between the keyframes makes the text appear to zoom in from a distance!

Create a Generated Media "Legacy" Text animation

Keyframes can be used to create animations as well as to create shifts in color, size and any other properties of your title or its background.

To demonstrate the animation possibilities, we'll create a **Media Generator** title clip in which the text appears to zoom in over a blue background – then the blue background dissolves to transparency, the text remaining on-screen over a video background.

1 **Add a Media Generators Text clip to your timeline**

From the **(Legacy) Text** category on the **Media Generators** window, select the **Solid Background** preset and drag it to your timeline.

It will appear, by default, as a 10-second event clip, and the **Video Media Generators** dialog window will open.

2 **Create your title's main look**

Under the **Edit** tab on the **Video Media Generators** dialog widow, type in your title's text, as described in **Customize a Generated Media title** on page 163.

Set your text's font, size and styles then, under the **Properties** tab on this dialog window, customize your text's color, tracking, etc.

3 **Open the Keyframe Controller mini-timeline**

Click the **Animate** button on the **Video Media Generators** dialog window.

If the **Timeline Cursor** (playhead) is positioned over the clip on your timeline, any changes you make will be displayed in the **Preview** window.

4   Set up your title's initial keyframe

Select a color for your background and ensure that the **Opacity** slider (left of the color picker) is set to 100%, as indicated in the illustration.

So that the text will zoom in, slide the **Scaling** slider for the **Text Properties** to 0.000. (Your text will shrink to nothingness.)

5   Open the Keyframe Controller mini-timeline

Click the **Animate** button in the lower left of the **Video Media Generators** dialog window to open the **Keyframe Controller** mini-timeline.

6   Animate your title

On the **Keyframe Controller** timeline that runs along the bottom of the **Video Media Generators** dialog window, move the playhead about half a second to the right.

Move the **Scaling** slider for **Text Properties** to 1.000 (or whatever is necessary) so that your title fills your **Preview** window's **Title Safe Area** (see page 155).

As illustrated at the top of the facing page, a new diamond-shaped keyframe will automatically be created on the **Keyframe Controller** mini-timeline, at the position of the playhead, representing this new setting.

Create an animation on a Titles & Text template

The principles for creating a keyframed animation on a **Titles & Text** template are essentially the same as those for creating an animation on a **(Legacy Plug-In) Title** template. However, the interface is slightly different.

The new Titles & Text Media Generator template has a slightly different animation workspace, which is launched by clicking on the clock icon to the right of any of the title's properties.

The function of this workspace is, however, virtually the same as in the legacy Keyframe Controller, except that it includes more advanced interpolation tools.

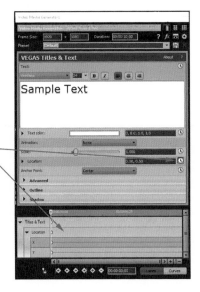

The main difference is that the animation workspace on the **Titles & Text** templates is launched by clicking on the clock icon to the right of each property rather than the **Animation** button. This means that animations can be controlled separately for each individual property.

The animation workspace is also slightly different, and it includes a higher-level tool for creating custom keyframe interpolations. (For more information, see **Create a custom interpolation with Curves** on the next page.)

7   Fade out the background

Move the playhead on the **Keyframe Controller** to the right on the mini-timeline.

In the **Background Color Properties**, drag the **Opacity** level slider to 0.000 (or type 0.000 in the **A** [for "alpha," or transparency] box under the color picker).

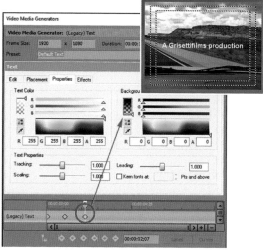

A new keyframe will be created at the position of the playhead on the **Keyframe Controller** timeline representing a transparent background for your title.

If your title clip is on a video track above another clip, the lower track's video will be now seen behind the text.

If there is no video on the track below the title, lowering the **Opacity** level will make the background appear black.

When you play your clip, you will see a plain blue background – then your text will suddenly seem to zoom in from a distance.

Moving the playhead and changing background opacity to 0.000 fades the background until is it transparent/black.

The background will then slowly fade from blue to transparent (or black).

Create a custom interpolation using Curves

You may notice that many of the **FX** and **Media Generators** dialog windows include two buttons in the lower right corner labeled **Lanes** and **Curves**.

These are keyframe interpolation tools (see the sidebar on page 225), but they are only available for a few effects and properties (e.g., the **Location** property of a **Titles & Text** template).

To activate this tool, click to select a keyframe on the **Titles & Text Keyframe Controller** timeline.

Click the **Curves** button to switch interpolation modes.

When in the **Curves** mode, **right-clicking** on a keyframe and selecting the **Manual** option activates a Bezier tool for customizing the variations of speed and motion between keyframes.

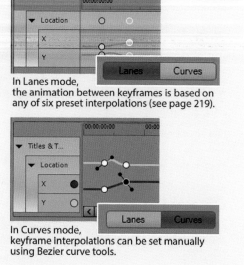

In Lanes mode, the animation between keyframes is based on any of six preset interpolations (see page 219).

In Curves mode, keyframe interpolations can be set manually using Bezier curve tools.

Use Video Envelopes to set levels at specific points

Envelopes are animations or changes that are keyframed to entire video tracks. They're called envelopes because, rather than these changes being applied to individual event clips, they're applied to a video or audio track and the changes shape how all of the clips inside it are affected.

Audio Envelopes are often used to raise and lower your audio tracks' volume levels at specific points or to balance or mix the sound levels of several tracks relative to each other. (For more information see **Use Audio Envelopes to adjust audio levels at specific points** on page 142.)

There are two video properties that can be adjusted and keyframed at various levels for a track of video using **Video Envelopes**.

   Fade to Color affects the overall level of color applied to the clips on your video track. Raising its levels shifts all of your clips' colors to white; lowering it shifts all of your video's colors to black.

   Composite Level sets the opacity level for the video on this track. By default this level is 100% – which means that the video on this track is 100% opaque (0% transparent). By lowering the level of this envelope, you can reduce your track all the way down to 0% opacity (100% transparent).

Envelopes can be used to change these levels, overall, for an entire video track. Or, using keyframes on a **Video Envelope** (or on an **Audio Envelope**), you can set these properties at specific levels at specific points in your movie.

To keyframe a **Composite Level Video Envelope**.

1   **Turn on a track's Composite Level Envelope**

   Select a video track.

   From the **Insert** menu at the top of the program's interface, select **Video Envelopes** and, on the sub-menu, **check** the option for **Track Composite Level**.

   You can also turn on this **Video Envelope** by **right-clicking** on a video **Track Header** and selecting **Insert/Remove Envelope** – then, from the sub-menu, checking the **Composite Level** option.

   A heavy purple line will appear along the top of the video track, as illustrated on the following page. This line is the **Composite Level Video Envelope**.

   When you hover your mouse over this heavy blue line, the cursor will become a hand with a pointed finger.

   If you click on this line and drag it down, you will lower the opacity level of the video track.

If you have video on a track below this track, lowering the opacity will reveal that video through this track's transparency.

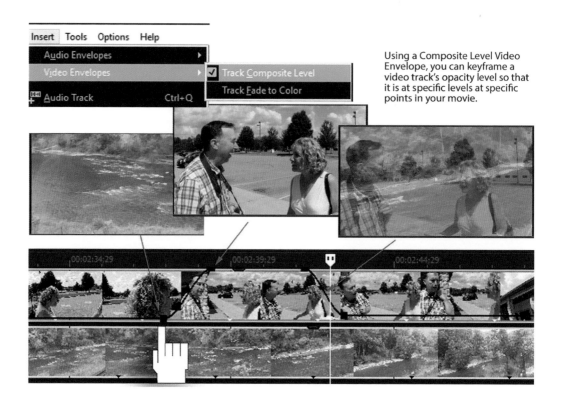

Using a Composite Level Video Envelope, you can keyframe a video track's opacity level so that it is at specific levels at specific points in your movie.

If you do not have video on a video track below, lowering the opacity will fade your video track to black.

2   **Keyframe a Composite Level**

Double-click on this line to create a keyframe point.

Drag the keyframe up or down to the level you'd like it to represent, as illustrated above.

3   **Create additional Composite Level keyframes**

Double-click on other places on this line to create as many keyframes as needed to create **Composite Levels** – various levels of opacity and transparency – at specific points on your timeline.

The result of this keyframing is a video track with various levels of transparency at specific points on the timeline.

Although this tool can be used to create fade ins and fade outs for your video, it's probably not the most common way to create this effect. That type of transition is more often created with the **Fade In** or **Fade Out** tool for an individual event clip (page 84) or a **Cross-Fade** transition (page 206).

Audio Envelopes are commonly used to control and mix the volume levels of audio tracks at specific points in your movie, as discussed on page 142.

Lock your keyframes to your clips or your timeline

Whether you're creating keyframes for an **Audio Envelope** or a **Video Envelope**, you can select whether these keyframe points are locked to the timeline or to the individual event clips.

This setting can be found under the **Options** menu at the top of the program's interface.

When the option **Lock Envelopes to Events** is unchecked, envelopes and their keyframes are locked to the timeline itself. This means that, if you move the event clips on your timeline left or right, the keyframed envelope line will remain in place on the **Timeline Ruler**.

However, when the option **Lock Envelopes to Events** is checked, any keyframes you create on a **Video** or **Audio Envelope** will shift right or left along with your clips as you edit.

When you select the option to Lock Envelopes to Events, any keyframes you add to an audio or video envelope remain locked to the event clip. This means that, if you move a clip on your timeline or even insert a clip between two event clips, the keyframe points themselves will shift positions or stretch the envelope between them so that the keyframes remain in position over the event clips.

Adding Markers for DVD or BluRay Disc

Other Timeline Markers

Optimizing Video Output for Disc Projects

Chapter 16

Prep Your Movie for Output to DVD or BluRay Disc

Putting your movie onto a disc

One of the most popular ways to distribute your movie is on a disc, sharing it on DVD or BluRay disc.

Vegas Movie Studio Platinum makes it very easy to prepare your movie for output to DVD Architect.

Vegas Movie Studio is a video editing program. It is primarily designed to take raw camcorder footage, edit it, add effects and transitions to it and then output it in a variety of ways.

DVD Architect is a disc authoring program. It is designed to take finished video, add menus and scene markers to it and then output it as a DVD or BluRay disc.

The two programs are designed to work together to create a DVD or BluRay disc. Your work should flow from one program to the other, taking advantage of the tools that each offers to handle its portion of your project.

Although DVD Architect can work with a variety of media, you'll get the best results – and the most efficient workflow – if you export your finished video from Vegas Movie Studio to DVD Architect in the most ideal source format possible. Fortunately, Vegas Movie Studio Platinum includes tools that make doing this as automatic as possible.

There are two types of playable discs:

DVDs. DVDs hold 4.7 gigabytes of data. (Dual-layer DVDs hold 8.5 gigabytes.) DVDs are designed to store standard definition (720x480 pixel) video. A 4.7 gigabyte DVD can hold approximately 80 minutes of full-quality video.

BluRay discs. BluRays hold 25 gigabytes of data. That's about 120 minutes of high-definition (1920x1080 pixel) video. Dual-layer BluRays discs hold about twice that.

Regions and other uses for Timeline Markers

Although the most common reason for adding **Markers** to your timeline is to create **Scene/ Chapter Markers** for your DVDs, it's not the *only* reason for using **Markers** in your project.

Many editors use **Markers** in larger projects as "bookmarks" to help them quickly locate certain segments in their movie.

When you click on an orange **Marker** flag, your **Timeline** playhead will jump right to it.

In addition to **Markers**, you can create **Regions** to "bookmark" certain segments of your movie project. Unlike **Markers**, **Regions** define both the beginning and end of a segment.

To create a **Region**, select a segment of your timeline, as described in **Create a Loop Region** on page 97. Then, from the **Insert** menu, select **Region** (or simply type **R**).

You can redefine a **Region** by clicking and dragging on either the green beginning or ending flags along the top of the **Timeline** window and dragging it to a new position.

Double-click on the green flag to redefine the **Region** area.

Region markers defining a timeline region.

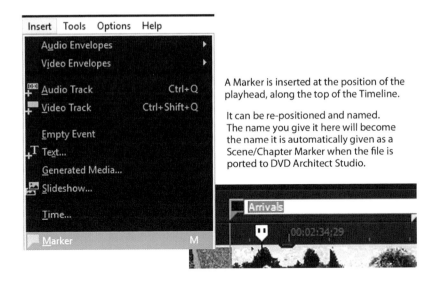

A Marker is inserted at the position of the playhead, along the top of the Timeline.

It can be re-positioned and named. The name you give it here will become the name it is automatically given as a Scene/Chapter Marker when the file is ported to DVD Architect Studio.

There are also hybrid uses for these discs. You can, for instance, put BluRay video on a DVD. However, a DVD can hold only about 20-30 minutes of full-quality, hi-def video – and this disc can only be played on BluRay disc players (*and not even all of them*).

But, for the most part, DVDs are assumed to be standard-definition video discs, while BluRays are assumed to be high-definition video discs.

Add and save Scene/Chapter Markers to your video project

Markers can be added to your video project's timeline in Vegas Movie Studio. If the file is saved with the option selected to save these **Markers** to the video, then, when the file is opened in DVD Architect, these **Markers** will automatically appear as **Scene/Chapter Markers**.

Scene/Chapter Markers allow your viewer to jump to specific points in your video, or they can be used to build **Scene Selection Menus**, from which your viewer can navigate directly to particular scenes in your movie.

To add a **Marker** to your video project's timeline:

1   **Position your Timeline Cursor (playhead)**

Position the **Timeline's** playhead to the approximate spot on your timeline that you'd like your **Marker** to appear. (Don't worry if you're not on the exact spot. The **Marker** can easily be dragged to any position on the **Timeline** after it's created.

2   **Create a Marker**

From the **Insert** menu at the top of the interface, select **Marker** (or just press **M** on your keyboard), as illustrated above.

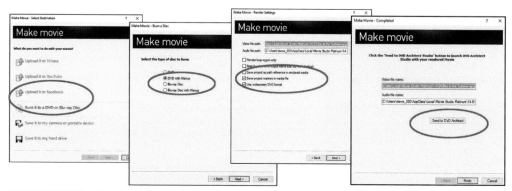

 Select the Make Movie option and save your movie as a DVD-ready or BluRay Disc-ready file. To send your video to DVD Architect for finishing, select one of the "with menus" options. Also ensure that the option to Save Project Markers in Media File is selected to include Markers.

An orange **Marker** will be added to your timeline, at the position of the **Timeline** playhead.

3   Name your Marker

Type a name in the blank to the right of the **Marker** (as illustrated on page 241). The name you provide here will also appear, by default, as the name of your **Scene/Chapter Marker** when your video is ported to DVD Architect.

To port your **Markers**, along with your video, to DVD Architect:

4   Make Movie

Click on the **Make Movie** button at the top of the program's interface, or select **Make Movie** from the **Project** menu.

On the first **Make Movie** dialog window that opens, select the option to **Burn To a DVD or BluRay Disc**. Click **Next**.

On the next **Make Movie** dialog window, select either the **DVD with Menus** or **BluRay Disc with Menus** option. Click **Next**.

5   Save your Markers to the video file

On the next **Make Movie** dialog window, **check** the option to **Save Project Markers In Media File**.

You may also browse to select a new location to save your video and audio files, if you'd like.

Click **Next**.

6   Send to DVD Architect

On the final **Make Movie** dialog window, click the button labeled **Send to DVD Architect**.

The Markers you add in Vegas Movie Studio are exported as metadata and become Scene/Chapter Markers in your DVD Architect project (bottom).

The program will transcode the file so that it is the ideal source format for your DVD or BluRay project. A new DVD Architect project file will open and your media will appear as a button on the main menu page.

If you **double-click** on this button in DVD Architect's Workspace window, the video will open in DVD Architect's **Timeline** window. Your **Markers** should be visible as **Scene/Chapter Markers** along the top of the **Timeline**, as illustrated above.

Edit and remove your Markers

Markers can easily be repositioned, renamed and removed from your timeline.

To rename a Marker, **right-click** on the orange **Marker** flag and select **Rename**.

To change the location of a Marker, click and drag on it.

To remove a Marker completely, **right-click** on the orange **Marker** flag and select **Delete**, or press the **Delete** key on your keyboard.

To remove all Markers and Regions from your timeline, **right-click** on the gray area above your timeline where the **Marker** flags reside (technically called the **Marker Area**) and select **Remove All**.

It's important to note that **Markers** and **Regions** are locked to the **Timeline** itself, not the individual clips – so, as events are added and removed, the **Markers** will remain in place.

For this reason, it's probably best to not add any **Markers** until your movie's editing is complete.

Markers can be renamed or removed one at a time or can be removed all at once via right-click menu options.

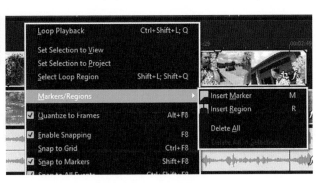

Output your video to a DVD or BluRay disc

Although DVD Architect can work with a variety of file formats, you'll get the best performance with the program if the video you're providing is of the optimal file format and codec. In fact, if the video you send to DVD Architect is of the ideal format – and you aren't trying to squeeze too much onto your disc – DVD Architect won't even need to transcode or recompress the video when it creates your DVD or BluRay disc. And this can reduce your DVD or BluRay production time to a few minutes rather than several minutes or even hours.

Fortunately, when you select the proper output options in Vegas Movie Studio, the program will automatically create the ideal video for your DVD Architect project.

For DVDs, the ideal source video is a standard definition (720x480 pixel) MPEG-2. (720x576 pixels in the PAL TV format.) Because television video is based on non-square pixels (see below), this video output's resolution is the same whether you're working with a standard 4:3 or a 16:9 widescreen video. Vegas Movie Studio outputs this video as a separate video (MPG) and audio (AC3) file.

For BluRay discs, the ideal source video is a 1920x1080 pixel MPEG-2. Vegas Movie Studio outputs this video as a separate video (M2V) and audio (W64) file.

When you follow the prompts in the dialog windows, Vegas Movie Studio not only produces these optimized video and audio files, but it even loads them right into a DVD Architect project automatically!

1   **Make Movie**

Click on the **Make Movie** button at the top of the program's interface, or select **Make Movie** from the **Project** menu.

Understand non-square pixels

Pixels are the tiny blocks of color that make up your digital photos and video.

For reasons that date back to the early days of television, the vast majority of standard definition video is made up of **non-square pixels**. This is true for PAL as well as NTSC video.

In standard NTSC video, these pixels are approximately 90% as wide as they are tall. Thus a 720x480 pixel video image becomes a 4:3 aspect ratio video (the equivalent of a 640x480 *square-pixel* video). A widescreen video is made up of the *same number of pixels* – however, because these pixels are 120% as wide as they are tall, a 720x480 pixel widescreen video has a 16:9 aspect ratio.

Many high-definition camcorders shoot their video in 1440x1080 *non-square* pixels. This produces exactly the same size video as a cam that shoots in 1920x1080 *square* pixels.

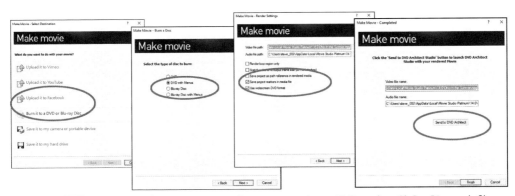

Make Movie Select the Make Movie option and save your movie as a DVD-ready or BluRay Disc-ready file. To send your video to DVD Architect for finishing, select one of the "with menus" options. Also ensure that the option to Save Project Markers in Media File is selected to include Markers.

On the first **Make Movie** dialog window that opens, select the option to **Burn To a DVD or BluRay Disc**.

Click **Next**.

You can burn a DVD or BluRay disc directly from Vegas Movie Studio. This disc will not have a menu system, however, and it will auto-play your movie when you load it into a disc drive or disc player.

To add a menu system to your discs, select the option to create your DVD or BluRay "**with Menus**." This will forward your finished project to DVD Architect for authoring.

If the "**with Menus**" options are grayed-out, it is because the format of your movie is not compatible with DVD Architect. In this case, check your **Project Properties** and ensure your video is not set up as a 3D project (page 85).

The Muvipix.com Guide to DVD Architect

If you'd like step-by-step instructions for using every tool in DVD Architect – as well as some tips for making the program do some very cool tricks – be sure to check out our *Muvipix.com Guide to DVD Architect*.

It's available on Amazon.com and at Muvipix.com.

For more information as well as some tutorials demonstrating the product, see Muvipix.com/vms14.php

The Muvipix.com Guide to
DVD Architect
Steve Grisetti

On the next **Make Movie** dialog window, if you would like to use your **Timeline Markers** as DVD or BluRay **Scene/Chapter Markers** (see page 241), check the option to **Save Project Markers In Media File**.

You may also browse to select a new location to save your video and audio files, if you'd like. Click **Next**.

2   **Send to DVD Architect**

On the final **Make Movie** dialog window, click the button labeled **Send to DVD Architect,** as illustrated on the previous page.

The program will transcode the file so that it is the ideal source format for your DVD or BluRay project. A new DVD Architect project file will open and your media will appear as a button on the main menu page.

Manually output DVD-ready or BluRay-ready files

You can, of course, also manually create DVD-ready or BluRay-ready files for your DVD Architect project. These options are made available by clicking the **Make Movie** button, then **Save It to My Hard Drive** – then, on the **Make Movie** option screen, clicking the **Advanced Options** button.

Traditionally, projects are ported from Vegas Movie Studio to DVD Architect as separate audio and video streams, which are combined in your DVD or BluRay project.

Video Stream:

To output a standard definition DVD-ready video stream:

Select the Main Concept MPEG-2 **DVD Architect Video Stream**. If your project is widescreen, be sure to select that output option.

To output a high-definition BluRay-ready video stream:

Select the Main Concept **Blu-Ray 1920x1080 25 Mbps Video Stream** (60i for NTSC, 50i for PAL).

Audio Stream:

To output the audio stream for your DVD or BluRay, select Dolby Digital **Stereo DVD** or, if your project includes 5.1 audio, **5.1 Surround DVD**. (Some people prefer to use Sony Wave64 Stereo or 5.1 audio outputs – although it's a matter of preference, since the results are virtually indistinguishable from the Dolby Digital files.)

If you'd prefer to output simplified files for DVD Architect that include both the audio and video streams in the same file, you can also use these **Render As** options:

Combined DVD-Ready Files: Main Concept MPEG-2 **Program Stream NTSC** or PAL

Combined BluRay-Ready Files: Magix AVC/MVC **AVCHD 1920x1080 60i** or 50i

Outputting Video to Your Computer
Outputting Video for the Web
Creating an Image Sequence
Uploading Video to YouTube
Sharing Your Video Online

Chapter 17
Make Your Movie
Sharing your project with the world

Finally – the edits, titles, effects and transitions are in place. It's time to share your masterpiece with the world!

Vegas Movie Studio includes a number of tools for outputting your finished movie – from outputting it as a DVD or BluRay disc to sharing it on a Web site to outputting it as a video optimized for a smartphone or tablet.

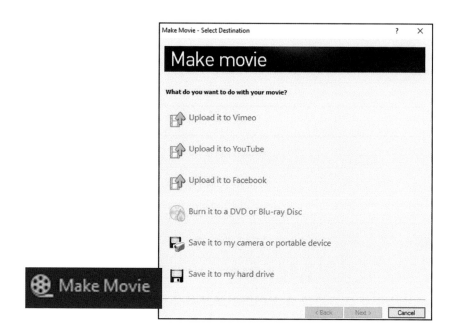

Selecting the right output options can be as important as selecting the right project settings (**Chapter 2**), when it comes to getting the best and most efficient results from your video editing project. This is why we often say you need to start at the end to get to the beginning.

How do you want to deliver your video to your audience? The delivery vehicle you plan to use will determine the best format for your delivery.

Video that's going to be viewed on a television, for instance, is best output as a DVD or BluRay disc. Video that's going to be viewed online is best output as a Windows Media, Quicktime, RealMedia or an MP4 file. Video that's to be viewed on a portable device, such as a Sony PSP, is best saved as an optimized Magix AVC file.

Fortunately, Vegas Movie Studio Platinum makes selecting the best output option as simple as possible. As you follow the screen prompts, the program will automatically provide you the best video format for the particular vehicle or device.

Output your video to a DVD or BluRay disc

Vegas Movie Studio and DVD Architect are designed to work together to create your movie and then build a disc menu system to present your finished movie on disc.

For more information on the best and most efficient way to send your movie to a DVD Architect for production as a DVD or BluRay disc, see **Chapter 16**.

Video output options

The **Make Movie/Save It To My Hard Drive/Advanced,** or **Render As,** screen offers 19 format options for output, nearly half of which are audio formats. This chart lists the best uses for the nine most common video formats.

Image Sequence (BMP, JPG, PNG, TIF, WMPhoto)	Outputs the frames of your video project as a series of still photos in one of five graphics formats. For information on creating and editing an Image Sequence, see page 253.
Main Concept AVC/AAC (MP4)	Saves your movie in the highly-compressed AVC/MP4 format. Main Concept is one of the most popular H.264 compressors, and it includes templates for producing video for Magix Tablets, iPods, iPads, Apple TV and both standard and high-definition files for the Internet.
Main Concept MPEG-2 (MPG, M2V, M2T, MPA)	The current MPEG standard, these options can be used to output both DVD-quality standard definition video (MPEG) or BluRay-quality high-definition video (M2T). An M2V is a video-only form of high-definition MPEG file and an MPA is an audio-only form. The Main Concept AVC MP4 can also be an excellent format for posting your videos online. This format includes a number of Internet templates that should provide excellent results.
Quicktime 7 (MOV)	Output settings in this category produce Quicktime (MOV) files that are optimized for display on the Internet.
RealMedia 9 (RM)	A Web delivery format that creates a streaming video or audio file. It's not as popular as the WMV and MOV formats, but it is still sometimes found online. The most efficient file for displaying an RM file online uses the 450 Kbps Video Template.
Sony AVC (MP4, M2TS, AVC)	An alternative to the Main Concept AVC option (above), Sony's AVC video matches the standard for all of its products, and it is the best choice for, say, outputting video for a Sony PSP. The AVC high-definition M2TS video is the best format to output your video if you plan to use it in another hi-def video project (See page 251.)
Sony XAVC S (MP4)	Also known as 4K, this is an extremely high-resolution video format, over four times the resolution of hi-def (3840x2160).
Video for Windows (AVI)	AVIs are the Windows video file standard. However, they can be made up of any of hundreds of possible codecs (compression systems). To output a finished video from a standard definition project for use as part of another standard def project, use the NTSC DV or PAL DV Template. (See page 251.) AVIs are rarely output as uncompressed or high-definition video files.
Windows Media Video V11 (WMV)	WMVs are the Windows compressed video file format and the most common format for posting to a Web site. (Less commonly, WMVs are also used as a source format – predominantly for Microsoft products.) To output the most efficient WMV format for displaying online, use the 512 Kbps Template.
XDCAM EX (MP4)	XDCAM EX is Sony's professional high-def camcorder format. Movie Studio outputs XDCAM video as an MP4.

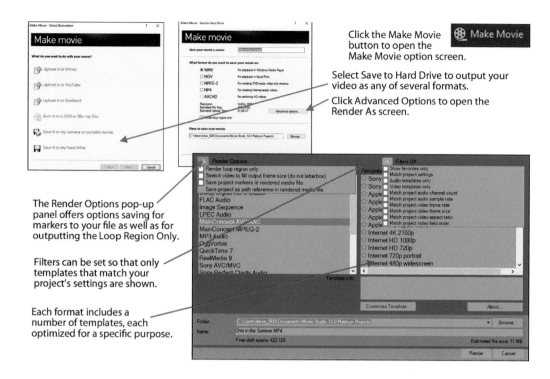

Click the Make Movie button to open the Make Movie option screen.

Select Save to Hard Drive to output your video as any of several formats.

Click Advanced Options to open the Render As screen.

The Render Options pop-up panel offers options saving for markers to your file as well as for outputting the Loop Region Only.

Filters can be set so that only templates that match your project's settings are shown.

Each format includes a number of templates, each optimized for a specific purpose.

Save your movie to your hard drive

There are a number of reasons for saving your movie to your hard drive:

- To save or archive your video in a high-quality format, or to save it for later use in another editing project.
- To finish and render a short video segment so that it can be included in a larger video project.
- To save your video in a format that can be viewed online.
- To save your video in a format that can be viewed on a portable device, such as a smartphone or a tablet.
- To output a segment of your video as individual frames (an "image sequence") in order to apply a complicated video effect.

Each of these output formats have different advantages and results in a file optimized for its specific purpose.

The **Render As** screen, illustrated above, launches when you select the option to **Save It To My Hard Drive** and then **Advanced Options**.

The **Render As** screen can also be reached directly by selecting the option from under the **Project** menu.

Archive a high-quality version of your movie for later re-editing

The native format for a standard definition video project is the DV-AVI. This is one of the formats that Vegas Movie Studio reads in its native format, without needing to re-render. This makes it the ideal format in which to store your standard definition video if you later plan to use it in a video project.

It is, in fact, it is the very format produced when you capture video from a miniDV camcorder. (See page 37.)

Based on the professional DV format, video that streams over FireWire into your computer from a miniDV camcorder arrives virtually unchanged, and the video is stored in the same DV codec that was created by the camcorder itself.

For this reason, in terms of standard definition video, the **DV-AVI** (an AVI using the NTSC DV or PAL DV codec) is considered the universal language of PC-based video editors. It can be used effectively in virtually any Windows-based video editing app.

The high-definition equivalent is the **AVCHD (H.264)**, which produces an M2TS file.

If you want to save your video for later re-editing, or for use in a future project, these are the ideal **Render As** templates to use.

Output finished video for use in a larger project

Likewise, if you're working on your project in shorter segments, the above formats are the ideal output formats for each segment.

Working on a large project in short segments and then mixing together the finished segments is a method most professionals use – particularly when their project includes an effects-heavy sequence or two. It's best to output the finished segments as short movies and then add them to your larger project as fully-rendered sequences.

Output the Loop Region only

A **Loop Region** is a segment of your timeline that you define (see page 97).

Loop Regions have a number of purposes, including defining areas of the timeline that you'd like to render.

Virtually every video output dialog window includes the option to **Render Loop Region Only**.

Selecting this option tells the program to output a finished movie of *only the segment of your timeline that's been defined as the Loop Region*.

Using this option, you can output a short segment from a longer movie. Or, as described on page 253, you can output a brief segment for some intensive special effects work.

Virtually every video output includes the option to output the Loop Region Only of your movie timeline.

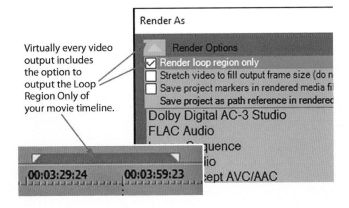

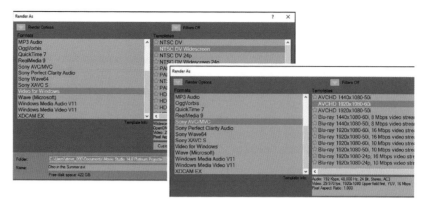

For standard definition video, the ideal format to output your segments to is **Video for Windows (AVI)** using the NTSC DV or PAL DV template. This is the ideal format to use as source media in a project set up for **DV** (see page 28).

For high-definition video, the ideal format to output your segments to is **Sony AVC** using the **AVCHD 1920x1080 60i (NTSC)** or **AVCHD 1920x1080 50i (PAL)** template. The resulting file will be an M2TS video. This is the ideal format to use as source media in a project set up for **AVCHD** (see page 28).

Save your movie in a format that's optimized for online viewing

The most common formats for displaying video online are the **WMV** (Windows Media Video), **MOV** (Quicktime) and the **MP4** (Sony AVC) formats. (Less commonly used is the **RM** [RealMedia] format.) See the chart on page 249.

Because Windows machines represent the vast majority of the world's computers, WMVs were once the most popular format for uploading to a Web site. However, because of the advanced H.264 compression system it uses, **MP4s** are becoming increasingly popular and can often provide even higher quality video in an even smaller file.

That said, the options for creating video for the web in each of these formats is:

WMV (Windows Media Video) or **MOV** (Quicktime) or **RM** (RealMedia Video): 512 Kbps

RM (RealMedia Video): 450 Kbps

Sony AVC (MP4)
Either of the Internet templates

For information about FTP software for posting your videos, see page 264 of the **Appendix**.

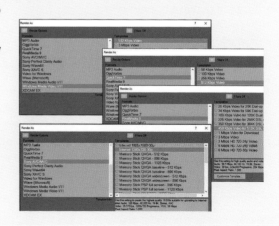

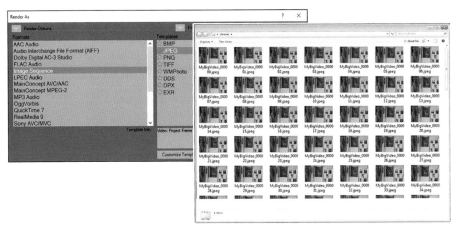

Outputting your video as an Image Sequence saves each frame of video as a separate photo file.

Create an Image Sequence

The **Make Movie** option to output an **Image Sequence** outputs *every frame* of your movie as an individual still photo.

The main purpose for outputting an image sequence is to allow you to create elaborate special effects in a graphics program by working on one frame at a time.

For instance, if you're adding glowing, electronic effects to a light saber battle, you may find that you get the best results when you draw each of the effects onto your movie one frame at a time. (A tedious process, yes, but one that produces amazing results!)

Since videos are made up of between 25 and 30 frames a second, you'll probably want to reserve this feature for outputting short movies or outputting only the **Loop Region** of a movie project (see page 251).

To output your movie as an **Image Sequence**:

1 **Select Make Movie**

   Click on the **Make Movie** button at the top of the program's interface, or select **Make Movie** from the **Project** menu.

2 **Open the Render As dialog screen**

   On the **Make Movie** option screen, click on **Save It To My Hard Drive**.

3 **Save your Image Sequence to your hard drive**

   On the **Render As** dialog window, select the **Output Format** for an **Image Sequence**.

There are a number of still image options for output. JPEGs produce the smallest files. TIFs and BMPs are uncompressed files, and can often produce cleaner, smoother images.

Instructions for converting the images back into a movie are on the following page.

Create a movie from an Image Sequence

Once you've finished adding your effects to the individual frames, you can bring them back into a project as individual frames and then output that as a video.

To create a movie from a sequence of individual photos:

1 **Open a new project**

   Set your project up as a **DV** (standard definition) or an **AVCHD 1920x1080** (hi-def) project.

2 **Set your still image duration to one per frame**

   Go to the **Options** menu and select **Preferences**, as illustrated.

   Under the **Editing** tab, set the **New Still Image Length (Seconds)** to 0.033. This means that each still photo you add will appear on your timeline for approximately one video frame. (For PAL this **Length** will be set to 0.040.)

3 **Import your photos into your project**

   Use **Import Media** to bring your photos into **Project Media** (see page 49).

   Your photos should appear listed, by name, in the same order as they were output from your movie.

4 **Add the photos to your timeline**

   Select all of these photos in the **Project Media** panel (**Ctrl+a**) and drag them to your timeline.

   They should appear on a video track in the same order as they were output from the movie – and they should also be sliver-thin, nearly 30 of them in every second.

5 **Make Movie**

   Output your timeline as either a standard definition **DV-AVI** or a high-definition **AVCHD 1920x1080 M2TS**, as described in **Output video for use in a larger project** on page 251.

Preferences

General | Video | Preview Device | Audio | Audio Device
VST Effects | Editing | Display | CD Settings

☑ Enable looping on events by default
☑ Preserve pitch when stretching audio events
☑ Cut, copy, and delete grouped events
☑ Do not quantize to frames for audio-only edits

JKL / shuttle speed: Medium

Quick fade length for audio events (ms):   10

New still image length (seconds):   0.0333   1 frames at 29.970 fps

Default time between CD tracks: 2:00

Cursor preview duration (seconds):   2.000   60 frames at 29.970 fps

☐ Automatically overlap multiple selected media when added

Cut-to-overlap conversion (seconds):   1.000   30 frames at 29.970 fps

Alignment: Centered On Cut

☑ Time selection envelope fades (ms):   50   1 frames at 29.970 fps

When the New Still Image Length (Seconds) is set to 0.0333, photos added to your timeline will appear for a single video frame.

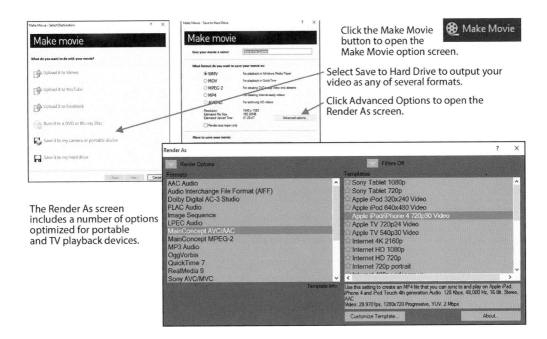

Click the Make Movie button to open the Make Movie option screen.

Select Save to Hard Drive to output your video as any of several formats.

Click Advanced Options to open the Render As screen.

The Render As screen includes a number of options optimized for portable and TV playback devices.

Output your video for a portable device

Vegas Movie Studio includes a number of templates for rendering your video or audio for viewing on a portable device like an iPod, iPad, smart phone or tablet.

To output your movie for a portable device:

1   Select Make Movie

Click on the **Make Movie** button at the top of the program's interface, then select **Save It To My Hard Drive**.

2   Open the Render As dialog screen

On the **Make Movie** option screen, click on **Advanced Options** to open the **Render As** option panel.

3   Select the appropriate output format

On the **Render As** dialog window, select the appropriate format:

For iPads, iPods, Apple TVs, smartphones and tablets, select the appropriate custom template under the **Main Concept AVC/ AAC Output Format**. These formats should, in fact, work for most portable devices, including smart phones.

For Zunes, the ideal format is the **Windows Media Player Output Format** using the **3 Mbps Video** template.

255

Upload your video to Vimeo, YouTube or Facebook

Included with Vegas Movie Studio is a tool for uploading your video directly to Vimeo, YouTube or Facebook. Your video will be sent to each site in an optimized format and will appear complete with search keywords.

To upload your video from Vegas Movie Studio:

1 Select Make Movie

Click on the **Make Movie** button at the top of the program's interface, or select **Make Movie** from the **Project** menu.

2 Select the Upload to Video, YouTube or Upload to Facebook option

On the **Make Movie** dialog window, select the option to **Upload to Vimeo, Upload to YouTube** or **Upload to Facebook**.

The **Upload** dialog window will open.

3 Title and tag your video

Give your video a title and description.

Supply a list of **Tag** or search key words, if the site uses them.

Selecting a **Category** and adding **Tags** can help people locate your video based on its subject matter or whatever other keyword criteria you supply.

You can also select whether your video is available to anyone or only to people you invite to view it.

4 Select Render Quality

Usually you'll want to select the higher render quality. However, at the writing of this book, YouTube has a file size limit of 2 gigabytes (or 15 minutes), so check the **Estimated Upload Size** listed on this dialog window to ensure you don't exceed it.

Loading a higher quality video can also mean that it streams more slowly and may stutter a bit over slower connections or during peak YouTube viewing hours.

So, although you can usually go with the higher quality setting, experience with your particular situation may show you a need to compromise in some cases.

5   **Select the option to Render Loop Region Only**

The **Upload to Vimeo, Upload to YouTube** and **Upload to Facebook** dialog windows include the option to **Render and Upload Loop Region Only**, which allows you to upload only a portion of your movie project. For more information on outputting the **Loop Region** only, see the sidebar on page 251.

If you'd like to send your entire movie to Vimeo, YouTube or Facebook, leave this checkbox unchecked.

The program will prepare an optimized version of your movie for the site.

This could take a few minutes or several minutes, depending on the length of your movie, the speed of your computer and whether your video is standard DV or high-definition video.

Because Vimeo, YouTube and Facebook re-encode any videos you upload, it can take several minutes for your uploaded video to actually appear on the site.

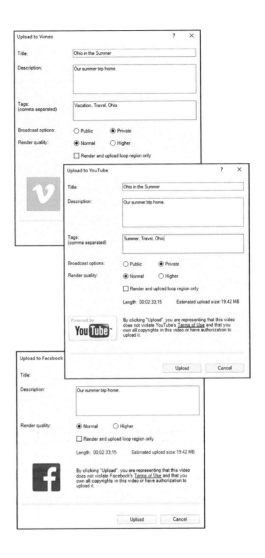

Create an Internet-ready video

In addition to uploading your video files directly to Vimeo, YouTube and Facebook, you can also create an Internet-ready file and load it manually to YouTube, Facebook, Vimeo or any other video sharing site.

To create an Internet-ready MP4, click the **Make Movie** button and select **Save To My Hard Drive**. Then, on the next **Make Movie** option screen, select the **MP4** option.

You can also create a high-resolution Internet-ready MP4 using the **Render As** instructions in the sidebar on page 252.

Save your video back to a miniDV or HDV camcorder

Saving your video back to your camcorder is a great, economical way to archive your project. Once I've finished a video project, I always save one copy as a DV-AVI or HDV video back to my camcorder. This back-up copy is in a full-quality, editable format – just in case I want to access the as-close-to-original-as-possible video for further editing or for use in another project.

You'll note that the two camcorder formats that allow for this kind of back-up are **tape-based**. (Both miniDV and HDV video record to miniDV video cassettes.) Which makes sense, since the tapes themselves can be kept in a cool, dry place as your back-up files.

To send your video back to your tape-based camcorder, first ensure your camcorder includes a VTR Record feature. (Most newer camcorders do not, unfortunately.) Then:

1 **Select the option to Save to My Camera**

   From the **Make Movie** dialog window, select the option to **Save It To My Camera or Portable Device**. Click **Next**.

2 **Select the DV or HDV Camera option**

   On the next dialog window, select either the **DV Camera** or **HDV Camera** option. The program will record your movie to your camcorder in real time over a FireWire connection.

Notable Program Preferences

Notable Project Properties

Set Where Captured Video is Saved

Recommended Computer Maintenance

Great Free Utilities

Proxy Editing Your Video

Keyboard Shortcuts Worth Knowing

Chapter 18

An Appendix

Advanced Vegas Movie Studio 14 tricks

Beyond the basics, there are a host of things worth knowing about how the program works and how to make it work better.

In this chapter we'll even introduce you to a few third-party apps that can work hand-in-hand with Vegas Movie Studio.

Most of this book is about getting to know the various tools in this great little program and learning how each works.

This chapter is about additional information that you may find useful – as well as a few tips and tricks that you may find helpful as you work with Vegas Movie Studio Platinum.

Key program preferences

Preferences determine how the program works. The program's **Preferences** are accessed under the **Options** menu.

Many of these preferences are pretty self-explanatory – particularly those listed as checkable options under the **General** tab.

If, for instance, you'd like the program to automatically open the last project you were working on as it launches, then check the option to **Automatically Open Last Project on Startup**.

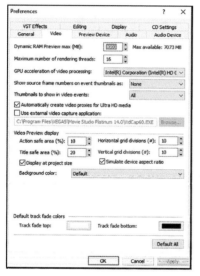

Or, if you'd like the playhead to stop where it's at when you stop your timeline's playback by pressing the **Spacebar** (rather than jumping back to where it was when your playback began – the more traditional way PC-based video editors function), check the option to **Make Spacebar and F12 Play/Pause instead of Play/Stop**.

Here are some other preferences worth knowing about:

The Video tab

As discussed in **Chapter 6**, we recommend that you set **Dynamic RAM Preview Max** to 3000-4000 MB less than whatever **Max Available** is listed to the right of this box. Dynamic RAM is one method of rendering an effects-heavy timeline, as discussed on page 91.

If you'd like to use a capture program other than the one included with Vegas Movie Studio, you can select it by browsing from the option to **Use External Video Capture Application**. We recommend a couple of our favorite video capture programs on page 263.

The Editing tab

As mentioned in the sidebar on page 80, if you're not careful, you can over-extend your clip and unintentionally create a loop rather than a single instance of the video. Unless you intend to create a looping clip, we recommend you uncheck the option to **Enable Looping on Events by Default**.

The **New Still Image Length** preference sets the default duration of any photos you add to your project. 5.000 seconds is the standard. But, as we discuss on page 254, there are situations when you may want your photos to appear as longer or shorter timeline events.

Key project properties

Unlike Program **Preferences, Project Properties** apply only to your current project.

Project preferences are accessed by selecting the **Properties** option under the **Project** menu or by clicking on the **Video Project Properties** button (the cog) on the **Preview** window (see the sidebar on page 155).

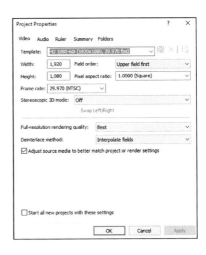

As we discussed in **Chapter 2**, for best results and performance, your project properties should, ideally, match your source video as precisely as possible. (Often, the program sets these automatically based on the first clip you add to your timeline.)

Additionally, we recommend that, under the **Video** tab, you set the **Full-Resolution Rendering Quality** to **Best** and the **Deinterlace Method** to **Interpolate Fields,** and that you **check** the option to **Adjust Source Media to Better Match Project or Render Settings**. These preferences will help smooth out any differences between your project's settings and the specs of your source video.

Under the **Audio** tab, you'll find the option for setting your movie project's audio as **Stereo** or as **5.1 Surround** sound.

Internal preferences

Finally, there are some deeper preferences for controlling how the program functions.

Generally, it's a good idea not to mess with these settings, unless you're sure you know what you're doing. But one preference here can help you out if you're seeing some buggy behavior that no other settings seem to fix.

To access your **Internal** preferences, hold down the **Shift** key as you go to the **Options** menu and select **Preferences**. When the **Preferences** dialog window opens, you'll note an **Internal** tab now included among the others.

Click on the **Internal** tab.

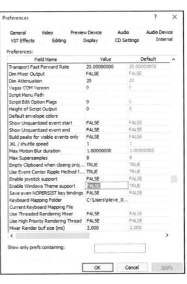

About three-fourths of the way down the list, locate the Field Name listed as **Enable Windows Theme Support**. Change this from TRUE to **FALSE**.

This will change, very slightly, how your program displays. However, it can also resolve some issues related to buggy Windows themes.

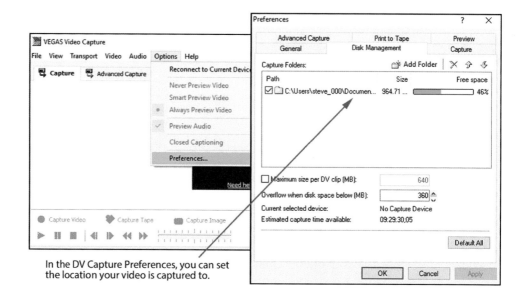

In the DV Capture Preferences, you can set the location your video is captured to.

Set where your captured video is saved to

By default, the video that is captured by the Vegas Movie Studio capture software is stored in your **Documents** folder.

However, it's very simple to change this default storage location.

For MiniDV video

To set the storage location for your captured miniDV footage:

1   **Open the capture utility**

   Click on the **Capture Video** button on the **Project Media** window or select **Capture Video** from the **Project** menu (see page 37).

2   **Select DV from the Capture Video dialog window**

   The Magix **Video Capture** workspace will open.

3   **Open Preferences**

   Go to the **Video Capture** window's **Options** menu and select **Preferences**.

4   **Set the Disk Management location**

   Click on the **Disk Management** tab. The default storage location for your captured video will be listed.

   Double-click on this folder and browse to set a new default location.

HDV video

To set the storage location for your captured miniDV footage:

1   **Open the capture utility**

Click on the **Capture Video** button on the **Project Media** window or select **Capture Video** from the **Project** menu (see page 41).

2   **Select HDV from the Capture Video dialog window**

The **HDV Capture** workspace will open.

3   **Browse to a storage location**

Click the **Browse** button on the right side of the **HDV Capture** dialog window and indicate where you'd like your captured video files saved to (as illustrated on page 42).

Valuable free or low cost tools and utilities

Capture utilities

In the event that Vegas Movie Studio won't capture your video no matter what you do, these free or low-cost tools will capture miniDV and HDV as perfectly compatible video files.

WinDV (free from windv.mourek.cz/) – A great miniDV capture utility with a simple interface.

HDVSplit (free from strony.aster.pl/paviko/hdvsplit.htm) – A great capture utility for HDV video.

Windows MovieMaker – Video captured from a miniDV camcorder into MovieMaker is perfectly compatible with Vegas Movie Studio.

Nero – Sometimes Nero's presence on your computer is the *reason* you can't capture from Vegas Movie Studio. However, if you've got it on your computer, you can use it to do your capture also.

Our favorite free audio editing utility

Audacity (audacity.sourceforge.net) is, hands down, the best *free* audio editing software you'll find anywhere. Easy to use, loaded with preset audio filters and yet extremely versatile.

Audacity can convert audio formats as well as adjust audio levels and "sweeten" your audio's sound. You can also record into it from a microphone or external audio device and edit audio with it. A real must-have freebie that you'll find yourself going to regularly!

It's no substitute for Sound Forge, of course – but, for a free program, it packs a lot of punch!

FTP software

FTP software uploads files from your computer to a web site and downloads files from a site to your computer. There are many great applications out there.

Here are a couple of personal favorites.

FileZilla Client is the current favorite FTP utility of a number of Muvipixers. Efficient, dependable and easy-to-use, sending files to a Web site with **FileZilla** is as simple as dragging and dropping.

FileZilla Client is available free from filezilla-project.org.

CyberDuck (a free download from cyberduck.en.softonic.com) – A very nice, easy to use FTP app that some people find even easier to use than FileZilla.

How to Proxy Edit your video

One of the great, advanced features in Vegas Movie Studio 14 is its ability to create and work with proxy video editing files.

Proxy files are lower resolution video files that the program automatically uses as temporary stand-ins for your higher-resolution video files, a process that puts less stress on your system's resources and allows for a smoother workflow. When it's time to output your finished movie, Vegas Movie Studio then applies the edits you made to the proxy files to your original higher-resolution files, giving you a full-quality output based on your proxy-edited project.

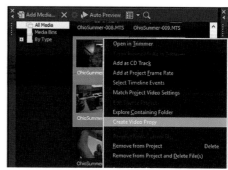

Most of this proxy editing is handled automatically and invisibly by the program. You don't even need to think about it! In fact, if you are editing a 4k or Sony XAVC video, the program even creates the proxy files automatically.

Otherwise, you will need to create your own proxy files. Then the program will automatically use them in your editing **as long as your Preview window's quality is set to Draft or Preview.**

To Proxy Edit a video:

1 **Create proxy videos of your source clips**

    Right-click on any clip(s) in your **Project Media** that you'd like to proxy edit and select the option to **Create Video Proxy**.

The program will generate a lower-resolution proxy file (a .sfvp0 file) of your selected media file.

You will not see this file in the **Project Media** window or in the program's **Explorer** window. But the program will automatically substitute it for your high-resolution file as you work.

2   **Set your Preview window quality**

Click the **Preview Quality** button at the top center of the **Preview** window. Ensure that it is set to either **Draft** or **Preview** quality (as described on page 153).

If your Preview quality is set to Good or Best, the program will work with your original high-resolution video files rather than your proxy media.

3   **Edit your movie**

Edit your movie as if your proxy video clips were your actual source footage.

4   **Make your movie**

Output your movie as described in **Chapter 17**.

The program will automatically use your original footage and, based on the edits and effects you've added to your project, it will produce a full-quality output of your finished piece.

Helpful Vegas Movie Studio keyboard shortcuts

Using keyboard shortcuts can help you work more efficiently. When you use a keyboard shortcut, you'll quickly launch or access a tool or feature without having to navigate to it with your mouse or open a series of menus.

There are dozens of keyboard shortcuts for Vegas Movie Studio. Here are a handful you may find pretty useful.

Project shortcuts

Ctrl+n	Start new project	**Ctrl+s**	Save project
Ctrl+o	Open existing project	**Ctrl+F4**	Exit Vegas Movie Studio

Editing shortcuts

Ctrl+Home	Jump to beginning of movie	**Ctrl+a**	Select all clips
		Ctrl+x	Cut selected clips
Ctrl+End	Jump to end of movie	**Ctrl+c**	Copy selected clips
Spacebar	Playback/stop	**Ctrl+v**	Paste clips
Enter	Pause playback	**Ctrl+b**	Paste multiple
J, K, L	Scrub playback (see page 76)	**Delete**	Delete selection
		g	Group selected events
Arrows Left, Right	Move one frame at a time	**u**	Remove selected event from Group
Arrows Up, Down	Zoom in/out on timeline		
Ctrl+g	Set playhead by timecode (see page 76)	**Ctrl+u**	Ungroup all
		Ctrl+z	Undo
Shift+click	Select range of clips by selecting first and last in a series	**Ctrl+Shift+z**	Redo
		/ (Keypad)	Convert cut to transition
Ctrl+click	Select several clips by selecting one at a time	**Ctrl+/ (Keypad)**	Convert transition to cut

Printed in Great Britain
by Amazon